Crowther to Warnock

How Fourteen Reports Tried to Change
Children's Lives

RICK ROGERS

H·E·B

Heinemann Educational Books
London

in association with
The Interna

Heinemann Educational Books Ltd
22 Bedford Square, London WC1B 3HH

LONDON EDINBURGH MELBOURNE AUCKLAND
HONG KONG SINGAPORE KUALA LUMPUR NEW DELHI
IBADAN NAIROBI JOHANNESBURG
EXETER (NH) KINGSTON PORT OF SPAIN

© Rick Rogers 1980
First published 1980

British Library Cataloguing in Publication Data

Rogers, Rick
   Crowther to Warnock
   1. Educational reports — England
   2. Education — England — History — 20th century
   3. Children — Care and hygiene — Great Britain —
     History — 20th century
   I. Title

   370'. 942   LB2901

   IS BN 0-435-80762-5
        0-453-80761-7 Pbk

Typeset by The Castlefield Press of High Wycombe
in 11/12pt Baskerville, and printed and bound in Great Britain
by Biddles of Guildford

Preface

During International Year of the Child each country was asked to think about all children. Not only about those children in developing countries where resources are inadequate to meet the most basic means to maintain life, but also those children here in our midst for whom we have a direct responsibility. Children here, too, have needs which are not being met — not because there are not sufficient resources available, but because we do not rate children's needs as a high enough priority to allocate resources to them (resources of time and political commitment as well as money).

What are those needs and what should be done to meet them? In the last twenty years, Governments have set about looking for answers to such questions. This book describes the questions that were posed and the answers that were suggested. It also describes what has been done to carry out the recommendations.

When the United Nations decided that 1979 should be the International Year of the Child, this is what they said the general objectives of the Year should be:

To provide a framework for advocacy on behalf of children and for enhancing the awareness of the special needs of children on the part of decision-makers and the public;

To promote recognition of the fact that programmes for children should be an integral part of economic and social development plans, with a view to achieving, in both the long-term and the short-term, sustained activities for the benefit of children at the national and international levels.

For anyone starting to construct such a programme for improving the lives of children, reading this book should be the first step. Here they will find blue-prints drawn up over the years for a better life for children. They will also see that planning and awareness are of little value unless they are backed up by sustained activity.

The UK Association for International Year of the Child is grateful to the Department of Education and Science for a grant which helped them to fund the preparation of this book.

Judith Stone
Director, UK Asssociation for
International Year of the Child
May 1980

Author's Note

A large number of people — professional and lay — have been kind enough to read through, comment and advise on each section of this book. I am immensely grateful to them all. Together they have greatly improved the book. Whatever errors, omissions or idiosyncrasies that may still remain are entirely mine.

The Department of Education and Science were generous enough to provide a grant to the UK Association for the International Year of the Child to help fund the preparatory work for this book. I should, of course, make it clear that at no time did they try to influence the content of the book, nor are they responsible for any of the opinions expressed herein.

Rick Rogers
May 1980

Contents

Timescale of the Fourteen Committees of Enquiry

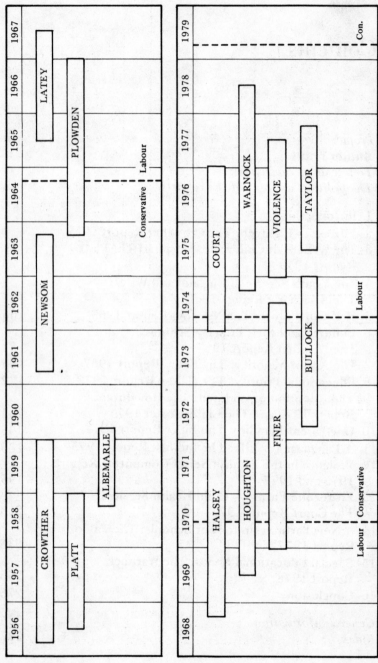

General Election	Parliament: assembled/dissolved	Government
5 July 1945	1 August 1945 – 3 February 1950	Labour
23 February 1950	1 March 1950 – 5 October 1951	Labour
25 October 1951	31 October – 6 May 1955	Conservative
26 May 1955	9 June 1955 – 18 September 1959	Conservative
8 October 1959	27 October 1959 – 25 September 1964	Conservative
15 October 1964	3 November 1964 – 10 March 1966	Labour
31 March 1966	21 April 1966 – 29 May 1970	Labour
18 June 1970	2 July 1970 – 8 February 1974	Conservative
28 February 1974	13 March 1974 – 19 September 1974	Labour
10 October 1974	29 October 1974 – 7 April 1979	Labour
3 May 1979	9 May 1979	Conservative

Education Minister/Secretary*

Ellen Wilkinson	July 1945 – February 1947
George Tomlinson	February 1947 – November 1951
Florence Horsburgh	November 1951 – October 1954
Sir David Eccles	October 1954 – January 1957
Viscount Hailsham	January 1957 – September 1957
Geoffrey Lloyd	September 1957 – October 1959
Sir David Eccles	October 1959 – July 1962
Sir Edward Boyle	July 1962 – March 1964
Quintin Hogg	April 1964 – October 1964
Michael Stewart	October 1964 – January 1965
Anthony Crosland	January 1965 – August 1967
Patrick Gordon Walker	August 1967 – April 1968
Edward Short	April 1968 – June 1970
Margaret Thatcher	June 1970 – March 1974
Reginald Prentice	March 1974 – June 1975
Fred Mulley	June 1975 – September 1976
Shirley Williams	September 1976 – May 1979
Mark Carlisle	May 1979

*In 1964, the Education Minister became known as the Secretary of State for Education and Science, when the Ministry of Education was reorganised as the Department of Education and Science.

Health Minister/Secretary*

Aneurin Bevan	August 1945 – January 1951
Hilary Marquand	January 1951 – November 1951
Harry Crookshank	November 1951 – May 1952
Iain Macleod	May 1952 – December 1955
Robert Turton	December 1955 – January 1957
Dennis Vosper	January 1957 – September 1957
Derek Walker-Smith	September 1957 – July 1960
Enoch Powell	July 1960 – October 1963
Anthony Barber	October 1963 – October 1964
Kenneth Robinson	October 1964 – November 1968
Richard Crossman	November 1968 – June 1970
Sir Keith Joseph	June 1970 – March 1974
Barbara Castle	March 1974 – April 1976
David Ennals	April 1976 – May 1979
Patrick Jenkin	May 1979

*In 1968, the Health Minister became known as the Secretary of State for Health and Social Security, when the Ministry of Health was re-organised as the Department of Health and Social Security. (S/he can also be referred to as the Social Services Secretary.)

Home Secretary

James Chuter Ede	August 1945 – October 1951
Sir David Maxwell Fyfe	October 1951 – October 1954
Gwilym Lloyd George	October 1954 – January 1957
Richard Austen Butler	January 1957 – July 1962
Henry Brooke	July 1962 – October 1964
Sir Frank Soskice	October 1964 – December 1965
Roy Jenkins	December 1965 – November 1967
James Callaghan	November 1967 – June 1970
Reginald Maudling	June 1970 – July 1972
Robert Carr	July 1972 – March 1974
Roy Jenkins	March 1974 – September 1976
Merlyn Rees	September 1976 – May 1979
William Whitelaw	May 1979

1 Introduction

This book looks at fourteen official Reports produced by Committees of Enquiry set up by Government. They considered key issues concerning the education, health and social well-being of children.

Each section on a Report is divided up into four: how the Committee of Enquiry came to be set up; what the Committee was asked to do (its official terms of reference); what the Committee recommended should be done, and why; and what has happened since the Report was published — legislation, changes in policy, subsequent reports and surveys, allocation of resources, educational or social developments, and so on.

The Reports span a period of some twenty years. They deal with a variety of issues — from the welfare of children in hospital and the educational opportunities available to secondary school children to the special educational needs of handicapped children and how schools should be governed. All the issues (even those covered in the Reports of the 1950s and 1960s) are still current today.

Four Government departments have been concerned with the Reports — either individually or jointly: the Department of Education and Science (DES), the Department of Health and Social Security (DHSS), the Home Office, and the Lord Chancellor's Office. Over the twenty-four years since the first Reports were commissioned (the Crowther Report in March and the Platt Report in June 1956), there have been eleven Secretaries of State for Health, fifteen Secretaries of State for Education, and eleven Home Secretaries. There have been four changes of Government.

Over the same period, some seventeen million children

have been born in England and Wales; some half a million have died for one reason or another (most in the first year of life). There are now some thirteen million children under eighteen; three million are under five years of age. These Reports are about their needs and aspirations.

How the Committees of Enquiry were set up

The Committees of Enquiry which produced the Reports covered here originated in two main ways. Four were part of existing advisory councils established by Act of Parliament to advise Government direct on educational and health issues. So Crowther, Newsom and Plowden (set up by the Education Minister) came under the Central Advisory Council on Education (there was one for England, and one for Wales), which had been established under section 4 of the 1944 Education Act 'to advise the Secretary of State upon such matters connected with educational theory and practice as they think fit, and upon any questions referred to them by him'. (The Councils have not been used since 1968.) The Platt Committee was a part of the Central Health Services Council set up under the 1948 National Health Act to perform the same kind of task as the Central Advisory Council.

Eight Committees were set up by the Secretary of State of a specific Government department as *ad hoc* or one-off committees, often through public or Parliamentary pressure, to investigate a particular issue or area of policy, and then disbanded. Thus the Albemarle, Bullock and Taylor Committees were set up by the Education Secretary of State; Finer by the Health Secretary; Court and Warnock jointly by the Education and Health Secretaries; Houghton by the Home Secretary and Latey by the Lord Chancellor.

The Reports on violence in the family came out of Parliamentary Select Committees comprising MPs of all the major political parties and able to call on evidence and witnesses to inform and advise them.

The Halsey Report was the result of an action-research project set up jointly by the Department of Education and Science and the Social Science Research Council (SSRC).

Where to find out more

Books

The Politics of Education Edward Boyle and Anthony Crosland in conversation with Maurice Kogan (Penguin, 1971)

Education, the Child and Society: A Documentary History 1900-1973 Willem van der Eyken (Penguin Education, 1973)

Advisory Councils and Commitees in Education Maurice Kogan and Tim Packwood (Routledge and Kegan Paul, 1974)

Educational Policy-making: a Study of Interest Groups and Parliament Maurice Kogan (George Allen and Unwin, 1975)

Much to do about Education: A Critical Survey of the Fate of the Major Educational Reports Anne Corbett (Macmillan Education, fourth edition, 1978). Looks at Crowther, Newsom, Robbins, Plowden, the Public Schools Commission, James, Russell, Bullock and Taylor

Educational Documents, England and Wales: 1816 to the Present Day J. Stuart Maclure (Methuen, 1979). Goes up to the Warnock Report on special educational needs.

2 Fifteen to Eighteen: The Crowther Report (1959)

Why Crowther was set up

The 1944 Education Act had established the principle that secondary education should be freely available to all children up to the age of fifteen[1] — and, as soon as was considered practicable, up to sixteen. The school-leaving age was duly raised from fourteen to fifteen in April 1947. Ten years later though it was still not thought possible to raise the minimum leaving age to sixteen.

However, a second key factor about secondary education was that, in most parts of the country, it was based on a selective system of entry to one or two (and, in some cases, three) types of school: grammar, secondary modern, and technical. The justification for the selective system was that children could be assessed to see which type of school most suited their educational needs. A 'pass' would mean a place at a grammar school; a 'fail' would mean attendance at a secondary modern school[2]. And, for many, the system was

[1] The 1926 Hadow Report on the education of the adolescent had recommended that the minimum leaving age be raised to fifteen. In 1929, proposed legislation to do so was defeated in the Commons. The 1936 Education Act included a section raising the age to fifteen from September 1939 — but the 1939-45 war prevented this.

[2] Secondary technical schools had been developed since 1944, but only just over half of the LEAs had them. Comprehensive schools were rare — in 1956 only 2 per cent of pupils went to a comprehensive.

By 1958, 60 per cent of pupils aged between eleven and eighteen went to secondary modern schools; 27 per cent went to grammar schools; 5 per cent to all-age schools (then being phased out); 4 per cent to technical schools; 3 per cent to comprehensive schools; 1 per cent to bilateral and multilateral schools. However, for fifteen- to eighteen-year-olds only, the proportions were: grammar 71 per cent, secondary modern 15½ per cent, technical 8½ per cent, comprehensive 3½ per cent.

4

an arbitrary and frequently unjust rule of thumb for success and failure, rather than a procedure to match ability or need with educational provision.

For these schools provided a very different kind of education and set of experiences — and received an uneven allocation of educational resources. What happened to a child's education after the age of fifteen was very much determined by this selection at eleven. For example, a grammar school offered an academic education right through to the sixth form with considerable emphasis on taking public examinations. In contrast, a secondary modern school provided few opportunities for gaining qualifications and gave little encouragement to pupils to stay on beyond the minimum leaving age of fifteen.

But it was becoming increasingly clear that the period between fifteen and eighteen was of crucial importance. It was another watershed that could determine a child's chance in life — for good or ill. By the mid-fifties, a growing number of educationalists and politicians were coming to realize that, for a child's own personal development and for the long-term economic good of the nation, more thought and more resources had to go into providing educational opportunities for academically-minded *and* practically-minded children. In short, more children had to be persuaded to stay on in full-time or part-time education after the age of fifteen.

In 1956, when the Crowther Committee of Enquiry was set up, a majority of children aged between fifteen and eighteen were getting no education at all — just over half the boys, and two-thirds of the girls. Only a quarter of all fifteen- to seventeen-year-olds (boys and girls) were staying on at school or going into some kind of full-time further education. At seventeen, the proportion was only 10 per cent; at eighteen, the proportion of boys staying in full-time education was below 8 per cent, and for girls under 6 per cent. Moreover, only an additional 21 per cent of boys received some form of part-time education; for girls, the proportion was 6 per cent.

A Government Report (*Early Leaving*) published in 1954 revealed how strongly family background determined whether a child stayed on at school beyond the minimum leaving

5

age. A large proportion of children were getting no encouragement at home *or* at school to pursue their education after fifteen.

In 1956, these problems of early leaving and inadequate provision were about to be made worse. The post-war baby boom in the late 1940s meant that a larger number of children were coming up to fifteen. And by 1965, the fifteen to eighteen age group would be a third larger than what it was in 1959.

What Crowther was asked to do

Consider, in relation to the changing social and industrial needs of our society, and the needs of its individual citizens, the education of boys and girls between fifteen and eighteen, and in particular to consider the balance at various levels of general and specialized studies between these ages and to examine the inter-relationship of the various stages of education.

What Crowther recommended and why

Social changes were profoundly affecting what could and needed to be done in schools. Men and women were living longer, marrying younger and having smaller families. The main consequences of these changes were threefold: the individual family was more able to support a lengthy education for its children; married women were more able to take up paid employment; for more girls marriage came soon after, or even preceded, the end of education. Other relevant consequences were that society had to support more old people; the family group covered a narrower age range thus limiting a child's intimate circle; birth and death were rare events in most children's lives.

Young people were more independent — partly through changed social attitudes, partly through being able to earn high wages. A different moral code existed for many of them and for their parents. The family was not such a stable unit; divorce had increased. Previously-accepted authority was being increasing called into question. Many established customs and attitudes had been discarded and new moral and sexual attitudes were taking their place. There was gain and loss in such changes. However, young people needed to develop new guiding rules of behaviour — and this did not always happen. The education service had to prepare children for adult life, but it could only function within the broad directives of right and wrong which society itself gave.

There was also concern about the level of juvenile delinquency and about the role of the school in helping young people to avoid 'getting into trouble'. The last year of compulsory education was the worst year for juvenile delinquency. The steadily rising rate of delinquency in the secondary school years declined when a boy went out to work.

Economic changes were having an effect too. The average standard of living had risen sharply since the second world war. There had been a great increase in the nation's wealth-producing capacity. Thus, there were more real resources to spend on education, and, in turn, there was a greater challenge for education to provide the brains and skills needed to sustain a high level of national productivity.

More young people were staying on in full-time education. However, the ability of young people to earn high wages was luring many promising pupils away from continuing their education. The demand for more education was conditional on whether young people saw it as meeting their specific needs. There was also a growing need to be properly qualified — and not just for the professions. Modern technology was creating many more jobs which required some special knowledge or experience. Many occupations were requiring evidence of an attested standard of general education.

The task of education in the technological age was a double one: to provide the opportunity to acquire qualifications; to develop the human personality.

There was a new emphasis on education as an investment. For it was believed that the nation could control its own economic development and that the prosperity and safety of the nation depended on keeping up in the economic race. It was not beyond the country's means to pay the cost of investing in a new education for fifteen- to eighteen-year-olds.

7

The development of the modern school

Four-fifths of the boys and girls in England had left school before they were sixteen. But there was a demand among both boys and girls for a longer education. It was insufficient opportunity rather than lack of desire for more education that made many children leave school at fifteen. Only a minority of secondary modern schools offered extended courses — those that went on into a fifth year of schooling.

Extended courses should be made available for all secondary modern school pupils. By 1965, half the number of pupils who needed them should be able to follow such a course. Wherever possible they should be available in the school a pupil had attended since the age of eleven.

There were two groups of children in the examinable minority of modern school pupils: those who had the ability to take subjects at GCE O-level; and those, probably a third of all the pupils over fifteen, who would find it useful to take an external exam below the level of the GCE (i.e. an examination set by an outside examination board rather than by the school itself). There were however some dangers in having large-scale national external examinations — for example, they could distort what was taught in school and how it was taught; the needs of the abler pupils could override those of the less able. Thus any external examinations that were devised should develop with regional or local, rather than with national, control.

Whether more examinations were devised or not, pupils in the lower half of the modern school should in any case receive regional or local leaving certificates. Those teachers who worked with below-average pupils should receive a due proportion of special responsibility allowances. Authorities and governing bodies should not judge their modern school by public examination results. Having fewer able pupils than selective schools, modern schools had to be concerned with producing more boys and girls capable of doing jobs which required a sound basic education of an academic kind. Their success in doing so was encouraging.

Secondary education for all

The period of compulsory schooling should be extended, and the minimum leaving age raised from fifteen to sixteen[1] in one of the school years 1966/7, 1967/8, or 1968/9. The additional year should offer new and challenging courses, and not simply be a continuation of what pupils had had before. Legislation should be brought in at once to reduce the three school leaving dates to two — at Easter and in July.

County colleges

Compulsory part-time education for all sixteen- and seventeen-year-olds not in full-time education should be brought in as soon as possible. This was the second priority, the first being the raising of the school-leaving age. This meant setting up a national network of 'county colleges' — based, in part, on further education colleges. The Education Act 1944 had provided for the establishment of county colleges, and the County Colleges Order 1947 had put a duty on LEAs to establish and maintain them — at some unspecified date in the future.[2]

A three-stage programme should be introduced over three or four years comprising initial intensive encouragement to extend day-release schemes by voluntary means; a compulsory attendance scheme in one or two selected areas; the phased introduction of compulsory attendance throughout the country. The Youth Service should be developed and strengthened as an essential complement to county colleges, so as to provide more contact with the least skilled and least able members of the young community once they had left school

[1] A survey of National Servicemen commissioned by the Crowther Committee found there was a large pool of untapped talent because so many children left school at fifteen. Half the recruits to the army who were rated in the two highest ability groups had left school at fifteen.

[2] Section 43 of the 1944 Act stated: 'It shall be the duty of every local education authority to establish and maintain county colleges, that is to say, centres approved by the Secretary of State for providing for young persons who are not in full-time attendance at any school or other educational institution.' The education provided would include 'physical, practical and vocational training, as will enable them to develop their various aptitudes and capacities and will prepare them for the responsibilities of citizenship'.

and to maintain their morale. Selecting and training the right kind of staff for county colleges was most important as was the suitability of the accommodation.

The sixth form

More pupils in maintained grammar schools, direct grant schools and independent schools were staying on into the sixth form. This trend would increase. However, a great wastage of talent still occurred through early leaving from grammar schools. More pupils would stay on if there was a greater variety of curriculum open to them.

Pupils should not specialize too early in their school career, as this usually meant dropping practical and aesthetic subjects, including English, in favour of foreign languages and science subjects. Fourteen was too soon for pupils to commit themselves to the subjects they would take at sixth-form level; nor should they be expected to sit for GCE O-level exams as early as fourteen. The curriculum should be broadened to ensure that pupils had a greater choice of subjects as they approached the sixth form.

Once in the sixth, pupils should then be able to specialize in a small range of subjects. But periods of 'minority-time' study ought to be organized to ensure that science specialists were literate and that arts specialists were numerate. More boys and girls would stay on at school if they were offered a greater variety of subjects to choose from.

The competition for university places was, and would continue to be, very strong. This had a detrimental effect on what was taught in schools. A growing number of pupils were 'qualified' to enter university, but were not 'selected' to do so. More higher education places should be planned for — particularly for girls. A standard system for dealing with applications for university should be set up. Pupils regarded as potential university candidates ought not to be separated from other sixth formers. The GCE A-level examination should be seen mainly as a school-leaving examination rather than as an examination for university entrance. It would, of course, continue to be used as an entrance qualification, but applicants should not be selected solely on the marks attained.

Many pupils found that staying on at school to complete a full eight years of secondary education (including three years in the sixth) created undue financial hardship for their families. Consequently, many left earlier than they would have wanted to. LEAs should be able to offer pupils substantial grants or bursaries for their eighth year of schooling.

More general courses needed to be developed, with some work leading to the A-level examination, to enable pupils to stay on in the sixth form and qualify for those professions which had started to recruit at eighteen rather than sixteen. No pupil should be allowed to take more than three A-levels.

Technical challenge and educational response

A quarter of all fifteen-year-olds left school but continued in some form of further education. More needed to be encouraged to do so; first because more technicians and craftsmen were required, second because only 12½ per cent of sixteen- to eighteen-year-olds were in full-time education. This proportion should be raised to half the age group by 1979. A coherent national system of practical education should be set up to replace the existing varied collection of vocational training schemes. There should be more integration between schools and further education, and between further education and apprenticeships. A new form of practical education should be developed in schools and further education colleges for the 'technicians and craftsmen of the future', with more time allocated to all further education courses. This should help to reduce the failure rate and enhance the courses provided. No one should be expected to follow a course by evening class only. Block-release schemes should be introduced wherever practicable in place of day release. Girls were under-represented on further education courses and more provision had to be made for on them on block and day-release schemes.

Until the school-leaving age was raised to sixteen, boys who left at fifteen and who found it difficult to get an apprenticeship with day release, should be given special help, including the offer of a one-year full-time introductory course in a local technical college.

Institutions and teachers

A fourfold expression of full-time further education was needed to ensure that some 50 per cent of boys and girls could make use of it. Much depended on successfully persuading them to take up further education opportunities. That meant enlarging the choice of provision available to them, including the freedom to choose what to study and where to study.

Secondary technical schools should be developed with a proportionately larger sixth form to allow for pupils transferring from other schools. Comprehensive schools should be developed in areas with particular characteristics — providing for the varied needs of children of all levels of ability and serving as a socially unifying force in the community. Colleges should be available which offered similar academic and practical courses to those in sixth forms in schools.

More teachers were needed to ensure that raising the school-leaving age was a success and to improve the quality of education generally. The size of classes should be reduced — the pupil/teacher ratio in secondary schools was 1 to 21. After raising the leaving age, it should never be higher than 1 to 17 or 1 to 19. More graduates, with high academic qualifications, should be encouraged into teaching, and especially into sixth-form teaching. Teachers' salaries should compare favourably with those of other professions. Teachers should receive more help with clerical and routine tasks. They should have a special responsibility allowance for working with below-average pupils and be encouraged to go into areas of teacher shortage or with a high teacher-turnover rate through financial incentives or special housing provision. Older men and women needed to be attracted into teaching; married women especially should be helped to stay in, or return to, teaching.

The best chance of success for these measures was for the Government to adopt a coherent and properly-phased long-term development programme. This should be backed up with funding for more research and statistical work to provide the policy-makers with detailed information about what was going on in schools and colleges, and what was going on in the minds of the pupils.

The cost of education had to be compared with other forms of welfare expenditure and with other forms of capital investment. The cost of these specific recommendations would not be very large when set against other items of national capital investment such as housing, plant and machinery, or against consumer spending on drink and tobacco.

What happened to Crowther

The Crowther Report, published in November 1959, was debated in the House of Commons in March 1960, and the 1959-64 Conservative Government announced that it would not take any immediate action on the key recommendations, including the raising of the school-leaving age and making part-time attendance in county colleges compulsory. Instead the Minister of Education, Sir David Eccles, accepted the principle that these measures should be carried out sometime in the future. No coherent or properly-phased development programme was adopted. It was a bad start for a Report that had been generally well received.

The school-leaving age was not raised to sixteen until September 1972 — some thirteen years after the Report was published and nearly 30 since the 1944 Education Act. No Government would consider it an over-riding priority, despite an even more urgent plea from the Newsom Committee in 1963. The intention was there, but it fell victim to the public expenditure cuts during the 1960s.

The development of comprehensives did not start in earnest until the mid- to late sixties. In 1960, only 4.7 per cent of maintained secondary school pupils went to a comprehensive; in 1965, 8.5 per cent; 1968, 20.9 per cent; 1978, 83.4 per cent; 1979, 85.9 per cent.[1]

The task of devising a new external examination was given to a special Government working party under Robert Beloe. In 1960, the working party proposed the Certificate of Secondary Education (CSE). The GCE O-level was intended for the top 20 per cent of the ability range; the CSE was designed to cater for the next 40 per cent. The examination system would be run by a series of regionally-based examination boards. There would be three modes to the examination, each one giving schools progressively more autonomy to devise their own syllabuses. This was a partial success for the Crowther Committee since it went a fair way to satisfying the perceived needs of flexibility and a greater control by the schools over the examination syllabus with less pressure from external, and sometimes inappropriate, interests.

The effect has been that many more children leave school with a qualification. In 1967[2], an estimated 51 per cent of pupils left school with one or more public examination grade; in 1977, the proportion had leapt to 84 per cent[3]. In terms of the actual number of pupils, the proportion has more than doubled — from an estimated 303,348 to 630,924 school leavers. The proportion of school leavers attempting CSE or GCE has also increased from about half to 86 per cent.

The CSE examination has made a significant difference to the educational opportunities of secondary school pupils. But the existence of a dual system of CSE and GCE could also work against the interests of those taking CSE. Many employers did not fully appreciate the structure of school examinations and would not readily accept the value of a

[1] The above figures do not relate to *all* children in secondary education. Also many comprehensives still do not operate with pupils from the full range of ability. One estimate has put the proportion of pupils in 'true' comprehensives at 67 per cent — and it could be as low as 50 per cent (see *Where* 158, May 1980 and *Forum*, Spring 1980).

[2] CSE was first examined in 1965.

[3] *Statistics of Education 1977: Vol. 2 School Leavers, CSE and GCE* (HMSO, 1979). These figures relate to England and Wales.

CSE grade. Often, the division was an artificial hurdle with many children finding that a clutch of GCE and CSE best met their needs. For example, in 1978 over 60,000 pupils were double-entered for GCE and CSE in particular subjects. Moreover, the exam system as a whole has been coming increasingly under fire for being an unreliable indicator of children's skills and attributes. In *Outcomes of Education* (Macmillan, 1980), Tyrrell Burgess and Elizabeth Adams criticize the system because it 'denies the public recognition of a 'pass' or higher grade to . . . well over three-fifths of all young leavers'. Nor does it provide useful information about the competence of school leavers. (See the section on the Newsom Report, page 77.)

In July 1978, the Report[1] of the Waddell Committee (set up in 1977 by the Labour Education Secretary Shirley Williams to consider a common system of examining at sixteen-plus) recommended that a single examination system replace GCE O-level and CSE. After consultations with interested bodies, the 1974-9 Labour Government accepted the recommendation. Its October 1978 White Paper *Secondary School Examinations: A Single System at 16-plus* proposed the GCSE — General Certificate of Secondary Education — to begin in the mid-eighties. The 1979 Conservative Government subsequently withdrew the proposals for further consideration.

In February 1980, the Conservative Secretary of State Mark Carlisle announced that a new single 16-plus examination scheme would replace the existing GCE O-level and CSE system. There would be one set of grades from one to seven, with alternative examination papers of varying difficulty. The GCE boards would be responsible for the top three grades and the CSE boards the remaining four grades. Candidates would not be sitting the new examination for at least five years.

What sixth-formers should be taught and what examinations they should take remain under active discussion. Many of the issues discussed by the Crowther Committee are of concern for schools today: how to broaden the curriculum;

[1] *School Examinations* (HMSO, Cmnd 7281, July 1978).

how to delay the moment of specialization; how to meet the demands of a more heterogeneous sixth-form population. The demands of university still exert a strong influence on sixth-form work (and on work below sixth-form level). Only 6 per cent of all school leavers go on to do a university degree course. This influence draws resources away from the non-degree sixth former and the 'new sixth former' — those who stay on for just one year in the sixth.

These problems were referred to in the 1977 Green Paper *Education in Schools: A Consultative Document*:

> Some narrowing of the range of subjects studied after sixteen is legitimate and perhaps inevitable, but traditional practice in England and Wales may have gone too far in this direction. Some of those who follow academic sixth-form courses devote almost all their time to only two or three closely related subjects, without even the substantial broadening element of general studies provided in many schools.
>
> The curriculum for the less academic sixth former is not well defined. The same general principles apply as at earlier stages in the secondary school but particular care has to be taken to ensure that the education given to this very wide range of pupils furthers their career prospects as well as their personal development.

The 1979 DES survey of local authority arrangements for the school curriculum confirmed the continuing difficulties in this area of schooling.[1] Further evidence of the need to make changes in the curriculum offered in many schools came from the HM Inspectorate's national secondary survey *Aspects of Secondary Education in England* published in December 1979. After the third year of secondary schooling, pupils studied a small number of subjects chosen from a wide range of optional subjects in addition to a 'core' curriculum of, primarily, English, mathematics, PE and games. More able pupils tended to concentrate on science or languages to the exclusion of aesthetic, practical or humanities subjects. Less able pupils, with less choice on offer, followed an even narrower curriculum, largely undemanding and lacking in coherence.

[1] The rapidly declining school population, due to the fall in the birthrate between 1964 and 1977, is now affecting the secondary schools. This has made decisions about the future of sixth forms more urgent. LEAs are proposing, and implementing, a range of measures including sixth-form colleges, fewer but larger secondary schools which are able to sustain a viable sixth form, and greater liaison between schools and further education colleges.

So complex were the option schemes and the curricular organization in many schools that it was difficult for pupils or their teachers to see an individual pupil's programme as a whole. Important areas of the curriculum were excluded, wholly or almost wholly, from many pupils' programmes. The loss of some subjects reduced the potential range of opportunities, whether for employment or for continued education, open to those pupils at the end of their fifth year. The loss of other subjects removed opportunities to enlarge experience and understanding in ways potentially valuable for the future quality of their lives as adults and citizens.

In January 1980, two official documents were published to begin consultations on the future of the curriculum in primary and secondary schools and the establishment of a 'core' curriculum. Government presented its views in *A Framework for the School Curriculum* (DES) and HM Inspectorate produced a discussion paper *A View of the Curriculum* (HMI Series: Matters for Discussion no. 11, HMSO).

In 1976, the Schools Council put forward proposals for a new examination at seventeen-plus for those pupils spending just one year in the sixth form (the new sixth formers) — the Certificate of Extended Education (CEE). Experimental schemes were set up in some schools and, in 1978, the Education Secretary Shirley Williams established a working group under Professor Keohane to consider the Schools Council's proposals. The working group's report was published in December 1979[1]. They recommended that the CEE be introduced on a national basis, and that CEE syllabuses should be geared to those pupils staying on for one extra year who were not interested in doing GCE A-levels, and should help to prepare them for employment.

Other proposals were put up during the 1970s for a replacement to the GCE A-level examination. There was concern that the A-level system encouraged pupils to study too narrow a range of subjects. The most recent scheme, proposed by the Schools Council, was the N (Normal) and F (Further) series of examinations. This would have increased the number of subjects to be studied by sixth formers to five, and was designed to accommodate three basic principles: curricular reform to meet the various needs of sixth formers; reducing

[1] *Proposals for a Certificate of Extended Education* (The Keohane Report, HMSO, Cmnd 7755).

specialization and broadening the scope of sixth-form study; delaying the time of specialization. The discussion of these proposals were again cut short by the change of government after the May 1979 General Election. The new Conservative Education Secretary, Mark Carlisle, rejected the proposals and stated that 'it would be wrong to replace A-levels for the foreseeable future'.[1]

Curriculum development was enhanced from the mid-sixties by the Nuffield science and mathematics teaching projects. These projects sought to improve the quality of GCE O-level courses in biology, chemistry and physics and of maths teaching in primary schools. From 1972, material was also produced for CSE syllabuses in science.

The three school-leaving dates were eventually reduced to two: the 1962 Education Act abolished the Christmas leaving date. A further change was made by the Education (School Leaving Dates) Act 1976 to allow pupils who reached sixteen after the Easter leaving date to end their schooling at the end of May, rather than having to wait until the end of the summer term.

By 1978, some 274,500 pupils were over the compulsory leaving age of sixteen (that is, 7 per cent of all children in secondary school). This was the largest number ever. But there was a small decline in the numbers deciding to stay on at seventeen and eighteen — and a larger drop in the numbers of sixteen-year-olds deciding to remain in school. A quarter of all sixteen-year-olds now decide to stay on. Part of the drop can be explained by a trend for these students to switch from school to a further education college to continue their education.

No action was taken after Crowther reported on setting up a grants scheme for pupils deciding to stay on in school, despite a similar plea from the Newsom Committee. A few LEAs have used their discretionary powers under the 1944 Education Act to award some grants to sixth formers. In 1974, a report[2] by the House of Commons Expenditure Committee suggested new ways of helping sixteen- to eighteen-year-olds financially to stay in education. At the end of 1978, the Government announced the introduction of a small-scale

[1] Report in *Education* 29 June 1979.
[2] Third Report from the Expenditure Committee *Educational Maintenance Allowances in the 16-18 Years Age Group* (HMSO, HC306, July 1974).

experimental scheme of grant-aid for over-sixteens who stay on at school. The estimated cost was an annual £10 million plus. A full national grants scheme had been vetoed by the Cabinet — that would have cost over £100 million a year. Following the May 1979 General Election, the new Conservative Government abandoned the proposed experimental scheme.

Education for sixteen- to eighteen-year-olds has developed along three lines: school, further education (with a variety of different colleges — tertiary, sixth form and separate FE colleges) and industrial training (run by employers and industrial training boards). The proposal for developing county colleges with compulsory part-time attendance was consigned to the museum of educational lost causes. The large-scale development envisaged by the Crowther Committee did not materialize as quickly or as coherently as had been hoped. In 1959 some 12½ per cent of sixteen- to eighteen-year-olds were in full-time education. Crowther had wanted 50 per cent by 1979.

By 1978, the proportion had risen to 29.2 per cent. An additional 12.7 per cent were involved in some form of part-time non-advanced further education (NAFE) — mainly day — or block-release schemes. In all, only 41.9 per cent of sixteen- to eighteen-year-olds were in full- or part-time education during 1978 (17.5 in schools; 9.7 in full-time NAFE; 12.7 in part-time NAFE; 2.0 in higher education).[1]

The destinations of those young people who reached the age of sixteen in the school year 1976/7, were (at the beginning of January 1978) as follows:

	%
unemployed	8
in school	28
in full-time FE	14
employed with part-time day FE	14
employed with *no* part-time day FE	36
	100

Source: Table 1 *Education and Training for 16-18 Year Olds: A Consultative Paper* (DES, February 1979).

[1] DES *Statistical Bulletin* 15/79 December 1979. See also DES Report on Education no. 94 *Non-advanced Further Education* (December 1978). (In January 1977, there were 1,983,000 sixteen- to eighteen-year-olds. In the 1970s, only 40 per cent of boys and 10 per cent of girls received any day-release training.)

19

In 1973, the Technician Education Council (TEC) and the Business Education Council (BEC) were set up to coordinate a variety of vocational and professional qualifications. They are gradually taking over as the national bodies for giving awards and setting standards for technical and business courses, replacing Ordinary National Certificate (ONC)/ Ordinary National Diploma (OND) and Higher National Certificate (HNC)/Higher National Diploma (HND), and some City and Guilds of London Institute courses.

Industrial training — the responsibility of the Department of Employment — also developed during the sixties. The 1964 Industrial Training Act had established 23 industrial training boards (ITBs) in Britain to organize and fund adequate training facilities in a range of key industries. The massive rise in youth unemployment during the 1970s[1] gave fresh impetus to the need to establish more and better training for school leavers. (During 1976, more than 800,000 sixteen- to eighteen-year-olds in Britain registered as unemployed.) In 1977, the Manpower Services Commission (set up in 1974 by the Employment and Training Act 1973) undertook a key review of existing training provision for young people. The result — the Holland Report *Young People and Work* — was published in May 1977. It proposed a more coherent programme of education, training and work-experience courses for school leavers to start in September 1978 at an annual cost of £160 million.

Out of the Holland Report came the Youth Opportunities Programme which offered all unemployed sixteen- to eighteen-year-olds training or preparation for employment. It planned to cater for 230,000 young people a year.[2]

In February and April 1979, the Education Secretary Shirley Williams issued two consultative papers on education and training for sixteen- to eighteen-year-olds[3] with the intention

[1] In March 1972, 2,000 school leavers (under eighteens) were registered unemployed; in March 1976, there were 22,000; in March 1978, 38,000. In January 1978, there were 205,000 under nineteens unemployed. *Manpower Services Commission*, June 1978.

[2] Public expenditure cuts in June 1979 reduced this target figure to 210,000.

[3] *16-18: The Education and Training of 16-18 Year Olds* (DES, February 1979) and *Providing Educational Opportunities for 16-18 Year Olds* (DES, April 1979).

of producing a White Paper setting out future Government policy on this age group. This attempt to formulate a coherent policy was interrupted by the May 1979 General Election.

Earlier, in March 1977, the DES-funded Further Education Curriculum Review and Development Unit (FEU) began reviewing and proposing curriculum policy in further education. Its latest report[1] recommended a set of national criteria, with a core curriculum, for pre-employment courses taken by sixteen-year-old school leavers who went into a further education college for one year before starting work.

In November 1979, a Government working party (the Macfarlane Committee) began to consider educational provision for 16- to 19-year-olds, following up on the consultations undertaken during the 1974-9 Labour Government's period in office. One proposal being investigated is allowing 15-year-olds to leave school before the minimum leaving age so long as they have apprenticeships to go to. The Committee is aiming to complete its work by the end of 1980.

Crowther's recommendation for more places in higher education to cope with the approaching 'bulge' in the age range and the consequent fast-growing sixth forms was taken up in the special Committee of Enquiry under Lord Robbins, set up by the Prime Minister Harold Macmillan in 1960. (There were many other bodies expressing concern about the future direction of higher education.) The Committee were asked to review the pattern and long-term development of full-time higher education. They started work early in 1961 and reported in 1963. They recommended a rapid expansion of places in higher education and helped to set the terms (if not the final outcome) of the debate on higher education through the 1960s and 70s, providing the rationale for the expansion of institutions and student numbers in the 1960s.

One final statistic: the Crowther Committee estimated that their recommendations would put £200-£250 million on the annual education budget. Crowther was not adopted as a coherent programme and little action was taken. Four years later, the Robbins Committee recommended a ten-year

[1] *A Basis for Choice: Report of a Study Group on Post-16 Pre-employment Courses* (October 1979).

21

development programme costing £3,500 million. It was accepted by the 1959-64 Conservative Government within 24 hours of the Report being published.

Where to find out more
Books

15-18 The Crowther Report (HMSO, 1959, two volumes: report and surveys)

A Guide to Learning after School Michael Locke and John Pratt (Penguin, 1979).

Aspects of Secondary Education in England (HMSO, December 1979). A national survey of secondary schools today carried out by HM Inspectorate.

Education and Equality David Rubinstein (ed.) (Penguin, 1979).

Outcomes of Education Tyrrell Burgess and Elizabeth Adams (eds.) (Macmillan, 1980).

Organizations

The Schools Council, 160 Great Portland Street, London W1N 6LL (01-580 0352). The Schools Council produces a series of books, pamphlets and other materials on examinations and the curriculum in schools.

Circulars

Key DES circulars on the education of fifteen to eighteen year-olds include:

9/63   The Certificate of Secondary Education
8/71   Raising the School Leaving Age to 16
7/73   Development of Higher Education in the Non-university Sector
2/76   Sex Discrimination Act 1975
4/76   The Education (School Leaving Dates) Act 1976
6/76   Government Statement on Unified Vocational Preparation
4/77   Race Relations Act 1976
10/77 Unemployed Young People: the Contribution of the Education Service
14/77 Local Education Authority Arrangements for the School Curriculum
1/80   Education Act 1980

3 The Welfare of Children in Hospital: The Platt Report (1959)

Why Platt was set up

The welfare of children in hospital has been a matter of professional concern since the 1920s, when paediatric work began to develop in hospitals. Under the then Child Guidance Council, new approaches for helping children with emotional and behavioural problems were tried out. More welfare services for children were established in schools and in the local community. At the same time it was being recognized that sick children had to be treated with great care — not just medically but in order to satisfy their emotional needs as well.

In 1946, the Care of Children Committee produced a report[1] on the difficulties faced by deprived children. It highlighted two of the most damaging elements that characterized their lives — an unfamiliar environment, and separation. These were just what children in hospital encountered, often with the additional strain of having to cope with 'painful and frightening experiences'.

When the National Health Service was set up in 1948, hospital treatment was made available to many more sick children. Hospitals became more a part of the community they served, and the differences in the way children were handled between home and hospital became more obvious. The results of further research (for example, the Nuffield Foundation's report on planning for children in hospital, and work on maternal deprivation carried out by the Tavistock Institute for Human Relations) underlined the need for

[1] The Curtis Report (HMSO, Cmnd 6922, 1946).

hospitals to cater as much for children's emotional needs as for their medical ones. This general concern was summed up by one of the major campaigners for change, James Robertson, who maintained that 'the greatest single cause of distress for the young child in hospital is not illness or pain but separation from mother'.

By the 1950s, some progress had been made. For example, a few hospitals did allow mothers to stay with their children. But such examples of good practice were rare. Pressure from a wide range of professional and voluntary bodies finally persuaded the Central Health Services Council to take action. In June 1956, the Council appointed a special committee under the chairmanship of Sir Harry Platt, president of the Royal College of Surgeons.

What Platt was asked to do

Make a special study of the arrangements in hospitals for the welfare of ill children — as distinct from their medical and nursing treatment — and make suggestions which could be passed on to hospital authorities.

What Platt recommended and why

Greater attention needed to be paid to the emotional and mental needs of the child in hospital, against the background of changes in attitudes towards children, in the hospital's place in the community, and in medical and surgical practice. The authority and responsibility of parents, the individuality of the child, and the importance of mitigating the effects of the break with home should all be more fully recognized.

The guiding principle for the care of children in hospital was that while children had, of course, to undergo the necessary investigations and treatment for the condition from which they were suffering, they should be subjected to the least possible disturbance of the routines to which they were accustomed.

Alternatives to in-patient treatment

Developments in medical and surgical practice meant that sick children did not necessarily have to go into hospital. Where possible, an alternative should be found to in-patient care, and children should not be admitted to hospital if it could be avoided. Special nursing facilities for looking after sick children at home should be extended. There should be separate out-patient departments for children, with suitable facilities and staff[1]. Waiting time should be kept to the minimum. Some simple surgical operations could be undertaken at the hospital, subject to certain safeguards, without fully admitting the child.

Hospital organization, design and staffing

When a child was admitted to hospital, the following criteria should apply. Children and adolescents should not be nursed in adult wards. Separate children's hospitals for all children were impracticable and for the general run of cases a small children's unit at the local hospital should suffice.

Children should be nursed in company with other children of the same age group. They should have facilities for inside and outside play and colour schemes should be cheerful. Children should be properly supervised and the prevention of accidents was important.

A children's physician should have a general concern with the care of all children in the hospital. The sister in charge of the ward should be a Registered Sick Children's Nurse (RSCN) as well as a State Registered Nurse (SRN), and have

[1] The Committee explained further by saying that many children required no more than a brief stay in hospital, either at the out-patient clinic or a daylong admission for an operation or investigation. The out-patient department attended by children should be near the children's ward and separate from the adult out-patient department, where children might be alarmed or upset by what they saw and heard. Children's out-patient departments should have adequate and comfortable accommodation for mothers and babies as well as for children: play-space, a canteen, a room to feed babies, suitable literature, ready information. Essential diagnostic services (such as X-ray and routine pathology) should be nearby and there should always be close liaison with the children's ward.

had previous experience as a staff nurse in a children's ward. A child in hospital should be handled by as few people as possible, and be able to get to know his or her own nurse. Nursery nurses could help with children under five. Social workers and occupational therapists had a valuable contribution to make.

Preparation for admission

It was important to prepare children for admission to hospital. The risk of disturbance to children could be reduced by proper preparation of both parents and children. For parents, this could be achieved through the promotion of a better understanding of the hospital's place in the community, explanations from the family doctor and local authority clinic staff, and through suitable measures adopted by the hospital in arranging admissions. These should include an explanation of the reasons for admission by the doctor who makes the decision; an interview with a suitably trained person to discuss details; and properly designed leaflets and letters. Talks between the ward sister and groups of parents might also be useful.

Children's confidence depended very much on the degree of security they sensed in their parents. The information suitable to be given to the children themselves would depend on their age and emotional maturity. A period in hospital should never be threatened as a punishment, nor promised as a treat.

Reception

First impressions on admission to hospital were important to both child and parents. The main admissions procedure should be carried out in the ward and there should be the least possible delay in reaching it. The ward sister should welcome the child in reassuring surroundings and find out from the parents about the child's idiosyncrasies.

Children admitted during the day should not be put

to bed unless this were medically necessary. Where children were admitted at bedtime, the parents should be allowed to help put them to bed. Clothes provided by the hospital should be attractive and well-fitting. The experiment of allowing children to wear their own clothes was worth considering; and they should be able to have with them a favourite toy or 'comforter'. Any readmission should be to a familiar ward.

A proper reception was especially important for emergencies. There should be separate accommodation for children in casualty departments and waiting parents should have suitable and comfortable amenities.

The child as in-patient

Children of different ages had differing psychological needs. Admitting mothers to stay with their children — especially if the child was under five and during the first few days in hospital — could go a long way to meeting those needs[1].

Visiting   A child in hospital had to be visited frequently to preserve the continuity of his or her life, and the arguments formerly advanced against frequent visiting were no longer valid. Parents should be allowed to visit whenever they could, and to help as much as possible with the care of the child.

Visiting was especially important in the first few days of a child's stay in hospital. Evening visits should be encouraged and visits on operating days allowed. Parents should be able to get authoritative information about their child's progress when they visited. Visitors other than parents should be permitted at certain times. Special arrangements should be made for children whose parents could not visit them. More amenities for visitors were needed. Parents in genuine need of financial assistance to enable them to visit frequently should be helped to get it.

[1] Other likely benefits mentioned by the Committee included: less emotional disturbance on a child's return home; both nurses and mothers could benefit from the experience, mothers gaining valuable experience in handling sick children; the creation of a happy atmosphere in the ward.

Education Providing educational facilities was important for short-stay as well as long-stay patients, and it was the hospital's responsibility to approach the local education authority for the purpose[1]. Children should not normally be admitted to hospital when they were about to take important examinations. Teaching required the cooperation of the hospital staff, suitable arrangement of the ward and the provision of space for teachers to prepare work and store books and equipment. It was important for children to be given organized activity outside the school term.

Other aspects of in-patient care The hospital day was long and there should be an organized programme of recreation with suitable toys and other diversions, with opportunities to play inside and out. Happy discipline depended not only on correct management but on harmonious relationships between all the staff, and between staff and parents. If there was sensibly organized diversion, disciplinary problems would be reduced. Safety was a major concern, but physical restraints should not be needlessly applied.

Children should be able to keep the personal possessions they treasured by their beds and all should have accessible storage space. Food should be attractively served and satisfying. Toilet needs should be adequately attended to; private vocabularies should be learned and children allowed to get up to go to the toilet if at all possible.

Parents should be able to get information about their children's progress from a knowledgeable and responsible person. They should be told if their child was to be transferred to another ward or hospital and should be given the opportunity to go with the child.

Daily prayers, Sunday school and visits by clergy were important.

---

[1] Under the Education Act 1944, LEAs had the power to make arrangements for teachers to work in hospitals where there were groups of children of school age (this included children from the age of two upwards). In September 1956 both Education and Health Ministries had issued circulars stressing the need for more liaison between hospital and education authorities over the provision of education for children in hospital.

Medical treatment

Unpleasant medical procedures should be kept to the minimum and carried out with tact and understanding of children's reactions. Time and care should be taken to explain to children (within the limits of each child's understanding) what was involved in their treatment. There should be separate treatment rooms and children should not be within sight of other children when they were being anaesthetized or coming round after an operation. Premedication should normally be used before operations. It would help the child if the mother could be present until s/he went to sleep and when coming round. Exceptional discretion was needed in the discussion of children's cases during ward rounds.

Special groups

In looking at different types of care and the various reasons why children were admitted to hospital, specific groups of children with special needs could be identified.

Most of the recommendations made applied equally to children in long-stay hospitals. There were additional comments on the need to ensure that these children (and their parents) were particularly well-prepared for admission, settling in and discharge, with special attention paid to visiting arrangements, accommodation for mothers, the children's education and recreation. Children should not be kept in long-stay hospitals for longer than their medical condition required and should be allowed to go home for short periods while they were under treatment.

Blind and deaf children and their parents had special needs, for example in relation to contact with home, leisure activities and education. If a child became blind or deaf in hospital, there should be no delay in providing the special services the child needed.

Isolation hospitals were being used for a wider range of children's ailments than formerly and this should be reflected in their staffing and management. In particular, restrictions on visiting should be lifted.

29

The welfare of the large numbers of children admitted for tonsil and adenoid operations merited particular attention, notwithstanding the shortness of their stay. They should not be nursed with adults and the recommendations about admission, reception, and in-patient care (including visiting) all applied equally to them.

Children admitted for eye operations should be nursed in a separate children's unit. Bandaging of children's eyes should not be lightly resorted to and if it was medically imperative it should be accompanied by special arrangements for the reassurance and occupation of the child concerned.

Discharge

The discharge of a child from hospital was a welcomed conclusion but also an important procedure and one which needed special consideration.

Parents should be warned about behaviour problems that might arise after discharge and be advised how to deal with them[1]. They should also be told of their part in any treatment required after the child's discharge from hospital.

The time of discharge should be convenient for the parents as well as the hospital, and a senior nurse should be available to speak to the parents. The family doctor should be told in advance when a patient was coming out of hospital and s/he should be provided with a full report as soon as possible. There should be adequate liaison with the local health and education authorities about any after-care or special educational requirements. Follow-up visits to the out-patient department should be reduced to the minimum.

Training of staff

The proper training of staff was one way to improve the quality of care of children in hospital. Nurses needed training

[1] The Committee pointed out that some children showed evidence of psychological disturbance after leaving hospital, such as regressive or aggressive behaviour, disturbed sleep, timidity, terrors, and difficulties at school.

30

not only in the special aspects of disease in children but in the factors that influenced the development of the normal child. Part of this training should take the form of practical experience in the care of healthy children whether in nursery schools or in their homes. The emotional needs of children in hospital should be stressed in refresher courses for ward sisters. Doctors generally also required more training in children's emotional needs. Ancillary hospital staff should be taught how to adjust their procedures to children's needs. An extention of the arrangements for training hospital teachers was required.

What happened to Platt

The 1955-9 Conservative Government accepted the Platt Committee's recommendations as soon as the Report was published in February 1959. The Ministry of Health issued a circular (HM(59)19) endorsing the recommendations, particularly those calling for an end to putting children in adult wards and urging unrestricted visiting of children in hospital[1].

Since 1959, numerous official circulars have been issued pressing for more widespread implementation of the recommendations. In March 1966 *Visiting of Children in Hospital* (HM(66)18) was published urging hospitals to abolish without delay any routine restrictions on visiting children, to provide accommodation for mothers to stay with their children in hospital, and to produce explanatory leaflets for parents on visiting arrangements. In February 1969, a further circular *Accommodation of Children in Hospital in Children's Departments* (HM(69)4) was issued asking hospital authorities to end the practice of putting children in adult wards by 1971.

In April 1971, a comprehensive paper *Hospital Facilities for Children* (HM(71)22) was published on the essential requirements of a hospital service for children. Hospital boards were asked 'to review existing provision and secure

---

[1] An earlier circular *Visits to Children in Hospital* (HM(56)6) had only pressed for hospitals to allow daily visiting.

further improvements at an early stage"[1]. Each circular followed closely the recommendations in *The Welfare of Children in Hospital*.

In the same year, another circular *Visiting of Patients by Children* (HM(71)50), asked hospital authorities to adopt a general policy of allowing children to visit parents and other close relatives in hospital frequently and regularly.

The need for unrestricted visiting and for close links between hospital staff and parents was reiterated in a 1972 circular advising hospitals how to deal with the problem of children abandoned in hospital (HM(72)2). The circular declared that 'visiting without restriction and positive encouragement of visits by all family members are essential safeguards [against abandonment]'[2].

In 1972, a special letter was sent out to hospital secretaries on *Meals and Accommodation for the Parents of Children in Hospital* (DS(218)72). This reminded hospitals of the circulars issued thus far on the welfare of children in hospital, stressed once again the need to ensure the well-being of the children, and specifically pointed out that hospitals must take responsibility for looking after parents who were staying with their children in hospital. The letter recommended that parents staying in hospital should not be charged for meals or accommodation, that it *was* reasonable to charge parents for meals if only visiting daily, and that hospitals should review their facilities for providing such meals.

Several official publications have been produced giving guidance on mentally handicapped children: the 1971 White Paper on *Better Services for the Mentally Handicapped*; the 1974 paper *Long-stay Children in Hospital* (DS182/74); the 1978 circular *Children in Hospital: Maintenance of Family Links* (HC(78)28); and the Report of the National Development Group for the Mentally Handicapped *Helping Mentally Handicapped People in Hospital*.

---

[1] This circular was revised and reissued in 1977 as HC(77)30. In it the DHSS stated that while the principles of the Platt Report were widely accepted, they were still not universally practised. They noted that 'serious mistakes have been made when specially trained paediatric medical and nursing staff have not been involved in the care of a young child'.

[2] This circular was updated and reissued in 1978 (HC(78)28).

THE WELFARE OF CHILDREN IN HOSPITAL

If conditions for children have still to be considerably improved in acute hospitals, the need is even greater in long-stay hospitals. It is now official Government policy to get as many children as possible out of hospital and into some form of community care, provided that suitable facilities exist in the community for them. It has been accepted that a small number of profoundly handicapped children will continue to need the specialist services of a hospital, although many will be able to receive treatment as out-patients.

The Jay Committee's Report on mental handicap nursing and care (March 1979, Cmnd 7468) brought together much of the current thinking on such care and has pressed for changes to be implemented quickly.

In December 1976, the Court Committee's Report on child health services *Fit for the Future* (Cmnd 6684) was published. It declared unequivocally:

It is our belief that children have special needs which they cannot articulate for themselves and that society has therefore a duty to ensure that these are identified and cogently represented.
(paragraph 16.19, page 279)

The Committee called for a child- and family-centred service capable of providing for the needs of all children, and for a powerful and legitimate advocacy of children's interests. One of the Committee's major criticisms of the health services was that much could have been done on behalf of children at little or no additional expense, but had not.

Some deficiencies may, at least in part, be the consequence of financial restrictions as with the urgent need for better care of mentally handicapped children. But this is by no means always so. Sometimes central recommendations which could be implemented without difficulty or great expenditure are overlooked or ignored by the peripheral authorities. For example, the DHSS accepted in 1959 the recommendations of the Platt Report on the Welfare of Children in Hospital that children and adolescents should not be nursed in adult wards and that parents should be allowed to visit whenever they could, helping as much as possible with the care of the child. Nevertheless these practices are still not universally accepted by hospitals, despite repeated Departmental exhortation and the pressure exerted by NAWCH. A deficiency of an entirely different scale is demonstrated by the failure of the three main services concerned — health, social work and education — to act in concert to meet the needs of children in long-stay hospitals. (paragraph 16.19, page 279)

The Court Report reaffirmed the principles of the Platt Report, and considered the existing structure of health care in relation to children:

The development of [district general] hospitals has been one of the most significant contributions by the NHS to the care of children. Their intended structure and function in relation to children have been expressed with clarity and conviction in the Department of Health's memorandum (HM(71)22) and its explanatory annexe Hospital Facilities for Children. We are in essential agreement with these recommendations and wish to see them fully implemented. The central conclusion of the circular was this: To make the most efficient and economic use of resources, the district services for acutely ill children should be centralised in one department, in one part of the main hospital, accommodating all children and providing paediatric and specialty services. This also implies, for example, that in urban areas where closely adjacent district hospitals may each maintain a children's department, every effort must be made, without ignoring all the complex geographical, human and other factors, to concentrate the paediatric services in one hospital only. In this way alone can duplication of staff, accommodation and equipment be avoided, and families seem on the whole prepared to recognise that greater inconvenience for some may be the price that has to be paid to ensure better care for all. (paragraph 12.20, page 183)

The Report concluded that:

. . . whilst much progress has been made in some hospitals, a great deal of evidence we received underlined that it is in the sphere of social understanding of their needs that children are least well cared for. Whilst this is particularly true of the long-stay hospitals our visits made it clear that the personal needs of children in acute hospitals were not always being met. Most of the staff are well aware of the difficulties, but tend to see them in terms of financial and manpower restraints. It is true that the current economic situation does place limits on what can be achieved, but at the same time we think it is important to recognize that whatever the financial position, progress will continue to depend most of all on the interest and initiative of those working within the individual hospital. (paragraph 12.39, page 190)

Thus despite consistent support for the Platt Committee's principles by successive Governments since 1959, progress towards full implementation has been slow. For Government action has been primarily concerned with issuing circulars, which can only advise and recommend. They cannot compel.

That progress would have been slower without the existence of the National Association for the Welfare of Children in Hospital. NAWCH was formed in 1961 to press for the implementation of the Platt principles and to inform and advise parents about becoming more involved in their child's experience in hospital.

Six years after Platt reported, fewer than twenty hospitals had made any satisfactory progress towards implementing the recommendations. James Robertson put down the lack of progress to 'the difficulty of changing long-established attitudes and practices within the hospital professions'. He concluded: 'We may have to wait for a change of generations before the Report is fully implemented'. (*The Times*, 18 February 1964).

A Health Ministry census of children and adolescents in normal NHS hospitals taken in 1965 and published in 1967 claimed that 85 per cent of hospitals allowed 'unrestricted visiting'. Only a minority of hospitals provided separate children's out-patient and casualty facilities. The same census also found that 18 per cent of hospitalized children were still being treated in adult wards. Special accommodation for adolescents (twelve- to sixteen-year-olds) remained rare — a third were in children's wards, well over half were in adult wards. NAWCH subsequently challenged the Government figures on unrestricted visiting. Their own survey based on 65 hospitals in one region put the level of such arrangements at only 57 per cent of hospitals (defining 'unrestricted visiting' as 45 hours a week, say 10 a.m. till 6 p.m. with 1½ hours for daytime resting). Over 25 per cent forbad morning visiting. Fifty-five per cent had no accommodation for mothers wanting to stay with their children. Of the rest, a quarter had some beds available for mothers, 15 per cent could provide a bed in an emergency, and 5 per cent catered only for private patients.

A follow-up NAWCH survey in 1975 noted a 'gradual

improvement' in unrestricted visiting provision since first beginning to monitor the arrangements in 1962. The 1975 survey revealed almost 20 per cent of all hospital wards for children had 24-hour visiting. A further 33 per cent allowed visiting through the daytime. Most of the rest allowed only from four to six hours daily and 2 per cent from nought to three hours. The survey also revealed that visiting on the day of operation was still the area most resistant to change and that limitations of all kinds were most strictly enforced for children coming into hospital for ear, nose or throat treatment. A quarter of all children's wards which provided general surgical care did not allow visiting on the day of a child's operation, before or after. Even in those wards which did have such arrangements, mothers were often not allowed to be present during a child's premedication or when a child was recovering from anaesthesia.

Many children, then, continued to be deprived of the benefit of unrestricted visiting by their parents: eight out of every ten children's wards forbad 24-hour visiting; almost seven out of ten forbad parental access through all the daytime hours; two out of ten permitted only up to six hours' visiting time. Moreover, a large number of hospitals did not allow visits by brothers and sisters — the recommendation made by the Platt Committee and extended by subsequent DHSS circulars was that children should be able to visit a brother or sister in hospital freely, to their mutual benefit.

The Platt Committee also recommended that financial aid be made available to parents who found difficulty visiting their children in hospital. Many hospital social workers recognize this as a continuing major need. The Platt suggestions were not implemented — and would now need substantial revision if they were implemented. For example, the poorly paid in full employment cannot be helped through any DHSS funding. NAWCH has suggested that since visiting is now officially regarded as an essential part of a child's treatment in hospital, parents who find the cost of regular visiting beyond their means should be eligible for funding as of right to enable them to visit as frequently as the child needs them to do so.

The other Platt recommendations have been subject to the same slow progress as have visiting arrangements. Most hospitals do now produce leaflets for parents on preparing children for admission to hospital. NAWCH also produces material, and there are currently several children's books available based on the experience of going into hospital which can help to ease a child's anxiety. Yet despite a greater awareness by both professionals and parents of the need to provide reassurance and understanding, admission to hospital remains for many children a frightening ordeal. A child's young age, an emergency admission, an ill-judged remark, a lack of communication can prevent adequate preparation or render such preparation useless. Equally worrying, hospital staff in general still do not tell parents that visiting is an essential part of children's treatment, whatever their age or condition.

The reception that children encounter on going into hospital continues to vary markedly. By no means all children will find an amenable and sympathetic reception geared specifically to their needs. There may be a lack of proper staff training on how to cater for children, no special facilities, a reluctance to involve parents fully in the numerous procedures that an admission can entail.

Some 50 per cent of children under seven are likely to spend a day or more in hospital. Although the pattern of childhood illness has altered dramatically since 1959, some three-quarters of a million children — about six per cent of the total child population — are admitted to hospital each year. Half are emergencies and about half need some kind of surgery. The average stay in hospital has fallen from two weeks in 1964 to under four days now. Some 73 per cent of the children admitted to hospital are there for less than five days. Many of the reasons why children go into hospital are new — an increasing parental concern for children and an awareness of illness and of hospital services; a greater use of hospital accident and emergency departments primarily because of inadequate GP services, especially in inner-city areas.

There are more 'social' reasons too for children being in hospital — the failure of a young child to thrive in the home environment; the admission of more disturbed children; the admission of victims of child abuse, and an increase in accidents at home and on the streets. Many children are admitted because the home environment is considered unsatisfactory for a child's welfare. It has been estimated that some 20 per cent of the children admitted to hospital are there for other than purely medical or clinical reasons.

The development of alternatives to going into hospital has also been patchy. The major change has been the large-scale switch from using GPs to going to the accident and emergency (A and E) department at the local hospital. This is particularly so in inner-city areas where the general practitioner service is at its most vulnerable with inadequate staffing, a preponderance of ageing, singlehanded GPs, a heavy reliance on deputizing services, and inconvenient appointments systems. However, most A and E departments still lack specific paediatric expertise and are ill-equipped for dealing with children — no separate waiting-room or examination rooms, no appropriate furnishing or facilities for children. The only detailed official survey was conducted in Wales in 1972. Of 50 A and E departments only two had separate facilities for children. Only 23 per cent of out-patients' departments had such provision.[1]

Few home-nursing or home-care programmes exist to enable parents to care for a sick child at home with adequate medical and nursing support. There are programmes in Birmingham, Edinburgh, Gateshead, Paddington in London, and Southampton. Not all operate on a 24-hour basis. Similarly, the use of day surgery for children is still available in only a minority of hospitals — surprisingly so since the cost of such surgery is much lower (less than half) compared with admitting a child as an in-patient.

Once settled in hospital, how well are children currently treated as in-patients? We have seen that unrestricted visiting will not yet be a part of every child's treatment — nor will many mothers be able to stay with their young children should they wish to. Accommodation for parents to stay with their children remains, according to NAWCH's most recent figures, generally

[1] *Children in Hospital in Wales* (Welsh Hospital Board, 1972) from Dept. of Child Health, Welsh National School of Medicine, Heath Park, Cardiff.

available in only six out of every ten wards. It is definitely
not available in two out of every ten. (There has been some
improvement: the 1972/3 NAWCH survey showed that only
one hospital ward in three could accommodate more than
one parent at a time; nationally, well over a third of all wards
— 37 per cent — provided no accommodation at all.)

All new hospitals built now must provide some such
accommodation and as early as 1964 the Government set
out guidelines on the level of provision to be established
per number of children's beds (four places per twenty children's beds). Often, though, where accommodation is provided, it fails to match the demands made on it by parents.
Sometimes hospitals do not inform parents that they are
able to stay or of the value of staying to the child. Incidentally, no recent official Government figures are available
— the information just is not collected.

The Platt Committee had, in effect, recommended separate
units for adolescents in hospitals.[1] But this is one proposal
that has rarely been acted on. There are a few examples of
special adolescent units, such as St Mary's in Manchester.
Others use special bays within children's wards or partition-
ing where the number of adolescents is very small. Too many
hospitals though fail to recognize the special needs of adolescents. The 1976 Court Report reiterated and expanded on
the Platt recommendations:

At hospital level, the services available for the treatment of illness
and injury in adolescence are generally those provided for children
or for adults. However mature adolescents have little in common
with the average child on a children's ward and the ward's routine may be inappropriate for them. Conversely an immature
adolescent of fourteen or more is often unsuited to the environment of an adults' ward. We feel that there is need for the establishment of more appropriate in-patient facilities in acute hospitals. A special unit for adolescent patients in Manchester is
proving successful; patients prefer separate accommodation, bed
occupancy is high and medical and nursing staff approve the
arrangements. We therefore recommend that consideration be
given to the provision of small adolescent units or failing that,

[1] Paragraph 33: 'Ideally, adolescents need their own accommodation, but if
the number admitted do not permit this it is better for them to be nursed with
children than with adults.'

of a partitioned adolescent area in a children's ward. Decisions on placement should be made on biological rather than chronological grounds and all rigid age limits for admission to children's wards should be abolished. Close collaboration between paediatricians and colleagues in surgical specialties and in adult medicine should be maintained to ensure proper attention to adolescents' needs. (paragraph 11.9, page 166)

The provision of education for children in both short- and long-stay hospital remains inadequate[1]. Many children receive little education. Some hospital schools are well-equipped and well-staffed; others have insufficient space, poor equipment, and backward teaching methods. The number of hospital teachers has declined, the number of children in hospital has not. Some teachers are not properly qualified. A NAWCH survey, which was included in the 1976 Report from the Expert Group on Play for Children in Hospital, found that only 60 per cent of children's wards provided any educational facilities at all; only 40 per cent made provision for the under-fives.

Handicapped children and children in long-stay hospitals, though, are considerably worse off than those children who have to spend only a brief period in hospital — as, for example, the work of Maureen Oswin has revealed. In December 1978, a report[2] by a group of HM Inspectors was published on sixteen hospital schools for mentally handicapped children (20 per cent of all such schools). The group found that staffing ratios were improving, more teachers were qualified, and there were improvements in equipment and materials. Every child over five was receiving some kind of education — 'though this is not always adequate in extent nor provided in satisfactory conditions'. Nevertheless, the HMIs documented that a quarter of the teachers had no

[1] The Education (Handicapped Children) Act 1970 transferred responsibility (as from April 1971) for the education of handicapped children from the health to the local education authorities. An LEA was already able — though not legally obliged — under section 56 of the Education Act 1944 to provide for children who could not go to school, for reasons such as having to go into hospital for an operation. A Ministry of Education circular in 1956 recommended that where a hospital school was available, every child in the hospital should be given the opportunity to join in the classes no matter how short a stay was expected.
[2] *The Education of Children in Hospitals for the Mentally Handicapped* (HMI Series: Matters for Discussion, no. 7).

professional teaching qualification; only sixteen out of 208 teachers had completed a specialized training course. The teachers were, in turn, inadequately supported by human and material resources, and the buildings used were mainly well below the standards required. Teachers and nurses rarely adopted 'an agreed and consistent approach to meeting the developmental needs of children'. While most schools officially cease to provide education for children once they reach sixteen, many adolescents stay on because there is nowhere else for them to go. Of the 42 children under five in the sixteen schools surveyed, only eighteen were receiving any kind of education. The Inspectors also concluded that 'the evidence of this survey suggests that the [LEA advisory] services available [to teachers] are uneven, almost invariably uncoordinated, and in some cases profoundly deficient'.

In contrast, one of the more heartening developments since the Platt Report has been the extension of play schemes into hospitals and the acceptance of the importance of play for children in hospital. In 1972, a DHSS-sponsored Expert Group on Play for Children in Hospital was set up to study the staffing, aims and resources for play in hospital. Their report was published in March 1976 along with a DHSS circular *Play for Children in Hospital* (HC(76)5). The report proposed a new profession – the playworker – to be an integral part of the hospital staff. However, the circular rejected this proposal and suggested instead that there should be more involvement by the nursing staff, in collaboration with teachers and voluntary workers. A senior nurse should be designated as having responsibility for play. Official DHSS policy remains that 'hospitals should recognize the need for play and make the best arrangements possible within the limits of existing resources'.

Hospital staff have become more sensitive when having to carry out unpleasant medical procedures on children and they do tend to involve parents more – up to a point. But, in general, current practice continues to fall short of the kind of support needed during what is for most children a traumatic experience.

Children are better catered for in terms of day-to-day

living; for example, having somewhere to keep their personal possessions, being occupied during the day, being able to wear their own clothes or attractive hospital clothes. One backward step though has been with food — the trend towards centralization has made it harder to cater for children's individual needs.

When children come to leave hospital, too many hospital staff still fail to explain to parents about probable behaviour difficulties or other problems of readjustment when the children return home. So widespread is this failing that NAWCH has produced a guide for parents (and for hospital staff, too) called *Has Your Child Been in Hospital?* (1978).

Two recent studies[1] in 1970 and 1974 concluded that the main cause for the slowness in implementing the Platt recommendations was a lack of preparation by hospital staff. There remained 'a fundamental lack of knowledge among nursing staff of the emotional needs of children and of the basic assumptions on which the recommendations were made'. For example, even where unrestricted visiting was allowed, the disapproval of the nursing staff would often deter parents from taking advantage of these arrangements.

Ironically, one of the key problems still seems to be 'the inability of senior nursing staff to adapt to new ways'[2] — precisely the reason given by James Robertson nearly fifteen years ago.

Certainly one of the biggest disappointments has been the poor progress made in ensuring that hospital staff are properly trained in the care and needs of children and given a proper understanding of child development. Lack of finance, insufficient training places or tutors, a low take-up of non-compulsory courses, an unattractive career structure for those wanting to specialize in paediatric nursing have all contributed to the slow development of well-trained staff. To make matters worse, there is now a shortage of sick

[1] *Hospitals, Children and Their Families: a Pilot Study* M. Stacey *et al* (Routledge and Kegan Paul, 1970); *Nurse I Want My Mummy* P. J. Hawthorn (Royal College of Nursing, 1974).

[2] Dr Desmond MacCarthy, formerly consultant paediatrician at Amersham General Hospital and currently honorary paediatrician for the Institute of Child Psychiatry (*Nursing Mirror*, 2 November 1978).

children's nurses. Not all children's wards are supervised by someone specially trained in the care of sick children; less than half of the registered nurses who care for sick children are qualified RSCNs (Registered Sick Children's Nurses) — even though, according to the General Nursing Council, some 600 RSCNs qualify each year.

Fundamental changes have yet to be made in medical and nursing training in general. The Joint Board of Clinical and Nursing Studies promotes some advanced courses in clinical nursing and there are several relating to pediatrics; there are few foundations courses on child development; basic nursing training courses vary in what and how much they cover in child development and the needs of children. In short, there are not enough courses and they are not comprehensive enough.

The lack of expertise in children's needs persists throughout the range of hospital staff, including hospital teachers, social workers and occupational therapists. The delay in ensuring that a children's physician has overall concern for all children in a hospital has frequently been put down to 'hospital politics' — in other words, staff fearing a loss of status by administrative changes, or believing that their proper role should not involve concern for children's needs. While some progress has undeniably been made in ensuring that professionals are made aware of and trained for the other-than-medical needs of sick children, surveys and much professional opinion reveal that a wide gulf remains between what is needed and what is actually happening.

The Consumers' Association Survey 1980

In June 1980, the Consumers' Association published the results of a national survey of *Children in Hospital*[1]. One of the aims of the project was to find out how far the Platt Report's recommendations had been adopted by hospitals.

---

[1] *Children in Hospital* (June 1980, available from the Consumers' Association, 14 Buckingham Street, London WC2N 6DS). An action-guide for parents is also available from the same address.

This, in brief, is what the Association found, based on a preliminary report of the data collected. Fifty-eight hospitals and 300 parents took part in the survey.

In general, there has been a marked change in the attitudes and awareness of hospital staff towards the emotional needs of children in hospital, notably by paediatric staff. However, non-paediatric staff who have not had specific training in the care of children remain considerably less aware of, and less responsive to, children's non-medical needs.

Alternatives to in-patient treatment Children generally stay in hospital for shorter periods and it is widely accepted that some ailments no longer require in-patient care. However, hospitals do not place great emphasis on avoiding admission by, for example, making more use of the out-patients department for treating children or by establishing home-visiting teams. Home treatment has not increased, specifically because of a lack of suitably trained staff and proper facilities. Few hospitals have a separate, permanent out-patients' department for children, although most make some kind of special arrangement for dealing with children (for example, specific days allocated for children only). Nevertheless, the departments tend not to be very welcoming to children. Paediatric nurses are not often on duty in the departments. Parents and children frequently have to put up with long waits and, sometimes, unsympathetic staff.

Hospital organization and design Many children continue to be admitted to adult wards. (Fifteen per cent of the parents interviewed in the survey said their child was in an adult ward.) The Consumers' Association identified three main reasons for this: lack of resources, conflict or poor co-ordination between paediatric and other staff, and administrative anomalies. Children admitted as ENT patients and adolescents are particularly prone to being placed in adult wards.

Most hospitals have at least one children's ward (usually bright and cheerful) with paediatric staff. Few see any need to ensure a child is nursed with other children of the same age group, although many have separate facilities for babies.

Many hospitals do not have special playrooms and fewer still provide the opportunity for outdoor play. Where playrooms are available, they seem adequately stocked with toys and usually have a playleader or voluntary helper in attendance. There are sometimes restrictions on the use of a playroom including denying access to ENT children, closing it at weekends or using nurses to supervise the room thereby limiting the times it can be open. Few hospitals organize special recreational programmes for children.

Hospital staffing All hospitals have access to a consultant paediatrician, although s/he will not always be responsible for all the children in a hospital. Most sisters who supervise children's wards are RSCN. But there is less awareness of the value of this kind of training in other wards, which sometimes have no staff trained in paediatrics. Children still tend to be looked after by a number of nurses, instead of being allocated just one or two. This is generally given a low priority, because of under-staffing and the shortness of many children's stays in hospital.

Preparation for admission Hospitals still need to communicate more with parents and to provide more information about what goes on in hospital and a child's medical treatment. Some hospitals offer pre-admission visits to parents and children, and most parents in the survey received a leaflet giving information about the hospital. Few leaflets are produced specially for children.

Reception Just over half the children whose admission has been planned go straight to the ward; only a quarter of emergency admissions do so. Most emergencies go first to the casualty department. Few hospitals have a separate casualty department for children, only a curtained-off area for treatment or examination. Children are rarely welcomed by the ward sister, mostly by a ward clerk or nurse. Parents usually have a discussion with hospital staff, and are sometimes asked about a child's eating habits, but hardly ever about any private toilet vocabulary. Hospitals no longer put children straight to bed when admitted during the day,

45

and parents are able to stay to settle the child in. Children can bring their own clothes and toys. They all get a locker for their personal possessions. If re-admitted, most children go back to the same ward.

The child as in-patient Most hospitals claim to have provision for parents to stay with their children. But the facilities are often limited: they may only be available in certain wards; be unable to cater for all the parents wishing to stay; be in a different building from the wards; or have poor amenities. Parents can be put off staying by hospital staff, many of whom believe the presence of parents disrupts hospital routine. Most parents do not know that they can stay in the hospital. Often the initiative has to come from the parents themselves.

Policy on visiting varies considerably and can differ not just from one hospital to another, but between wards in the same hospital. 'Open visiting' is defined in various ways — 24-hour visiting, daytime only and so on. Official times are usually relaxed for children, but in turn a policy of open visiting can be altered in practice to suit the convenience of the hospital staff. Whatever the arrangements, parents may be unaware of when they can visit and under what conditions. Few hospitals tell parents of the value of early and frequent visiting; few have real 24-hour unrestricted visiting; most discourage visiting in the evening, say after eight. Parents can usually visit a child on the day of operation, though generally not immediately before or after the operation. Visits from other members of the family, especially brothers and sisters, are often not encouraged or restricted to certain times. When parents do visit, most are able to get all the information they want from hospital staff about how a child is progressing and the medical treatment involved. Few *formal* arrangements exist for children whose parents do not visit them, although they do tend to get much more attention from staff and other parents.

Most hospitals provide some kind of education for children. But teachers usually work independently of a child's school or current curriculum; they have to cope with a wide age-range and are not able to give children much individual attention. Only a minority of hospitals have a schoolroom and equipment can be poor. Staff cooperation is good in paediatric wards but poor in adult wards; some staff tend to see a teacher's job as merely keeping children occupied. ENT children and adolescents are catered for worst of all.

Medical treatment Hospitals are not always careful of children's sense of modesty or personal privacy when carrying out unpleasant procedures. One in four hospitals do not have a separate treatment room and such procedures are often carried out in the wards. All children fear an operation most of all, but hospital staff rarely explain adequately to children about tests and operations.

Discharge On the whole, hospitals liaise well with parents when a child comes to leave. Parents usually talk with the sister or staff nurse and then liaise with a paediatric health visitor. A child is normally discharged at a time to suit the parents. Parents receive adequate information about a child's medical treatment, but hospitals are much less aware of the emotional difficulties that can follow a stay in hospital. The family doctor is rarely told in advance that a child is leaving hospital; most hospitals generally make contact on the day with a detailed report being sent a week or two later.

Training of staff The training of hospital staff in child development and children's diseases is often poorly organized, with less training being given to staff lower down the hospital hierarchy. There is little attempt to introduce non-paediatric staff to paediatric aspects of medicine. Nurses generally have to rely for additional training (beyond the paediatric element in their basic training) on informal tuition by the ward sister or learning on the job. Ancillary staff with no special training as part of their initial qualification are unlikely to receive any further training from the hospital.

Where to find out more

Books

The Welfare of Children in Hospital the Platt Report (HMSO, 1959, reprinted 1975)

Children in Hospital: Studies in Planning (Nuffield Foundation /Oxford University Press, 1963)

Young Children in Hospital James Robertson (Tavistock, second edition, 1970)

The Empty Hours Maureen Oswin (Penguin, 1971)

Play in Hospital Susan Harvey and Ann Hales-Tooke (eds) (Faber, 1972)

Children in Hospital: The Parent's View Ann Hales-Tooke (Priory Press, 1973)

Hospital Schools: A Challenge for Education? (National Union of Teachers, 1977)

Children Living in Long-stay Hospitals Maureen Oswin (Spastics International Medical Publications, 1978)

Children in Hospital (Consumers' Association, 1980)

Organizations

National Association for the Welfare of Children in Hospital (NAWCH), 7 Exton Street, London SE1 8VE (01-261 1738). Provides an information and counselling service for parents and publishes a range of useful booklets including Has Your Child Been in Hospital?, The Under Fives in Hospital and What is a Children's Ward.

Circulars

The key DHSS circulars for the welfare of children in hospital are:

HM(66)18 Visiting of Children in Hospital

HM(71)22 and HC(77)30 Hospital Facilities for Children

HM(72)2 and HC(78)28 Children in Hospital: Maintenance of Family Links

DS(218)72 Meals and Accommodation for the Parents of Children in Hospital

HC(76)5 Play for Children in Hospital

4 The Youth Service in England and Wales: The Albemarle Report (1960)

Why Albemarle was set up

The Albemarle Committee was appointed in November 1958. At the time British society was undergoing rapid and radical changes. These changes were having a direct effect on those organizations which provided leisure and recreational opportunities for young people — in other words, the Youth Service. This Youth Service was a combination of recreational facilities and funding by central and local Government and by a range of voluntary bodies.

The post-war baby boom ('the bulge') was reaching the stage of adolescence. For every five young people between the ages of fifteen and twenty in 1958, there would be six by 1964. Young people were maturing faster than before; they were taller and heavier; they were meeting physical and emotional demands earlier. The ending of National Service (conscription into one of the armed services for a period of two years for men aged between eighteen and twenty) meant more young people looking for alternative sources of challenge and entertainment. The role of women was changing with earlier marriage, a shorter period of childrearing, and a growth in the desire, need and opportunity for full-time employment.

Increasing affluence meant that adolescents generally had more money to spend. This affluence though was unevenly distributed. For example, many families still had to put up with bad housing. Even some families who had been rehoused on new estates faced problems because of a lack of amenities and isolation from an established network of relatives and friends. For many 'affluence' meant social

49

and physical upheaval. There was a jump in the rate of juvenile delinquency. With more money being spent by the fifteen- to twenty-year-olds, commercial interests were skilfully exploiting the role and image of the 'teenager'.

Developments in education following the gradual implementation of the Education Act 1944 were enabling more children to stay on at school after the minimum leaving age of fifteen. But they were still a minority of the age group. A split was developing among young people. There were those who went out to work and had money to spend, and those who stayed in full-time education with little money of their own. As the Albemarle Committee pointed out, there was 'a striking contrast between what is provided for those young people — the minority — who continue their formal education, full-time or part-time, and what is available for the remainder who have only an impoverished Youth Service to turn to'.

The Youth Service clearly had to respond to those fundamental social changes and try to cater for the different life-styles and life-chances which young people possessed. But the Youth Service was in 'a state of acute depression'. (There were a few notable exceptions; for example, Essex, Derbyshire and Glamorgan had invested heavily in their Youth Service, though the patterns they established were often inflexible.) The Albemarle Committee found when they started their work that: '. . . those who work in the Service feel themselves to be neglected and held in small regard, both in educational circles and by public opinion generally'.[1]

Since 1939, overall responsibility for the Youth Service had rested with the Ministry of Education (in 1964, renamed the Department of Education and Science). The Education Act 1944 had put a clear duty on local education authorities to provide adequate leisure and cultural opportunities for young people. The extent and type of provision made available were mainly matters for the LEAs to decide in the light of local needs, but working closely with voluntary organizations 'in full partnership in a common enterprise'. However, voluntary organizations frequently tended to make their

[1] From the introduction to the Albemarle Report.

own independent contribution as they saw fit.

Sufficient central Government funds had never been made available to encourage LEAs to carry out these duties. A combination of chronic financial restrictions and a lack of ministerial policy towards the Youth Service made sure that provision was grossly inadequate for and unappealing to young people.

Government grant-aid was patchy, cumbersome and inconsistent. The lack of leadership at national level was reflected locally. An unattractive career structure for youth leaders made recruitment very difficult. Those already working in the profession were demoralized. There was little attempt at innovation or development in the services provided. Most youth organizations had not kept pace with the social developments going on around them.

In 1957/8 the total direct expenditure on the Youth Service by central and local Government amounted to just over £2¾ million. This meant that for every pound spent on education, only one penny went to the Youth Service. Funds for the Youth Service specifically from central Government came to a mere 0.1 per cent of all Government expenditure on education.

A new framework — administrative, financial and philosophical — was needed for the Youth Service. In 1958, the Youth Advisory Council (which had been set up in 1939 to advise the Education Minister when he took over responsibility for the Youth Service) was disbanded. In its place, the Education Minister, Geoffrey Lloyd, appointed a Committee of Enquiry under the Countess of Albemarle.

What Albemarle was asked to do

Review the contribution which the Youth Service of England and Wales can make in assisting young people to play their part in the life of the community, in the light of changing social and industrial conditions and of current trends in other branches of the education service; and to advise according to what priorities best value can be obtained for the money spent.

What Albemarle recommended and why

The Albemarle Committee divided its recommendations into four key areas: the Youth Service tomorrow (what it should be providing and how it should be organized); activities and facilities; staffing and training; and finance.

The Youth Service tomorrow

When the Youth Service was established, the assumption was that it would cater principally for those who had left school and its range was set for young people between fourteen and twenty. When, in 1947, the school-leaving age was raised to fifteen, the official Youth Service age range was duly amended to fifteen to twenty. However, the Service had never adhered strictly to these criteria, catering for children still at school as well as for those who had left, and as much for children below the age range. The Committee therefore recommended that the Service should officially be available for all young people aged between fourteen and twenty inclusive.

The Committee concluded that the Service was facing two emergencies: having to cater for more young people because of the 'bulge' and the ending of National Service; and the disquiet generated by the apparent estrangement from society of some sections of young people. These could only be dealt with by a rapid growth in the Service; improvements in the training, quality and conditions of service of youth leaders and workers; and by new approaches towards the young. A strong sense of urgency was also required at the top to produce the appropriate machinery for these developments – and to encourage a new Government circular from the Ministry of Education.

A ten-year development programme should be initiated, divided into two stages of five years each. Stage one would deal with the need to catch up with the current situation of young people; stage two would securely establish a permanent structure.

A Youth Service Development Council (YSDC) should be

set up for the duration of this programme to act as an advisory committee monitoring new policies, suggesting changes and promoting plans. It should be composed of men and women with special qualities and experience to offer, but not appointed on a representative basis. It should meet frequently, and be adequately staffed. It should work in close collaboration with the Ministry and HM Inspectorate, and with the Standing Conference of National Voluntary Youth Organizations (SCNVYO). The current situation called for organization which created more concern for enquiry, the sharing of ideas and promotion of new activities than for administration. Government decisions about the Youth Service should be taken at a high level and be implemented quickly.

The function of local education authorities should be to determine a policy for their areas in consultation with voluntary bodies; to establish machinery for cooperation and the coordination of development, servicing and training; to encourage and give financial aid to voluntary effort through existing voluntary organizations and in other ways; and to ensure that adequate and varied facilities were provided. Every LEA should establish a subcommittee of its education committee to be responsible for the development of the Youth Service in its area. This should have executive and spending powers. LEAs' further education schemes should be brought up to date. Particular attention should be given to the special needs of new housing areas, new towns and 'tough' areas.

The principle of voluntary help should be encouraged at every level of Youth Service activity, with a national campaign for more voluntary helpers. Clubs should be associated more with the life of the neighbourhoods through the creation of supporters' clubs.

Young people should be given more responsibility for originating and organizing their own activities, becoming partners in the running and development of their groups and clubs.

Local authorities and voluntary groups should consider effective approaches to young people 'who find it difficult to come to terms with society' and who become known as 'the unattached'.

Activities and facilities

There should be opportunities in the Youth Service for association (that meant being part of a group which offered commitment, counselling and self-determination), training and challenge.

The development envisaged would need a generous and imaginative building programme by both central and local government. There should be better buildings, furniture, equipment, lighting and decoration. Residential accommodation should be expanded and more facilities provided for indoor and outdoor physical recreation.

LEAs should cater for Youth Service provision in any plans for new secondary schools and for renovations due to secondary reorganization. They should encourage young people to take up some kind of physical recreation, by helping with finance, equipment and coaching, and by recognizing the contribution to be made by sports clubs and specialist groups.

Staffing and training

The Youth Service needed more and better-trained leaders, instructors and helpers. They should be either full-time or part-time, salaried or voluntary. The most urgent need was for full-time professional youth leaders, who were well-trained and well-paid and had a proper life-long career structure.

Long-term training schemes for ful-time youth leaders should be established, with easy transfer from youth leadership to other related professions. These schemes should cater for the three main sources of youth leaders: teachers, social workers and mature people with a natural gift for leadership. Four schemes were suggested: youth leadership as an option in three-year teacher-training courses; three-and four-year courses for social workers; three-month 'transfer' courses for those who already had suitable professional qualifications; and one- and two-year courses for mature

THE YOUTH SERVICE IN ENGLAND AND WALES

students. More grants should be made available by the Government for mature people and social workers wishing to attend these courses. National voluntary organizations wishing to have their own training schemes recognized as providing a professional qualification should submit the schemes for approval by the Minister, who would obtain the advice of the Youth Service Development Council.

The Government should set up a negotiating committee for salaries and conditions of service for youth leaders.

The number of full-time youth leaders needed to be increased quickly to cater for the larger number of young people. The number of leaders had to go up from 700 to 1,300 by 1966. An emergency training college should therefore be opened to offer one-year courses in youth leadership. There should be more part-time paid leaders in areas of genuine need. LEAs and voluntary organizations should cooperate closely to provide training schemes for part-time leaders, both paid and voluntary. After 1966, LEAs should be able to appoint more teachers specifically to spend half their time in school and half in club leadership.

All full-time leaders should eventually be properly qualified — experience alone would not be enough. LEAs without Youth Service Officers should reconsider whether they needed them after all.

Finance

The money for the Youth Service was provided from public funds, from voluntary sources, and from contributions paid by young people as members of youth groups. Public funds were administered centrally in two ways: through direct grants under the Social and Physical Training Grants Regulations 1939, which remained in force under section 121 of the Education Act 1944; and through direct grants under the Physical Training and Recreation Act 1937. Public funds were also administered locally.

Three types of grant were available under the 1939 Regulations: annual grants to national voluntary youth organizations

55

for organization and administration costs; annual grants for training youth leaders; grants to local voluntary bodies to cover the capital cost of premises and equipment for youth clubs and centres.

The Committee recommended that two types of grant should be payable under the 1939 Regulations: one for headquarters administration and training expenses (up to 75 per cent of the whole cost of provision); the other for experimental and pioneering work with fourteen- to twenty-year-olds. The capital grants currently available should after the first five years of the proposed development programme be payable by LEAs, with any such aid being matched from central Government funds. The limits on the size of these grants should be raised or abolished altogether. LEA financial support should be increased and be more consistent towards those voluntary bodies that merit it.

The denominational allegiances of organizations should not be a factor in the awarding of grant-aid; the sole criterion should be the value of the social and educational work being done.

Grants should also be made available for coaching schemes by the governing bodies in sport, under the 1937 Act. The 1937 Act was primarily concerned with adults, but LEAs should be encouraged to use the powers that did exist under that Act to provide grants and loans for the benefit of young people.

LEAs should ensure their Youth Service departments were adequately provided with administrative and clerical staff so as to keep trained organizers in the field. Similarly, voluntary youth organizations should relieve skilled leaders of the burden of raising funds, leaving them to concentrate on providing practical help to young people. The task of fund-raising should be given to management committees and supporters' councils.

Many of the charges for services provided by voluntary youth groups were unrealistically low and should be reviewed. However, a sliding scale of charges should be adopted so that no-one was excluded because of an inability to pay the full charge.

Priorities

The Committee based their recommendations on two cardinal assumptions: that the Government intended to make the Youth Service adequate to the needs of young people; and that the development of that Service required action on a broad front since so much of the work was interdependent. There were however three priorities: setting up the arrangements for both the proposed emergency and the long-term training programmes for youth leaders; beginning work on materially improving the Youth Service with better premises and facilities; and establishing the Youth Service Development Council.

What happened to Albemarle

The Government accepted the Albemarle Committee's main recommendations on the day the Report was published in February 1960. A Youth Service Development Council was subsequently set up to advise the Education Minister on the implementation of the ten-year development programme. A Youth Service building programme was initiated which was allocated some £3 million for 1960-2 and £4 million for 1962-3. This included funds for both new youth clubs and youth wings attached to secondary schools. Two relevant DES building bulletins (nos. 20 and 22) were published; the second was devoted entirely to Witheywood Youth Centre in Bristol. The DES made a concerted effort to influence Youth Service building, especially to ensure that commercial-style social amenities were given a central place in the programme. In all, building work costing some £28 million was authorized in the eight years after the Albemarle Report — the equivalent figure for the seven years before was only £½ million. Similarly, in the years following the Report, the value of central Government grants rose from just under £300,000 to £1.9 million; local authority spending went up from £2.6 million to £10 million.

A National College for the Training of Youth Leaders was opened in Leicester to provide the 600 extra full-time youth leaders by 1966. In 1960 there were 700 full-timers; six years later, the number had more than doubled to 1,465. A Government committee dealt with the training needs of part-time leaders. Their report (*The Training of Part-time Leaders and Assistants*, the Bessey Report, HMSO, 1962) recommended a 'common core' element to the training needs of all part-time and voluntary leaders with joint co-ordination between voluntary and statutory bodies in the provision of training. A second Bessey Report in 1965 made further proposals on the training of part-time leaders. A negotiating committee for the salaries and conditions of service of youth leaders was established. More experimental projects were set up, though not always closely monitored.

The Albemarle Report certainly fared better than many of the other official Reports of the sixties. The recommendations it contained about the structure and staffing of the Youth Service were largely taken up before the beginning of the public expenditure cuts of the late sixties and through the seventies. The cuts did eventually affect the level of provision — grants, building programmes, the number of leaders. But the basic 'revitalized' structure remained, as did the philosophical benchmarks created by the Albemarle approach to the Youth Service. The Service had been made more professional; had been provided with more purpose-built and better premises; had been given the opportunity to try new ways of working with young people. Statutory and voluntary cooperation had been confirmed and strengthened. The voluntary organizations underwent a reappraisal of their role and, in some cases, their aims too — though little radical change occurred. The Albemarle Report was a watershed for the Youth Service.

But at the end of the 1960s, the Youth Service was under increasing criticism again — on direction and policy. The further rapid social developments of the sixties meant that much of the Youth Service continued to lag behind in providing for the needs of many young people. The adoption of Albemarle's practical recommendations had meant that a Youth Service continued to exist through the 1960s, but how far it was more able to cater for the needs of young people was still in doubt. Had Government's approach to young people changed fundamentally or not? How relevant was the 'Albemarle' approach to the young people themselves?

Subsequent criticism of the Albemarle Report centred on the fact that it had emphasized the traditional view of service to youth, going along with the more established form of voluntary organization, and with the idea that young people needed to be in 'clubs'. In short, it was claimed that Albemarle encouraged a paternalistic approach to young people. More to the point perhaps, to some observers it seemed that more money was being spent on fewer members. For the social and cultural developments through the sixties — the way young people lived, thought and behaved — were making the traditional form of youth service, however 'flexible', even more unattractive.

One major survey of who used the Youth Service and similar provision found that 65 per cent of fourteen- to twenty-year-olds went to a club, society, team or similar grouping; that the prevalence of 'attachments' had not changed markedly since the 1940s; that only 26 per cent attended youth clubs; that, more significantly, the least likely to use clubs were those who intended to leave or had already left school at the minimum age, girls, older teenagers and those at work and working-class youngsters.[1]

Little of the Youth Service was able to provide for or attract young people after they reached the age of sixteen — there was a massive fall-off in membership after that age. The bulk of the older members of youth groups were between fourteen and sixteen, still at school, and relatively well able to cope with life. The unattached remained just that — unattached.

In October 1969, the Youth Service Development Council produced a report *Youth and Community Work in the 70s*[2] calling (once again) for a 'new and imaginative approach' to youth work. The report criticized the 'segregation' of the

[1] *The Youth Service and Similar Provision for Young People* Margaret Bone (OPCS/HMSO, 1972).
[2] The Milson-Fairbairn Report (HMSO, 1969).

Youth Service into clubs and from the adult community; highlighted the trend for more young people to be involved in community and environmental issues; downgraded the voluntary element; recommended more mixed organizations as opposed to single-sex ones; repeated the observation that only a small part of the total provision for young people was actually handled by the statutory Youth Service; recommended that a Youth and Community Service be set up. The report also raised other issues: the need for integrating ethnic minorities; for developing closer contact with social services to help young people at risk. (The Children and Young Person's Act 1969 had taken up the concept of intermediate treatment for young people 'in trouble' or 'at risk', putting an emphasis on youth work and youth club membership.) Finally, it saw the Youth Service's key role as giving young people education and experience for membership of 'the active society' — 'we are concerned to help young people to create their place in a changing soceity and it is their critical involvement in their community which is the goal'. It was a different philosophy from the one expressed in the Albemarle Report of 'association, training and challenge'.

This report created a good deal of controversy — and not just for the ideas expressed. In parts, it was itself confused about quite what it meant. Consequently, the report sparked off a variety of policy responses. Many LEAs changed the name of their Youth Service to the Youth and Community Service. But intentions frequently differed as to what was to be done by such a Service. Some LEAs integrated the Youth Service and adult education services; some allowed or required their Youth Service staff to sponsor adult community activities, playgroups, young mothers' clubs; while others encouraged youth workers to work more with young people out in the community — on the streets, in pubs, and so on.

An official Government response to the report was delayed — partly by the controversy aroused, and then by the June 1970 General Election. Denis Howell, the Minister for Youth in the 1966-70 Labour Government, had been closely identified with the report and favoured its approach to services for youth. The incoming 1970-4 Conservative Government was less sympathetic. On 29 March 1971, the Education Secretary,

Margaret Thatcher, said in a parliamentary statement: 'The Government do not think it would be right to change the nature of the Service in England and Wales radically by setting up a Youth and Community Service with not very clearly defined responsibilities.' At the same time, Mrs Thatcher announced the winding up of the Youth Service Development Council following the completion of Albemarle's ten-year development programme and the transfer of a substantial part of the fundings for the Youth Service building programme to the urban programme.

The Youth Service Development Council had, in its time, produced a number of reports — on immigrants and the Youth Service (the Hunt Report, 1967), which had little impact and dated fast; on community services by young people (1965) and on the training of part-time youth leaders. A Youth Service Information Centre, established in 1964, was reconstituted as the National Youth Bureau in November 1973, to act as a resource centre for those working with young people.

In 1972, the Government had commissioned a study from the research institute Political and Economic Planning (PEP)[1] to try to find a better way of funding youth organizations from central Government sources,[2] given the newly stated official aims of shifting the balance of Youth Service efforts towards helping areas of high social need and young people with economic, social, physical or mental handicaps. The eventual report (*National Voluntary Youth Organizations*, PEP, February 1975) declared that no consistent or fair way of distributing grants could be found under the existing system; that Government had to arrive at a clear youth policy and decide which groups of young people it wished to help and how it wanted to do so; and suggested an independent grants committee should be formed of representatives from the national voluntary youth organizations and the Department of Education and Science, on a

---

[1] Now renamed the Policy Studies Institute.
[2] Then operating through the Social and Physical Training Grant Regulations 1939, which were brought into the subsequent Further Education Regulations 1969. See also DES circular 13/71.

50-50 basis. In fact, no major changes have been made in the way central Government grant-aid is administered.

Over this time then, neither Government had come up with a coherent, long-term policy for developing and funding the Youth Service. In terms of the 'clientele', the Service was finding it just as difficult to break out of the narrow age range it was officially obliged to cater for — or the narrow range of needs it provided for. Moreover, different Government departments continued to be responsible for the range of issues concerning young people — education, the transition from school to work, careers and employment, sport, delinquency, children at risk, and so on. These departments operated separately with their own aims and policies. Liaison between them was slight; policy decisions were rarely if ever coordinated[1]. Further, Government went along with the conventional view of the Service which was still unable to cope with the very people Government claimed should be especially catered for — the unattached, the youngster in 'high social need'. Grants for experimental work were small, and hard to get.

Through the seventies, there was increasing uncertainty about just what role the Youth Service should or could play. In February 1975, the DES published a discussion paper *Provision for Youth* which suggested a dual role for the Service: a main educational role and a secondary role based on the social and community needs of young people. It saw the Service as providing a wide range of facilities (particularly for disadvantaged young people), planned in consultation with young people themselves which would offer them experience, opportunity and support to assist their development to full and responsible adulthood. It saw the youth worker as one of a multi-disciplinary team across the social and educational services catering for these needs, and referred to the consequent need for opportuni-

[1] In 1968, the Seebohm Committee on local government reorganization had said: 'There has been no completely comprehensive enquiry covering all aspects of their needs and such enquiry is overdue. We recommend that it should be undertaken urgently'. It has not. At central government level, at least five Departments continue to have major responsibilities for young people — the DES, DHSS, Home Office, Department of Employment and the Department of the Environment.

ties for appropriate training. The paper also reaffirmed the commitment to the existing statutory/voluntary balance and hoped that the Service would not adhere strictly to the official fourteen to twenty age range definition. The paper put its argument this way:

> There is a wide, but not comprehensive, range of services now available for the welfare of the community and for youth within the community, and many of these services are the ultimate responsibility of other government departments. The education service cannot, in terms either of its statutory responsibilities or of its available resources, preside over a comprehensive service meeting the special needs of disadvantaged young people in addition to providing the facilities for recreation and social education which are its main concern but neither can it disclaim all responsibility for the disadvantaged.

It described the dual role thus:

> . . . to develop a wide range of activities for leisure-time recreation and social education to meet the changing needs of those able to enjoy and to benefit from the facilities offered. Secondly, it would offer its particular skills and resources, along with those offered by other social services, to a cooperative and coordinated approach to the problems of the disadvantaged whether individual or general.

In 1977, the Youth Service Forum (set up by the DES in 1976 to act as a 'voice' for young people themselves) endorsed the DES's concept of the dual role.

Training for the Youth Service has now diversified into colleges of education and polytechnics following the closure in 1970 of the emergency National College for the Training of Youth Leaders which had been set up after the Albemarle Report. In September 1978, a review[1] of 'the policy, structures and provisions for the training and support' of part-time and voluntary workers was published by the Consultative Group on Youth and Community Work Training, which had been established in 1972 by the DES. In-service training for full-time youth workers was the subject of the DES circular

---

[1] *Realities of Training* (National Youth Bureau, 1978).

13/78 (September 1978) following a study by the In-service Training and Education Panel (INSTEP)[1] which recommended ways of setting up an established and comprehensive system of in-service training.

In October 1979, a national survey[2] conducted by the National Youth Bureau revealed that in the five years between 1975/6 and 1979/80 local authority spending on the Youth Service had declined by eight per cent — and that this decline was accelerating.

In November 1979, a private member's bill (the Youth and Community bill) had its second reading in the Commons and went into the Committee stage for more detailed discussion. If enacted, the bill would oblige local authorities to 'prepare a scheme for providing or making provision for a comprehensive range of services for young people in their area' (that is, provide a youth service), to set up joint committees with local voluntary services to coordinate the service, establish youth councils, and to make housing available to homeless young people. This would, in effect, make the discretionary or 'permissive' sections (41 and 53) of the 1944 Education Act obligatory.

By the end of 1979, the new Conservative Government had still to produce a detailed policy for the Youth Service. One of its first acts had been to abolish the Youth Service Forum, regarding it as too elaborate a body for discovering the views of young people. Instead, the Government intends to rely on 'frequent meetings' with individuals and to operate more through the National Youth Bureau to obtain opinion and ideas.

The Youth Service remains a disparate grouping of statutory and voluntary provision which has so far been unable to find definitive answers to mahy of those problems posed by the Albemarle Report. While a consensus on aims or needs has never been fully reached through the 1970s, new prob-

[1] INSTEP was set up in 1976 through the Consultative Group on Youth and Community Work Training (itself established to be responsible for in-service education and training of youth officers and youth and community workers). In 1977, there were 3,218 full-time youth and community workers.

[2] *Education Spending and the Youth Service: The Last Five Years* (NYB, 1979).

lems are emerging for the 1980s — 'adolescent unemployment, inequalities centring on race and sex; alienation from conventional forms of schooling, and political powerlessness'.[1]

Where to find out more

Books

The Youth Service in England and Wales The Albemarle Report (HMSO, 1960)
Youth and Community Work in the 1970s Fred Milson (Routledge and Kegan Paul, 1970)
Britain's Sixteen-Year-Olds Ken Fogelman (National Children's Bureau, 1976)
Adolescence and Community John Eggleston (Edward Arnold, 1976)
The Youth Service: Past and Present (NYB, 1978)

Organizations

National Council for Voluntary Youth Services, 26 Bedford Square, London WC1B 3HU (01-636 4066) provides services and acts as a voice for voluntary youth organisations and local youth services (formerly SCNVYO).
National Youth Bureau (NYB), 17-23 Albion Street, Leicester LE1 6GD (0533 554775) produces many pamphlets, reports and magazines on youth work, as well as annotated booklists.

Circulars

Key DES circulars on the Youth Service include:
10/63 The Training of Part-time Youth Leaders and Assistants
8/67 Immigrants and the Youth Service
3/70 Basic Training of Youth Workers and Community Centre Projects
13/78 In-service Training in the Youth and Community Service
18/78 Juveniles: Cooperation between the Police and Other Agencies

[1] *Policies for Youth into the Eighties* Bernard Davies (*Rapport*, September 1978).

5   Half Our Future: The Newsom Report (1963)

Why Newsom was set up

The Crowther Report had concentrated on the education of children and young people after the age of compulsory schooling. Its emphasis had been on the more able — those in grammar schools who went into the sixth form, those in secondary modern schools thought capable of taking public examinations, those who had left school but wanted to pursue their education or training in some other way.

Official consideration then turned to those children of average or less than average ability (the majority) and to the education they were receiving, largely in secondary modern schools. In March 1961, the Central Advisory Council for Education (England) was asked to look at these children's needs. The new Committee of Enquiry was chaired by John Newsom. The concerns that had encouraged the setting up of the Crowther Committee were also the motivating forces behind the Newsom Committee — the needs of the nation's economy and the personal needs of the children.

What Newsom was asked to do

Consider the education between the ages of thirteen and sixteen of pupils of average or less than average ability who are or will be following full-time courses either at schools or in establishments of further education. The term education shall be understood to include extra-curricular activities.

What Newsom recommended and why

The Committee considered that their most important recommendation was 'implicit in the whole of our report': that young people of average or less than average ability should receive a greater share of the nation's educational resources.

Since the second world war, there had been a great improvement in the kind of education children received and the buildings they were educated in. A massive building programme between 1954 and 1961 (due to continue until 1965) had created over 1,800 new secondary schools in England and Wales[1] — most of them secondary modern schools. There was more variety in the curriculum available to children. Educational equipment and materials had improved. There were more out-of-school activities. Essentially, the record of secondary education since 1944 had been one of progress in the face of formidable obstacles.

Nevertheless, many average and below-average pupils still suffered considerable disadvantages in the education they received — overcrowded and inadequate school buildings, playing fields a good distance from the school, frequent changes of teaching staff. They would be set less homework, their curriculum would be more traditional. Moreover, the contrasts in educational provision were growing sharper.

Some 20 per cent of secondary modern schools were in problem areas; 7 per cent were in slum areas and a further 13 per cent suffered from the same kind of disadvantages. Some 79 per cent of the schools in slums had seriously inadequate buildings; overall 40 per cent of secondary modern schools suffered from inadequate buildings.[2]

The Committee's more specific recommendations were divided into four main areas of concern: the pupils; the curriculum; the buildings; and the teachers.

The pupils

There was little doubt that there were reserves of ability

[1] In 1962, there were 3,688 secondary modern schools in England.
[2] From a survey conducted by the Newsom Committee.

among the nation's children which could be tapped, if the nation willed the means. One of the means was a longer school life. Since 1958, the percentage of pupils voluntarily remaining at secondary modern school beyond fifteen had doubled. Many of those who left at fifteen would also have benefited from staying on. Both for children's personal development and in the national economic interest, the school-leaving age should be raised.

An immediate announcement should be made that the school-leaving age would be raised to sixteen for all pupils entering secondary school from September 1965 onwards. Full-time education to sixteen should be school-based although the final year could be spent in part off the school premises, say in a college of further education.

The Ministry of Education[1] should establish a programme of research into teaching techniques designed particularly to help pupils whose abilities were artificially depressed by environmental and linguistic handicaps. An inter-departmental Government working party should also be set up to deal with the general social and educational problems in slum areas. Particular attention should be paid to the need for a stable teaching staff, the size of schools, and to the design and function of school buildings in slum areas as part of the general community provision.

The curriculum

Pupils should be helped and stimulated to enlarge their understanding and practise their skills, often using direct experience as a starting point for discussion. More demands should be made on them, both in the nature of work required and the amount of it. There was a need to stimulate intellectual and imaginative effort, and to extend the pupils' range of ideas so as to promote a fuller literacy. All children should be given homework.

[1] The Ministry of Education was renamed the Department of Education and Science in 1964.

Basic skills in reading, writing and calculation should be reinforced throughout the curriculum. But the value of the education offered should also take account of a pupil's own skills, qualities and personal development. Fourth- and fifth-year pupils should be offered a choice in what they learnt which related partly to occupational interests. Schools should be adequately equipped to offer this sort of choice — as well as providing imaginative experience through the arts and helping pupils' personal and social development. The personal advisory and welfare services available for school leavers should be improved.

Pupils should not be narrowly streamed. Groupings should be based on subjects. The status of older pupils should be enhanced, particularly through the way the school was organized and in the design of the buildings these pupils used. School hours for fourteen- to sixteen-year-olds should be extended, with more time given to both mainstream and extra-curricular activities. The implications for the staffing of schools should be examined as should the demands likely to be made by extending the use of school premises. There should be more experiments in joint appointments of the teacher/youth-leader type.

The officially-agreed syllabuses for religious instruction should be made more relevant to the problems and interests of older pupils. They should also be given positive guidance on sexual behaviour, including biological, moral, social and personal aspects. The school act of worship was valuable as a potent force in pupils' spiritual experience.

Corporal punishment for the older pupil was likely to delay rather than promote the growth of self-discipline. It was humiliating for pupils and staff alike, and was particularly deplorable when applied to adolescent girls. Schools should get to know their pupils and should devise a system for supervising their personal welfare. Home/school links should be encouraged and improved with staff having special responsibility for liaising with and visiting pupils' homes.

A school's programme in the pupils' final year should be outgoing, with the emphasis on providing an initiation into the adult world of work and leisure. Contacts with other educational sectors, such as further and adult education, the Youth Service and the Youth Employment Service (later to become the Careers Service) should all be strengthened. Pupil involvement in community service projects should be encouraged. Work-experience courses should be set up and carefully monitored. Many pupils would benefit from going on short residential courses. A joint Ministry/LEA survey should be undertaken to find out the availability of such courses and the cost of expanding such provision.

Schools should resist pressures to extend public examination to those pupils for whom they are inappropriate. A large part of the curriculum should be unexamined and public examinations including the new Certificate of Secondary Education, should not be allowed to shape the whole education offered by the schools. Pupils should not be entered for an external examination before their fifth year of secondary schooling. All sixteen-year-old school leavers should receive an internal leaving certificate, combining assessment and a general school record. The format of the certificate could be related to local needs and agreed between schools, employers and further education staff. There was an urgent need to keep parents, employers and the general public well informed on the nature of new examination schemes.

The building

Schemes to make good the deficiencies in school buildings and to replace inadequate schools — particularly in slum areas — should be accelerated. Some deficiencies were due to overcrowding; others were caused by the buildings being wholly unsuitable and inadequate. Improvements in provision for practical subjects, science and libraries should be a priority. Workshop and technical facilities should also be upgraded. Modern audio-visual aids should be available in all secondary schools. Experimental building programmes should be encouraged so that different ways of organizing a school and of teaching the children could be tried out. The design and equipping of school building should allow for extended use, including use by other educational and social services — such as youth work and adult education.

The teachers

A substantial proportion of secondary school teachers should receive what was known as 'concurrent' training, where academic studies and professional training were taught together over the three-year training period. Teachers should be trained to teach in one main subject, plus one or two other subjects. They should have a choice of subjects which enabled them to cut across the conventional divisions of 'practical' and 'academic' subjects. Graduates should be professionally trained to teach, and there should be an emergency interim training programme for graduates and other teachers who had acquired a qualified teaching status without training. Training for the demands of the raising of the school-leaving age should begin immediately. All teachers should have training in sociological and environmental studies, with special reference to the problems of pupils in culturally-deprived areas.

The system of graded posts should be made more flexible to include salary and promotion incentives for work with average and below-average pupils. Particular attention should be paid to devising incentives for teachers to serve and stay in slum areas. Schools should have more non-teaching ancillary help.

What happened to Newsom

The Newsom Report, published in October 1963, highlighted the considerable disadvantages suffered by many of the children who had to go to secondary modern schools — particularly those of average ability. Their needs, both academic and social, were rarely being adequately provided for. While 'Newsom children' made up half of all pupils in secondary schools, they came nowhere near receiving half the country's educational resources.

For example, 40 per cent of secondary modern schools had seriously inadequate buildings. For schools based in slum areas, this figure jumped to 79 per cent. There was a rapid turnover of teachers — half the male teachers left a school before three years.

71

The Newsom Committee recommended more money, a change of attitude by policy-makers and the general public, and a reorganized curriculum. Like the Crowther Committee, they did not discuss in any detail the concept of the selective system which put so many children into these disadvantaged schools, thereby often labelling them (or leading them to label themselves) as failures.

The Newsom Report had as much luck as the Crowther Report in persuading Government to raise the school-leaving age as a matter of urgency. It was not carried out until September 1972, even though the 1958-64 Conservative Government (once again) accepted the principle and announced in January 1964 that it would raise the leaving-age from September 1970. (The Committee had recommended 1969 as the best year, in terms of pupil numbers.) However, in January 1968 the proposal was delayed a further two years by the 1964-70 Labour Government (DES circular 6/68) following the 1967 economic crisis and devaluation of the pound. Finally, the detailed arrangements were set out in August 1971 in DES circular 8/71.

(There are long gaps in the history of extending compulsory schooling: the minimum leaving-age was set at ten in 1880, raised to eleven in 1893 and to twelve six years later. In 1923, it went up to fourteen, then to fifteen in 1947. Twenty-five years later the minimum leaving-age became sixteen.)

The White Paper *Secondary Education for All* (Cmnd 604, December 1958) had announced a five-year building programme of £300 million from 1960 to meet basic needs; improve facilities for science, technical and practical subjects in secondary schools; and phase out all-age schools. However, many of the schools housed in substandard buildings had to wait for the special building programme associated with the plan to raise the leaving-age (which became known as ROSLA or RSLA) and for local schemes for comprehensive reorganization. In 1969, a three-year programme worth £125 million was announced for 1970-3 specifically for ROSLA. Many LEAs linked their ROSLA plans with comprehensive reorganization schemes.[1] Both these developments had been

[1] The DES circulars 10/65 and 10/66 put forward the 1964-70 Labour Government's plans for ending selective education. But they pointed out that, at the time, most of the schemes for reorganization would have to be carried out 'within the constraints of existing stock' (i.e. buildings).

set back by the 1968 public expenditure cuts. (The elements
of the education budget that were, and still are, consistently
cut first when economies had to be made were the maintenance and replacement of buildings, in-service training for
teachers and spending on school and library books.)

The 1970-4 Conservative Government subsequently
approved the ROSLA building programme. But in 1972
the Education Secretary Margaret Thatcher announced a
significant switch in priorities, and resources, to the expansion
of nursery education and improvements in primary-school
accommodation (firstly to replace many of the schools built
before 1903, but secondly — and more 'politically' — to move
resources away from comprehensive reorganization schemes).
This tended to slow down developments in those schools
attended by the 'Newsom' pupils.

Both DES and LEAs concluded that adequate preparations
had been made for ROSLA. The DES reported 'a general
picture of considerable activity and of soundly-based preparations'.[1] However, a 1972 national study by the National
Union of Teachers found that only 17 per cent of LEAs
had set out positive proposals for reviewing the school
curriculum to satisfy the needs of ROSLA children and
none had plans for initiating or expanding work-experience
schemes for schools. An additional problem in raising the
school-leaving age was that the birth rate, unexpectedly,
continued to rise. Despite the expansion of teacher training
during the sixties, the teacher shortage was not ended as
quickly as was hoped. Raising the leaving-age to sixteen
would, it was thought, merely make matters worse.

The principle of ROSLA itself came in for some criticism, even from within the teaching profession itself. Many
people felt that the preparations for the transition to the
higher leaving-age *were* inadequate, although the education
world was better prepared for this rise than the earlier one
to fifteen. One fear was that many children kept at school
against their will would become a disruptive element in
the school, increasing vandalism, violence and truancy. To
some extent, these fears have been justified. A DES survey

[1] DES Reports on Education, no. 73, *Progress Report on RSLA* (March 1972).

73

in 1975 found that on one particular day out of 647,000 fifteen-year-olds absent from school a third were 'unjustified absentees'. A later survey[1] in 1977 estimated that 800,000 pupils were absent from school without good cause. The cost in terms of wasted resources has been estimated at £200 million a year — 2½ per cent of what was spent annually on education. In 1977, it was reckoned that vandalism and arson in British schools cost over £15 million a year.[2] Teachers' unions have produced claims and some evidence that violence in schools has also markedly increased, although neither the DES nor LEAs keep official statistics. It is debatable how far the raising of the school-leaving age is largely to blame; or whether children are responding to more general social factors beyond the scope and influence of the schools. There is however now growing evidence that both vandalism and violence can be reduced by the quality of caring and of the environment in a school.[3]

The DES survey[4] of the first year of ROSLA noted that catering for the 'non-examinable, the uninterested and the hostile' was 'perhaps the main area of difficulty' for schools. Absence among fifth-year pupils had increased. The survey spoke of 'a core of dissidents, probably less than 10 per cent, who have created problems out of all proportion to their numbers'.

The 1975-8 national survey of secondary schools by HM Inspectorate, published in December 1979 as *Aspects of Secondary Education in England* (HMSO), found most schools were 'orderly and hardworking'. In the majority of schools, if there was a problem, it was most likely to be the absence of pupils with the apparent acquiescence of parents. Just over a fifth of the schools in the survey (384) were troubled by this form of absenteeism. Truancy and vandalism were considerable problems in a small number of the schools.

[1] Report in *The Guardian* 31 May 1977.
[2] *Vandalism in Schools* Judith Stone and Felicity Taylor (Save the Children Fund publication, February 1977).
[3] *Fifteen Thousand Hours: Secondary Schools and Their Effects on Children* Michael Rutter *et. al.* (Open Books, 1979).
[4] DES Reports on Education, no. 83 *The First Year after RSLA* (April 1975).

74

Comprehensive education is now the rule rather than the exception it was when the Newsom Committee was set up. In 1960, only 4.7 per cent of secondary-age children in the maintained sector went to a comprehensive school. In 1965, some 8.5 per cent did so, and in 1970 the proportion had grown to 32 per cent. In 1973, 50.7 per cent. Today, it is up to 85.9 per cent (but see footnote 1, page 40).

A second key factor has been the expansion of the external examination system through the development of the Certificate of Secondary Education (CSE). The flexibility of this examination enabled many schools to develop suitable courses for average and less-able pupils with the incentive of a qualification at the end. Most pupils have entered for public examinations, and been successful in them, than ever before.

Between 1973 and 1976, the number of CSE entries for all modes in England and Wales increased from 1,426,000 to 2,543,000 — a jump of 78 per cent. Over 1.5 million candidates took CSE and GCE O- and A-level exams in 1977 — an increase of 90 per cent since 1967. Some 260,000 took CSE alone. An examination target tended to raise both pupil and teacher expectations and increase pupils' motivation. A larger proportion of pupils were going in for CSE and GCE than had been originally intended either by the Newsom Committee or by the Beloe Committee, which devised the CSE examination. The 1960 Beloe Report had recommended the CSE examination for the 40 per cent of pupils below the ablest 20 per cent for whom the GCE O-level had been intended.

Many non-examinable courses were developed for less able pupils, with varying degrees of quality and success. In 1964, the Schools Council for the Curriculum and Examinations was established to monitor, research and produce work on the curriculum. The Council provided a substantial amount of material for courses for the 'extra year', for young school-leavers, and for those needing some form of compensatory education. Local Government reorganization in the 1960s hampered some schemes for curriculum development, although many schools and authorities (notably the North West Curriculum Development Project) did go ahead with imaginative and valuable schemes. The establishment of teachers' centres also helped with the development of suitable courses as well as providing essential opportunities for in-service training and contact between teachers at different schools.

Linked courses (between schools and further education colleges) were set up although many suffered from problems of liaison and planning between school and college. Work-experience courses also had difficulties and were even less widely developed than linked courses. The 1975 DES survey of how ROSLA was progressing noted 'insurance problems, problems of supervision, and some truancy; . . . opposition from local trade union branches and from employers'.[1] Subsequent legislation and official guidance from the DES (circular 7/74) did not solve the problems involved. The 1977 DES survey[2] indicated a continuing low level of availability and success of both types of courses.

The 1977 survey found a 'marked emphasis was placed on the development of basic skills of numeracy and literacy' in the schools visited. But problems remained with the 'least able pupils'. Evidence was found of differing policies on how to handle them and what kind of course to offer. Some schools did not wish to mark them out as separate from the abler pupils; others felt it essential to adopt a policy of positive discrimination. The demands made on a school with limited resources sometimes meant that the least able pupils 'could suffer from relative isolation at this stage of their school life and from the effect this could have on their own and their teachers' expectations'. Some schools had also had to overcome the lack of interest and lack of status that accompany non-examinable courses.

The warping of a school's organization and curriculum because of an emphasis on examination courses was also in evidence — 'the desire for examination success was seen to have undesirable effects in some cases on curricular balance, teaching methods, and timetable organization'.

The national secondary survey[3] carried out between 1975 and 1978 by HM Inspectorate, and published in December 1979, concluded that examinations still tended to dominate and distort pupils' work, and that virtually all schools

[1] DES Reports on Education, no. 83 *The First Year after RSLA* (April 1975).
[2] DES Report on Education, no. 95 *RSLA — Four Years On* (October 1979).
[3] *Aspects of Secondary Education in England* (HMSO, December 1979).

let down the less able pupils by offering them inappropriate programmes of work. The Inspectorate also stated that there was no neglect of basic skills and much effort went into responding to pupils' needs and public expectations. However, the range of options or subject choices offered to pupils at the end of their third year was considered to be too wide and lacking in coherence, with the number of subjects studied considerably reduced: 'The more able pupils tended to have narrow programmes heavily weighted towards science or languages and often omitting aesthetic, practical or humanities subjects, careers education, health education and other courses important to their personal development. The less and least able pupils, often presented with little real choice, mostly followed a different, sometimes even narrower programme which tended to be undemanding and also lacking in coherence . . . The loss of some subjects reduced the potential range of opportunities, whether for employment or for continued education, open to those pupils at the end of their fifth year. The loss of other subjects removed opportunities to enlarge experience and understanding in ways potentially valuable for the future quality of their lives as adults and citizens'.

In January 1980, two official documents were published to begin a series of consultations on the future of the curriculum in primary and secondary schools and the establishment of a 'core' curriculum. The Government presented its views in *A Framework for the School Curriculum* (DES) and HM Inspectorate produced a discussion paper on a possible curriculum for schools in *A View of the Curriculum* (HMI Series: Matters for Discussion no. 11, HMSO).

However, despite the massive growth in GCE and CSE exam participation, concern is growing that too many school leavers fail to gain adequate public recognition for their years at school through the existing GCE/CSE system. Tyrrell Burgess and Elizabeth Adams point out in *Outcomes of Education* (Macmillan, 1980) that 'the present system denies the public recognition of a 'pass' or higher grade [at GCE or CSE] to . . . well over three-fifths of all young leavers'. They conclude that 'the present elaborate and costly system of external examinations is not designed to inform

77

young leavers, their parents, employers or other educational establishments about the competence of young leavers or even about the range of experience which they have had'.

Several experiments are underway in schools which are seeking to provide pupils and teachers with greater responsibility for compiling, assessing and recording pupil performance and attributes — the outcomes of education — without having to rely on the external exam system. They are, in effect, extensions of the idea of the internal leaving certificate. The experiments (for example, the Sutton Centre scheme in Nottinghamshire, the Scottish Council for Research in Education project, the Record of Personal Experience developed at Totnes) are tending to concentrate on producing 'pupil profiles' or statements which combine pupil self-assessment, teacher assessment and a dossier of pupils' work through the school.

Burgess and Adams maintain:

> The division into examined and non-examined at the age of 16 is not required in law nor supportable within the principle of comprehensive education as secondary schools up and down the country try to interpret it. It now behoves educators everywhere to look closely not only at school examinations — which has been done already *ad nauseam* — but at positive efforts to cater educationally for the non-examined group and to explore alternatives to examinations for the examined group.

A recent DES survey[1] of LEA policy on the curriculum found that many LEAs (40 per cent) had no systematic arrangements for regular review of the agreed syllabus for religious education. The survey also noted a shortage of well-qualified teachers for the subject. Most LEAs relied on in-service training for providing practical help for teachers. The growth of multi-ethnic communities was seen as a stimulus for teaching about aspects of world religions, which in turn could contribute to racial harmony and an awareness of general religious understanding.

Almost half the LEAs linked moral with religious education. Most saw moral and health education and education for personal relationships as being taught more through the

[1] *Local Authority Arrangements for the School Curriculum: Report on the Circular 14/77 Review* (DES/Welsh Office, HMSO, November 1979).

'hidden curriculum' and through the medium of a range of other subjects. Thirty per cent of LEAs had an adviser with special responsibility for health education or for education for personal relationships.

Corporal punishment[1] remains a frequent sanction in many secondary schools. By the end of 1979, only one LEA (Haringey) had banned the punishment from all its schools. Three other LEAs have decided to ban it: the Inner London Education Authority by February 1981, Brent by July 1980, and Waltham Forest.

In the late 1950s and through the sixties, there was a large expansion of the number of teachers trained. In 1960, the teacher-training course was extended from two to three years' duration. A DES report[2] on the first year of ROSLA concluded that staffing had been 'sufficient to allow the implementation of plans for dealing with the extra pupils'. But the report also referred to shortages of teachers in particular subjects (e.g. maths, science, home economics, handicrafts) and of teachers experienced in the 'skill to handle and inspire the middle- and lower-ability range of pupils'.

Moves to improve the standards of entry into teacher-training colleges and the quality of training received were slow in coming. Only in 1970 did it become compulsory for graduates to be professionally trained as teachers. Even then, the 1970 date only applied to primary school teachers; secondary schools had to wait another four years (but not for maths or science teachers, where a shortage exists). Students going into teacher training were not obliged to have GCE O-level passes in Maths and English until the September 1980 intake. In 1971, the Government set up a Committee of Enquiry under Lord James. This followed a trebling in the number of student-teachers in the colleges between 1961 and 1971 and a growing dissatisfaction with the status and quality of teacher training. The basic principles of the Report[3] were accepted by the Government, but little immediate action taken. There followed a major contraction in the number of colleges of education

[1] See also the section on the Plowden Report.
[2] DES Reports on Education, no. 83 *The First Year after RSLA* (April 1975).
[3] *Teacher Education and Training* The James Report (HMSO, 1972). See also *Colleges in Crisis* David Hencke (Penguin, 1979).

79

and the number of teachers trained — a combination of the dramatic fall in the birthrate between 1964 and 1977 and the public spending cuts.

The teaching force in schools is now more stable and more experienced than in the 1960s and early 1970s. Pupil/teacher ratios have steadily improved. In 1977, the Government Green Paper *Education in Schools* repeated the need for higher standards of entry into the profession and for more in-service training for teachers. It also called for closer links between teachers and industry — a gap criticized by the Newsom Report.

A report by the DES on schools which had responded to the raising of the school-leaving age through their curriculum, organization and examination policies was published in October 1979.[1] It was based on an HMI study carried out in 1977. The report noted again a shortage of maths and science teachers;[2] a more stable teaching force; and a need for more teachers experienced in dealing with less able pupils. The idea of the 'ROSLA' pupil and of the 'Newsom' pupil had gone — and 'the additional year has given teachers the opportunity to plan substantial courses for all their pupils whatever their ability, and in the fifth year there was evidence of only a small proportion of pupils showing the boredom and alienation once characteristic of some fourth-year leavers'.

The 1977 HMI survey concluded that, in general, accommodation was adequate for the 'observed needs of the pupils', although there were problems for some areas of the curriculum, notably through the increased demand for practical facilities. Careers work fared badly, and there was frequently inadequate library space. Difficulties also existed over the availability of suitable learning materials and, more so, of books.

The 1977 DES *Study of School Building* had put the same problems more strongly:

> . . . the great majority of secondary schools have insufficient practical accommodation and a substantial minority have insufficient large spaces, for the sort of curriculum expected today . . . The deficiencies in practical accommodation, damaging in any

[1] DES Reports on Education no. 95 *ROSLA — Four Years On* (October 1979).
[2] The shortage of maths, physics and chemistry teachers was further confirmed by figures produced by the Royal Society (November 1979). Since 1975, the number of physics teachers entering secondary schools has fallen from 627 to 256; of chemistry teachers from 664 to 359; of maths teachers from 2,338 to 1,052.

circumstances, may critically inhibit progress in the comprehensive reorganization of some areas, and may also limit the development of that part of the curriculum which has particular technical and industrial relevance.

A Government inter-departmental committee was set up soon after Newsom reported to look at general social problems in slum areas, and various minor research projects were started. But a major assault on improving education in deprived areas did not take place until the Home Office urban-aid programmes and the recommendations of the 1967 Plowden Report on positive discrimination and educational priority areas.

Both the Crowther Report and the Newsom Report had undertaken surveys and made detailed use of official statistics to produce a valuable profile of the availability of educational opportunity for particular groups of children and of some of the causes of disadvantage. They had pinpointed the influence that home circumstances, parental attitudes and environmental factors could have on children's educational chances. The question of selection was not dealt with by either Committee despite the existence of much research evidence on the damaging educational consequences of the selective system. All these issues were to be taken up in more detail, and to greater effect, by the Plowden Committee — and subsequently by the EPA projects under A. H. Halsey.

Where to find out more

Books

Education and the Working Class Brian Jackson and Dennis Marsden (Penguin, 1963)

Half Our Future The Newsom Report (HMSO, 1963)

All Our Future J. W. B. Douglas, J. M. Ross and H. R. Simpson (Panther, 1968)

In and Out of School Roger White and David Brockington (Routledge & Kegan Paul, 1978)

The School Debate Adam Hopkins (Penguin, 1978)

Fifteen Thousand Hours: Secondary Schools and Their Effects on Children M. Rutter *et al.* (Open Door, 1979)

The Comprehensive School Robin Pedley (Penguin, third edition, 1979)

Aspects of Secondary Education

in England (HMSO, 1979)
*The Condition of English School-
ing* Henry Pluckrose and Peter
Wilby (eds.) (Penguin, 1979)
Education and Equality David

Rubinstein (ed.) (Penguin,
1979)
Outcomes of Education Tyrrell
Burgess and Elizabeth Adams
(eds.) (Macmillan, 1980)

Organizations

The Schools Council, 160 Great Portland Street, London W1N 6LL
(01-580 0352) produces a series of books, pamphlets and other materials on examinations and the curriculum in schools.

Circulars

Key DES circulars on the education of thirteen to sixteen-year-olds
include:
9/63 The Certificate of Secondary Education
8/72 Raising the School Leaving Age to 16
7/74 Work Experience
11/76 The Education Act 1976
14/77 Local Education Authority Arrangements for the School Curriculum
18/78 Juveniles: Cooperation between the Police and Other Agnecies
1/80 Education Act 1980

Two administrative memoranda (AM) concern GCE:
4/60 General Certificate of Education
5/75 The General Certificate of Education Ordinary Level Examination: Grading of Results

Key DES circulars and administrative memoranda (AM) on the teaching profession include:
11/73 The Qualification of Teachers
5/75 The Reorganisation of Higher Education in the Non-University
Sector: The Further Education Regulations 1975
9/78 Entry to Initial Teacher Training Courses in England and Wales
4/78 (AM) Training and Retraining of Teachers in Mathematics,
Physical Science and Craft Design and Technology

Comprehensive reorganization

The circulars concerning the organization of secondary education
were numbered 10/65, 10/70, 4/74, and 11/76 on the Education Act
1976. The latest change occurs in the Education Act 1979 (no circular).

6   Children and Their Primary Schools: The Plowden Report (1967)

Why Plowden was set up

In August 1963, the Central Advisory Councils for Education were given another task: to enquire into the state of primary schooling in England and Wales. The last official surveys[1] of primary education had been carried out by Sir Henry Hadow in 1931 and 1933. His Reports had formed the basis for subsequent official thinking on the needs of primary-age children. The underlying philosophy of the Hadow Reports was summed up as 'what a wise and good parent will desire for his own children, a nation must desire for all children' — which meant equality of opportunity and a determined effort to reduce inequalities. The next 30 years showed too little of either.

Since the introduction of the Education Act 1944, Government Reports had concentrated on the secondary and further-education sectors of the maintained system — Crowther and Newsom on secondary-age pupils, Albemarle on a Youth Service for fourteen- to twenty-year-olds, Robbins on higher education. As a consequence, substantially more Government finance, time and concern had gone into those parts of the education service than into primary schooling. Yet many exciting and innovative ideas were being developed in English primary schools. They were frequently referred to, by other countries, as the envy of the Western educational world. But how widespread was the availability of a good primary education for the nation's children? And what comprised a 'good' primary education?

[1] *The Primary School* (1931) and *Infant and Nursery Schools* (1933).

Lady Plowden chaired the Committee investigating English primary schools; Professor Gittins chaired the one for Welsh schools.

What Plowden was asked to do

Consider primary education in all its aspects, and the transition to secondary education.

What Plowden recommended and why

The Plowden Report presented a detailed picture of English primary schooling in the sixties. It included descriptions of the existing structure of and ideas current in primary education; looked at how children grew and developed; and considered the effects that particular home and neighbourhood conditions could have on children's development.

The Committee considered the primary school not just in its educational context but as part of society and of the country's economy. While the cost of the proposals made by the Committee was large, some of the recommendations required changes of attitude, understanding and knowledge by teachers, rather than the allocation of more public money. Moreover, the Report set out an order of priorities for the years ahead for implementing the recommendations which would, according to the Committee, bring 'a system designed for "other people's children" up to the standard which "a good and wise parent" would accept for his own children'.[1]

The Committee concluded that the differences between children — their endowment and rates of development — were too great for them to be neatly assigned to streams or types of schools. Children had to be treated as individuals and whatever form of school organization was adopted, teachers had to adapt their methods to individuals in a class. Only in that way could the needs of gifted and slow-learning children and all those between the extremes be

[1] This referred to the 1931 Hadow Report's comment that 'what a wise and good parent will desire for his own children, a nation must desire for all children'.

met. The more progressive and imaginative methods that were being used to help children learn and develop their skills were encouraged by the Committee. 'Finding out' was proving better for children than 'being told'. Such methods could be used without losing the more 'established' skills (the 'older virtues') of 'neatness, accuracy, care and perseverance'.[1]

Children's capacity to create in words, pictorially and through many other forms of expression, was astonishing. The third of the three Rs was no longer mechanical arithmetic, French had made its way into the primary school, nature study was becoming a science. There had been a dramatic and continuing advance in reading standards. While there were still dismal corners of primary education (displaying parochialism, lack of understanding of the needs of children and of the differing homes they came from, lack of continued training of teachers and lack of opportunities for professional contact), English primary education was 'very good indeed'. Only rarely was it very bad; the average was good. Most of what was best came straight from individual teachers. A child could have no happier fate than to encounter, as many did, a good teacher.

The Report made the point that much of what is described was merely a reflection or reporting of current ideas and practices. But it launched — or at least gave a much needed boost to — two key concepts: the need for positive discrimination and the educational priority area; and the importance of parental involvement in a child's education.

Educational priority areas

As things were, there was no reason why the educational handicaps of the most deprived children should disappear. Though standards would rise, inequalities would continue and the potential of many children would never be realized. The range of achievement among English children was wide, and standards of the most and the least successful began to

[1] Paragraph 506, page 188.

diverge very early. Steps should be taken to improve the educational chances and the attainments of the least well-placed, and to bring them up to the levels that prevailed generally. That would need a new distribution of educational resources.

Neighbourhoods which were socially and economically disadvantaged should be given extra resources to help those children most severely handicapped because of bad home conditions. This programme of 'positive discrimination' should be phased to make schools in the most deprived areas as good as the best in the country. A start should be made as soon as possible (in 1968/9) by giving priority to the most severely deprived pupils, beginning with 2 per cent of pupils and building up to 10 per cent within five years. The purpose of the short-term programme would be, in part, to discover which measures best compensated for educational deprivation. Every LEA having schools in which children's educational handicaps were reinforced by social deprivation should be asked to adopt the measures outlined in this Report for these 'educational priority areas' (EPAs).

The extra resources should pay for more teachers, for teachers' aides, for urgent improvements to inadequate buildings, and for more books and equipment. The areas should receive more central Government grant-aid. The provision of nursery education should be expanded in EPAs. Classes in the primary schools should be reduced in size, so that none exceeded a ratio of 30 children per teacher. Other Government agencies in the social and education fields should become more involved in providing for schools in EPAs: for example, colleges of education should establish links and arrange for their students to do teaching practice in EPA schools; teachers' centres should be set up for in-service training; social workers should maintain contact with EPA schools; the idea of community schools should be tried out first in these priority areas. All these activities should be closely monitored to find out, and then to encourage, those schemes that worked best for the children and the schools.

Teachers working in schools in educational priority areas should receive an addition to their salary of £120 a year.

Children of immigrants

The curriculum of primary schools with large intakes of immigrant children[1] should take account of their previous environment, and prepare them for life in a different one. There should be more initial and in-service opportunities for teachers to train in teaching English to immigrant children and to increase their knowledge of the children's origins and cultural background. Remedial courses in spoken English for immigrant teachers should be expanded. The development of suitable materials and methods for teaching English to immigrant children should continue. Schools with special language problems or with high numbers of immigrant children should be generously staffed, possibly experimenting with help from student volunteers.

Participation by parents

An outstanding trend in recent years had been the growing awareness of the importance for the individual of family and social background. The last three Reports of the Council[2] and the Robbins Report on higher education had produced evidence showing the close association between social circumstances and academic achievement. Further research (instigated by the Plowden Committee) suggested that the most vital factor in a child's home was the parents' attitude to school and all that went on there.

All schools should encourage parental interest and involvement in their children's schooling. There should be a programme of contact with children's homes: more personal and written contact between school and parents; ensuring

---

[1] DES circular 7/65 had advised LEAs to avoid high concentrations of immigrant children in a school and encouraged a policy of dispersal of children into several schools. Some LEAs did not agree with the idea of dispersal, preferring to provide extra staffing, smaller classes and an enriched curriculum. Others went for a scheme of partial dispersal. The DES had also increased the quotas of teachers for areas with large numbers of immigrant families. Grant-aid was also available.

[2] *Early Leaving* (1954); *15 to 18* The Crowther Report (1959); *Half Our Future* The Newsom Report (1963) — all produced by the Central Advisory Council for Education.

parents saw their children's work and received written reports at least once a year; making contact with parents who did not visit a school; arranging open days; ensuring there was a regular system of parent/teacher discussion both before and during a child's school career; encouraging greater parental involvement in out-of-school activities; more use of school premises (rooms, equipment, sports areas) by the local community, with the head having a say in the evening use of the school. The DES should encourage this process of involvement by issuing a booklet containing examples of good practice in parent/teacher relations.

Parents should be able to choose their children's primary school whenever this was possible, and local authorities should improve those schools shown to be consistently unpopular with parents. Schools should prepare booklets about the school to help parents make a choice and to show how the children would be educated.

Community schools should be developed in all areas, but especially in educational priority areas.

Pre-schooling

There should be a large expansion of nursery education for children from the age of three until they reached the age of compulsory schooling. A programme of expansion should begin as soon as possible, but first of all in EPAs.

Children ought to be introduced gradually to primary education without any sudden transition from spending the day at home to spending the day at school. Nursery schooling should be part-time because it was considered best for young children not be be separated from their mothers for long periods. There were, however, a number of children who needed full-time nursery education, and 15 per cent of the places made available should be full-time.

Part-time places should be made available for as many as 90 per cent of four-year-olds and 50 per cent of three-year-olds.[1] Nursery schooling should be provided in groups

[1] The Committee suggested that by 1977 all four- and five-year-olds should have access to nursery schooling, subject to a single date of entry to primary school being introduced.

of up to twenty children; more than one and up to three groups could together form a unit called a nursery centre or be combined with day nurseries or clinics in children's centres. There should be one qualified teacher for every 60 places, with the day-to-day work done by two-year trained assistants in the ratio of at least one to every ten children.

The responsibility for the education of children over three in day nurseries should be transferred from the Health Ministry to the DES.

Until enough maintained places were made available, LEAs should be given powers to provide financial and other help to nursery groups run by non-profit making associations. All such groups should be open to inspection by LEAs and HM Inspectors.

Teachers' aides

A new group of staff — teachers' aides — should be recruited for primary schools. They would help overworked teachers and understaffed schools and be under the supervision of a qualified teacher. They should work in the ratio of one full-time aide to every two infant classes, and one to four junior classes (except in EPAs, where the ratio should be one to two junior classes). All teachers' aides should have one or two years' training (mainly 'on the job') and have equal status with nursery assistants. The introduction of aides should not be allowed to worsen the staffing ratio of unqualified teachers in a school.

The schools

Once provision for nursery education had been expanded to give all children one year's nursery schooling, there should be a single date of entry for children starting primary school — the September term after a child's fifth birthday. The date of a child's birthday could be a serious disadvantage since existing local authority practice meant some children getting two terms less of primary schooling than others.

The most suitable way to organize primary education was in separate first (i.e. infant) and middle (i.e. junior) schools. Every child should have three years in a first school and then four years in a middle school. There should be greater flexibility over entry to school and in the ages of transfer between different stages of schooling so as to cater for the special needs of individual pupils. For example, children could attend school half-time up to the age of six, if considered appropriate. There should also be flexibility in the length of the school day and the school term depending on children's needs. As a general rule, children should transfer to secondary school at the age of twelve instead of eleven. The trend of the abolition of selection procedures at eleven for secondary education was to be welcomed.

The best size for first schools would normally be two-form entry — about 240 children, and for middle schools two or three form entry — 300 to 450 children. There should be further studies on how schools of different sizes progressed educationally. Combining first and middle schools was not recommended except for small schools in rural areas, and for voluntary schools.

The class should remain the basic unit of school organization. However, there should be a combination of individual, group and class work, and the trend towards individual learning was to be welcomed. Children should have access to more than one teacher. Teachers should work together more. Streaming children in primary schools according to ability should be abolished.

Primary school classes should be reduced in size, and the maximum number of children brought below 40. There should be experiments to test the effects of small classes and generous staffing. Experiments should also be made with the grouping of classes of older children into larger groups for some lessons, say about 100 children in the care of three teachers.

In rural areas, schools with an age range of five to eleven should usually have at least three classes, each covering two age groups. If the age range were to be extended to twelve, further teaching help might be needed to provide an adequate education for the older children. The ages of transfer should be flexible and one- or two-class first schools kept open to suit the needs of isolated rural areas. Teachers in rural schools required extra help from advisers and teachers' aides, plus opportunities for regular contact with other teachers and schools.

There should be more continuity and contact between the various stages of schooling — pre-school, primary, secondary — for children, parents and teachers. The training of teachers should span more than one stage of education.

Schools should keep a detailed folder on every child, to include medical record, test results, basic family background material, information on illnesses and on attendance at school, examples of work, and a rundown of special skills and handicaps. This folder should accompany the child through middle and secondary school, and be used to keep parents in touch with how their child was getting on.

Decisions about discipline and punishments should generally be left to the professional judgment of the individual teacher acting within the policy of the school. However, the infliction of physical pain as a method of punishment (corporal punishment) in primary schools should be forbidden.

Handicapped children in ordinary schools

A detailed enquiry should be made into the needs of handicapped children, including slow learners, and adequate provision made by them. Children with a handicap should be identified from birth on.

Teachers needed to be alert to those children showing difficulty in learning, and ready to arrange expert examination without delay. Assessment of handicap should be a continuing process in which teachers, doctors, psychologists and parents cooperated as a team. Parents should have the support of a special counselling service. The term 'slow learner' should be used instead of 'educationally subnormal'.

Health and social services and the school child

All children should have a medical examination when they entered school to assess their developmental and medical needs. As they progressed through school, they should have selective (but thorough) medical examinations.

Observation registers should be kept on children to record perinatal information, developmental test results and other procedures to identify any disorders. More personal information should also appear on these registers. Social workers concerned with school health services should be told, in confidence and with parental consent, of a child's needs and problems. Family doctors, school and community health services and the social services should all cooperate more closely over providing for children's needs.[1] All branches of the school health service were in need of more staff.

Trained social workers should take on cases too complex for teachers to deal with. Schools should be able to call quickly on more specialized social services. The work of the education welfare officer (EWO) should be reorganized so that some of the routine work could be done by new welfare assistants and clerical staff. EWOs themselves could be trained in those social conditions which affect how children performed at school and in the way the social services operated. Some training could be done alongside social workers.

Independent primary schools

The DES should consider requiring all independent schools to state in their prospectuses whether they were 'recognized'

[1] The Seebohm Committee had been appointed in December 1965 jointly by the Home Secretary, Education, Health, and Housing and Local Government Ministers 'to review the organization and responsibilities of the local authority personal social services in England and Wales, and to consider what changes are desirable to secure an effective family service'. The Committee's Report published in July 1968 (Cmnd 3703) made the important recommendation that local authorities should have a unified social service department with a central Government department responsible for overall planning – drawing some responsibilities away from the Home Office.

or 'registered' with the DES. More informative terms could be devised. More stringent criteria should be worked out to ensure that such schools were paying sufficient attention to the children's welfare. All heads should be qualified teachers. More in-service training courses should be available to teachers at independent schools.

Staffing and training

There should be a full enquiry into the system of training teachers. More trainee teachers should have passed GCE O-level mathematics; more should have specialized in maths and science in the sixth form. More teachers — particularly men and graduates — should be encouraged into primary schools. The number of in-service training courses should be increased. Part-time teachers should be used to release more full-time teachers to go and work in difficult areas and to help understaffed schools. Headteachers ought to teach. Better use should be made of meals assistants, school secretaries and welfare assistants. Schools should make greater use of parents and other members of the local community both school and for out-of-school activities — provided it was at the invitation of the head and under his or her control.

The entry qualifications to training courses for nursery assistants and teachers' aides should be the same, and the Government should consider setting up a central examining body for both.

The existing system of inspecting schools should continue. Local authority advisory services for primary schools should be expanded.

Buildings and equipment

The Government should fund a new minor works building programme to get rid of the worst environmental aspects of some primary schools (e.g. outside lavatories, lack of heating). An extra £7 — £10 million should be allocated every year for a seven-year period starting in 1971. There should be more flexibility for LEAs and heads to carry out small projects quickly and efficiently. In future, schools should be planned so they were more accessible to parents and the local community, and free from traffic and other dangers.

Status and government

All primary schools should have their own managing body. Managers should be appointed on the basis of their genuine concern for education rather than their political allegiance. Parents should be represented on the managing body of their children's school.

Managers should be fully involved in selecting a headteacher (calling on expert advice if needed). In turn, heads should be equally involved in the selection of other teaching staff for the school. They should also have more say in the building programmes that affected their school and in how their school was used outside normal hours. Primary school teachers should be represented on local authority committees concerned with primary education.

The Committee, conscious of the economic problems of the country, attempted to cost their proposals; suggested economic, educational and social criteria by which they felt their proposals should be judged in relation to other demands on the country's resources; and set out a list of priorities for implementing their major recommendations.

The first priority was setting up the educational priority areas; second, the recruitment of teachers' aides; third, improving primary school buildings; fourth, the expansion of nursery education; fifth, planning the changes in the national dates of entry to primary school and the ages of transfer between the different stages of primary education.

What happened to Plowden

The Plowden Report, published in January 1967, had a profound effect on the way both professionals and parents viewed primary education. The Committee placed great importance on the power of a good primary school to enhance a child's life. They wanted more involvement of parents in the life of the school; greater cooperation between all those groups who were concerned with children at school — teachers, parents, LEA officials, governors, health and social service staff; more help for teachers in the classroom. They called for positive discrimination in allocating resources to children in deprived areas. They believed they had produced proposals that could radically change children's lives.

Some of their recommendations were controversial within the educational world — both philosophically and administratively; others were calling on additional resources at a time of economic crisis, although the Committee had taken all this into account in outlining their strategy for the future. None of this fully explains away why the optimism and commitment reflected in the Report was not translated into more energetic political action.

In August 1967, a special two-year allocation of £16 million was announced by the Education Secretary for school building projects in educational priority areas. A DES circular (11/67) set out the criteria for taking up the funds, and asked LEAs to submit projects for approval. An additional £18 million was made available for 1971/2. Official figures[1] had revealed that in 1962 some 44 per cent of primary school children were being educated in buildings erected before 1903, and 19 per cent in pre-1875 buildings. By 1967, earlier building programmes had certainly reduced those 1962 figures, but it was estimated that some £200 million would be needed to replace or improve all pre-1903 buildings — substantially more than the total amount allocated for all school building programmes in a year. In 1967, the projected school building programmes in England and Wales totalled £120 million for 1967/8, £138 million for 1968/9 and £138 million for 1969/70.

The 1970-4 Conservative Government made primary building improvements a key element in its education policy. Funds for 1972/3 were increased to £38.5 million (later raised to £44 million) and the aim was for a five-year programme at

---

[1] *The School Building Survey* (DES, 1965).

an annual £50 million to 'bring within sight the elimination of primary schools built in the nineteenth century'. Money was switched from comprehensive reorganization building schemes, from subsidies for school milk and meals, and further education fees were raised to pay for the projected programme of improvements. It was hoped to improve 500 nineteenth-century schools. Public expenditure cuts towards the end of the Government's period of office reduced the funding available.

By 1976, it was estimated that a million children (20 per cent of all primary school children in England and Wales) were still being educated in some 8,300 schools with some pre-1903 accommodation (36 per cent of all primary schools; but 20 per cent of total primary accommodation in terms of buildings). In 5,450 primary schools (23 per cent, or nearly one in four) *all* the permanent accommodation was pre-1903 — affecting well over ½ million children. Some 21 per cent of primary schools had more than 20 per cent temporary accommodation; 7 per cent of schools had over 40 per cent temporary accommodation. 7,000 schools (30 per cent) had outside lavatories.[1]

Two other Government responses to the Plowden recommendations came soon after the Report's publication. A special flat-rate allowance for teachers in difficult schools was announced. This was to come into force from April 1968 and to start at £75 a year — Plowden had wanted £120. In October 1967, the Education Secretary agreed to consider a proposal for setting up five action-research projects in specially designated educational priority areas. A grant of £175,000 was allocated in May 1968 and the projects got underway between September 1968 and January 1969 (see the section on the Halsey Report).

The Plowden Committee had hoped, with certain qualifications, for a comprehensive pre-school network by 1977 (serving part-time 90 per cent of four-year-olds and 50 per cent of three-year-olds). But a 1960 DES circular (8/60) issued by the 1959-64 Conservative Government had put a

---

[1] *A Study of School Buildings: A Report by an Inter-departmental Group* (DES/Welsh Office, HMSO, 1977) and the DES Statistical Bulletin 5/78 *School Building Surveys 1975 and 1976* (October 1978).

ban on LEAs providing any additional nursery places. That instruction was not lifted until 1973 (except for priority area programmes between 1968 and 1973) when the 1970-4 Conservative Government gave a firm commitment to expand nursery education (DES circular 2/73), based largely on the estimates given by the Plowden Committee.[1] The 1972 White Paper *Education: A Framework for Expansion* (Cmnd 5174) which preceded the more detailed circular declared: 'Within the next ten years (by 1981) nursery education should become available without charge within the limits of demand estimated by Plowden to those children of three and four whose parents wish them to benefit from it.'

This nursery programme has been criticized for encouraging provision primarily through nursery classes attached to infant schools (thereby discouraging 'a diversity of provision'), for not allowing LEAs sufficient time to assess local needs (as had been advocated by the 1972 Halsey Report), and for not allowing scope for providing full-time places for the growing number of mothers with children under five who were going out to work. For economic and social factors were already changing the pattern of demand for pre-school and day-care provision.

This first major response to Plowden's call for nursery education was found often to be working to the benefit of the more advantaged child. Moreover, the funds made available for building programmes (£30 million) tended to be taken up by the more aware, and more well-off LEAs, and not always by those LEAs most in need of the provision they would establish. Nevertheless, more places were provided, and the programme did at least provide some evidence[2] of official awareness of the need for a national policy on pre-school provision. Subsequent events proved that it was not regarded as an over-riding priority, for the public expenditure cuts following the 1973 economic crisis curtailed the plans for expansion.

[1] The circular stated that to provide full-time education for 15 per cent of three- and four-year-olds and part-time education for 35 per cent of three-year-olds and 75 per cent of four-year-olds would require up to 250,000 additional full-time equivalent places in 1982.

[2] It also allowed the Government to divert money away from comprehensive reorganization schemes.

The pre-school playgroup has been one of the key elements in provision during the 1970s: voluntary-based provision that involved parents as helpers and was funded through session fees and some LEA help. (A Government survey[1] published in 1977 found that 18 per cent of all under-fives and 35 per cent of all four-year-olds went to a playgroup; the Pre-school Playgroups Association claimed that for 1977/8 some 46 per cent of three- and four-year-olds attended a playgroup.) A drawback of the playgroup is the length of the sessions — too brief for many working parents and many of those children found to be most in need of provision by Plowden and Halsey. Advantages are the cheapness of providing playgroups and the level of parental involvement.

Capital expenditure on nursery provision declined after 1973. In 1977/8, the nursery building allocation was £2.7 million.[2] In 1978/9 it stood at £4.4 million. In January 1979, the 1974-9 Labour Government announced an expanded nursery building programme starting with £5.9 million for 1979/80. Since 1974, some £60 million had been made available for building programmes.[3] Between 1979 and 1982 a further £14.3 million would be made available. It was hoped that half of all three- and four-year-olds would be provided with a nursery place by 1982/3. The 1978 percentage was 39 per cent (which included 30,000 places at DHSS-sponsored day nurseries).

By January 1978, about 17 per cent of three- and four-year-olds (201,662) were in nursery schools or classes (in 1974, it was 8.5 per cent); a further 36 per cent of four-year-olds (213,728) were in reception classes in infant schools.[4] However, the Government accepted that 'there is still a great unmet need for educational and other facilities for the children of working women'.[5] The estimates recommended by the Plowden Committee were also 'unmet' — either in 1977 or by 1982.

The new 1979 Conservative Government stated in its public expenditure plans in November 1979 that it hoped

[1] *Pre-School Children and the need for Day Care* (HMSO/OPCS, 1977).
[2] and [3] Official DES statistics.
[4] and [5] Hansard: House of Commons, 20 February 1979, col. 122/3.

to keep the nursery programme going 'at about the present level'. However, it cut the nursery school building programme back to £1.9 million for 1980/1 and aims to rely on the decline in the birthrate to keep up the level of provision. Unfortunately, its policy of substantially reducing public spending from 1979/80 on has meant that some LEAs are already cutting back severely on existing nursery provision.

Pre-school education and day-care provision still remains divided between the DES and the DHSS.

Parental participation in education has substantially increased[1] in spite of frequent teacher opposition and much official indifference. Parent/teacher associations (PTAs) and parents' groups have proliferated. Few schools would now openly deny the value of parental involvement and parental knowledge of what goes on in school. However, there does remain much argument over how far parents should be (or have become) part of the decision-making process in education.

Until the late seventies, successive Governments side-stepped or ignored any firm commitment to parental participation. Unsympathetic LEAs were not actively encouraged to change their ways. One major parental complaint — the lack of information about local schools — was not taken up by Government until November 1977 when the DES circular (15/77) was published advising LEAs what sort of information they should provide parents with about schools.[2] Earlier in 1977, the consultative Green Paper *Education in Schools* had spelt out the importance of the parental role in schools

---

[1] The 1978 HMI survey *Primary Education in England* (HMSO) found that: 'parents helped teachers in nearly a third of the seven-year-old classes and in just under a fifth of nine- and eleven-year-old classes. The proportion of classes receiving parental help was lower in the inner-city areas than in 'other urban' or rural areas. Typically, where parental help was given, an average of two parents a week visited the class. In over three-quarters of the classes where help was given, parents assisted teachers in matters concerning the children's welfare and the supervision of children on visits outside the school. Teachers reported that parents were also involved with children's learning in over two-thirds of the classes where help was given. This type of involvement most commonly took the form of assisting with practical subjects or hearing children read'. (paragraph 3.16).

[2] Section 8 of the Education Act 1980 puts a statutory duty on LEAs, and governors of aided schools, to publish details of school admission procedures, parental preference arrangements, appeals procedures and the number of places available at each school. DES regulations will be published in due course on other information that must be made available to parents.

('the group most deeply involved with the school must always be the parents') and echoed much of what Plowden had said ten years before. Members were appointed to the Court, Taylor and Warnock Committees specifically to represent the parents' point of view. There are more parent-governors on school-governing bodies and the principle of parent-governors is now widely accepted if not always acted on in full. National bodies representing the interests of parents and pupils, such as the Advisory Centre for Education, the Campaign for the Advancement of State Education, the National Confederation of PTAs, the National Consumer Council — are consulted more frequently about educational issues. However, there are still no detailed guidelines about secondary school transfer; no local advice centres on education; no statutory obligation for national or local Government to consult parents over crucial issues that affect a school. Nevertheless, this is one Plowden recommendation that Governments no longer ignore in *talking* about education policy and the arguments now centre more on the level and form of parental participation rather than on whether or not there should be participation.

Some problems still exist over starting at primary school. The legal requirement remains that a child must start school at the beginning of the term after the child's fifth birthday. LEAs vary in their policy on starting school. Some stick strictly to the law, which can mean unnecessary 'lost' schooling for children born in the summer, who have the longest wait for a new term. Others adopt a 'rising-fives' policy, letting four-year-olds start school at the beginning of the term in which they will become five. Some children continue to lose out at transfer periods later on, say in moving from infant to junior school, or from first to middle school.

Problems like this may be resolved by the dramatic fall in the birthrate and consequently fewer children coming into school. On the other hand, rising-fives policies, like nursery provision, are falling victim to public spending cuts.

The flexibility urged by the Committee over the organization of primary schools did not develop to the extent hoped for by the Committee. Subsequent public anxiety about educational standards, fuelled partly by a vigorous

100

campaign under the aegis of the Black Paper movement against progressive methods in primary schools, was shown to be largely misplaced. The 1978 HMI survey found that, in general, a balance of progressive and traditional methods was being used in the majority of primary schools; that standards were rising; that an over-emphasis on traditional ways of teaching in some schools was detrimental and restrictive to the children's education. The HMIs recommended that teachers learn about a range of teaching methods and adapt according to 'what is best for their immediate purpose'. An earlier survey carried out by Lancaster University had come up with similar findings (*Teaching Styles and Pupil Progress* Neville Bennett, Open Books, 1976).

Few primary schools now organize classes by streaming children according to ability. The HMI survey found that one per cent of seven-year-olds' classes were streamed; three per cent of nine-year-olds'; and six per cent of eleven-year-olds'. (In 1962, some 87 per cent of schools streamed children at the age of eight.) It is more frequent for children to be streamed for specific subjects — nearly three-quarters of maths classes and well over half of all reading and writing classes were streamed.

Pupil/teacher ratios in primary schools have steadily improved. In 1967, the national average was 27.9 pupils per teacher (which included unqualified teachers); in 1979 it was 23.1 pupils per teacher. According to the 1978 HMI survey, most classes contained between 20 and 35 children. By January 1977, only 1.4 per cent of primary schools had an average taught class size of more than 40 pupils.

The recommendation about what size a primary school should be did not settle the debate about the 'best' size for a school. A rigid adherence by some LEAs to the Plowden guidelines has been a factor in the closure of many rural primary schools. Few LEAs adopted constructive policies for helping these schools (also suggested by the Committee) and made decisions strictly on economic grounds. Many LEAs took the opportunity to cut costs by putting children into larger educational units. Consequently, the closure of these schools often eliminated valuable schooling for rural-based children and a vital resource for the local community.

101

Corporal punishment persists in primary schools.[1] In January 1968, the Labour Education Secretary Patrick Gordon Walker issued DES circular 1/68 which declared that corporal punishment should gradually die out in all schools; a second circular forbad corporal punishment in special schools for the handicapped. In May 1968, the new Labour Education Secretary Edward Short withdrew the Gordon Walker circulars, leaving decisions on corporal punishment up to the individual teachers in ordinary and special schools. In 1972, the Inner London Education Authority (ILEA) became the first LEA to ban corporal punishment in primary schools. Elsewhere there remains no official sanction to prevent the beating of children as young as five. The 1977 Green Paper *Education in Schools* reopened the question when the Education Secretary invited views on beating from the interested groups. The teacher unions remained opposed to any ban, although at the end of 1979 the National Union of Teachers was reconsidering its position.

At the same time, three further LEAs (Brent, Haringey and Waltham Forest) decided to ban corporal punishment in primary schools. The view of the current Conservative Government is that schools should have the right to administer corporal punishment if they considered it necessary.

There has been no change in the legal requirement for a daily act of worship in schools.

All LEAs now keep some kind of record of a child's school career. There is currently controversy about the quality and effectiveness of those records, the accuracy of information held, and the right of parents to see the records that are kept on their children.

A national survey[2] in 1975 conducted by the Advisory Centre for Education (ACE) found that only three LEAs claimed to give parents a right of access to their child's school record. The Government's consultative document *Education in Schools* (published in July 1977) acknowledged the need for keeping school records and recommended that 'the keeping

[1] See *Corporal Punishment* Peter Wilby (Discussion Paper no. 2, UK Association for the International Year of the Child, 1979) and *Abolition Handbook* Peter Newell (Society of Teachers Opposed to Physical Punishment — STOPP, 1978).

[2] *Where* 109, October 1975.

and transmission of records should be systematic and understandable; they should be subject to clearly understood and agreed controls on what information is kept and what is not; and on what is disseminated and to whom; and full regard must be paid to the rights of parents, as well as those of teachers and pupils, to know what material is included'. As part of a general review of the curriculum, the Government asked[1] LEAs 'to examine and report on their existing practices in relation to records of pupils' progress', covering the records themselves, arrangements for parents to see records, and the currency the records should have.

The results of the review were published in the report *Local Authority Arrangements for the School Curriculum* (HMSO, November 1979). According to this review most LEAs require schools to keep some form of record; others encourage rather than require it. Record cards vary widely in the degree of detail and styles of recording information. 'Some three-tenths' of LEAs (about 30) have no overall policy on access to records; most leave it up to the head-teachers' discretion. 'Slightly over one-tenth' of LEAs specifically deny access to parents. Most record cards document a child's performance in literacy and numeracy, exam and test results, a child's behaviour and personality, and significant medical information. 'Somewhat fewer' had information on family background.

However another ACE survey[2] in 1979 found that no LEA in fact guarantees parental access to *all* information held on a child. Seven LEAs (out of the 80 replies received from 119 LEAs in England, Wales and Scotland) guarantee access to certain records. A further 35 leave parental access to headteachers' discretion.

The trend towards non-selective transfer to secondary school, much approved of by the Committee, had begun in earnest in 1965 with the publication of DES circular 10/65. This *invited* LEAs to submit plans for comprehensive reorganization: and many did so. This circular also, indirectly, established a flexible policy for the age of primary/secondary

[1] DES circular 14/77.
[2] *Where* 148, May 1979.

103

transfer. LEAs wanted a ruling on the kind of schemes for reorganization that would most likely meet with Government approval. In 1966, the Education Secretary announced that the Government would accept schemes with trasnfer at eight or nine, twelve or thirteen — as well as at eleven. Plowden had wanted twelve as an eventual national transfer date, and while some first and middle schools were established, the most usual age for transfer remains eleven. In 1977, just under 16 per cent of primary school children attended first or middle (deemed primary) schools in England.

The 1970-4 Conservative Government withdrew the 10/65 circular and pursued a different policy of maintaining selection where LEAs wanted it but still approving some comprehensive schemes (DES circular 10/70). The Government though did reduce the funds available for building programmes associated with reorganization. The Education Act 1976 brought in under the 1974-9 Labour Government *compelled* LEAs to reorganize schools along comprehensive lines. However, when the Conservatives regained power in May 1979, the policy was again reversed by the Education Act 1979, which repealed sections 1 to 3 of the 1976 Act, thereby abolishing the statutory duty on LEAs to reorganize schools along comprehensive lines.

Nevertheless, by January 1978 over 83 per cent of secondary-age children in England and Wales were being educated in schools designated as comprehensive (compared with 60 per cent in 1974 and 30 per cent in 1970).[1] Just over 5 per cent attended grammar schools and 10 per cent went to secondary modern schools. In July 1979, there were 253 grammar schools operating in 49 LEAs. At the time of the 1979 Act becoming law, 79 of those grammar schools had received approval to go comprehensive. Some are likely to remain selective, while a few LEAs are intending to return some comprehensive schools to a selective basis.

The question of handicapped children in ordinary schools received detailed attention from the Warnock Committee set up in September 1974 and which reported in May 1978. Both the Warnock Report and the earlier Court Report on child health services in 1976 highlighted the continuing inadequacy of procedures for preventing handicap, identi-

---

[1] DES figures for 1979 put the proportion at 85.9 per cent.

fying it where it occurs and for providing the right kind of advice to parents and teachers on how to cope. Both Reports called for greater efforts and resources to cater for these children's needs.

Children regarded as gifted received some attention; they were reckoned to make up 2 to 3 per cent of the seven to eleven age range. In 1969, a Schools Council working party was set up to make a special study of gifted children. Its report in 1973 recommended that they receive more attention, with special provision and a closer monitoring of their needs. In the same year, the National Children's Bureau brought out a report of a long-term study of gifted children (*In Search of Promise*). In May 1975, a group of HM inspectors embarked on a study of opportunities for gifted children in maintained schools and reported in 1977 — *Gifted Children in Middle and Comprehensive Secondary Schools* (DES/HMI Series *Matters for Discussion*).

In June 1977, the Education Secretary announced that the arrangements whereby the DES recognized independent schools as efficient[1] would cease from April 1978 (DES circular 6/78), although independent schools still have to register with the DES and remain subject to inspection requirements under parts 3 and 4 of the 1944 Education Act.

In 1970, the 1964-70 Labour Government had made a first attempt to look at the training of teachers. Teachers' own area training organizations were asked to review the current situation. The 1970/1 Parliament established a select committee to do the same job. Then, the new 1970-4 Conservative Government appointed a special committee under Lord James to 'enquire into the present arrangements for the education, training and probation of teachers in England and Wales'. The Committee reported in 1972 (*Teacher Education and Training*). They recommended an all-graduate profession, more in-service training, a training system more closely linked with the needs of schools, a common general course for all teachers with specialization later, better qualified trainees, closer integration with the higher education sector.[2]

---

[1] Published as *List 70* — the last was in 1974.
[2] For a detailed but succinct rundown of this Report, see *Much to do About Education* Anne Corbett (Macmillan, 1979).

Plowden's specific recommendations about teacher training and staffing progressed slowly. Graduate teachers still comprise only 25 per cent of the total teaching force of England and Wales — in primary schools it is 10 per cent. The requirement that entrants to teacher training should have GCE O-level in maths and English will come into force for the September 1980 intake of students. Women teachers in primary schools still substantially outnumber men: 3 per cent of teachers who take seven-year-olds are men; for nine-year-olds a third of the teachers are men; for eleven-year-olds half are taught by men.[1]

Teachers' aides have never been introduced into schools — despite a further recommendation that such a group be established by the Bullock Committee on the teaching of literacy skills in 1975. Some non-teaching paid adult help does occur, in about a third of all primary school classes, but with in the main only one helper per class.[1]

The procedures for inspecting schools have been maintained through the HM Inspectorate and through a further development of LEAs' advisory services. Demands for a closer monitoring and assessment of standards in the early and mid-seventies (a combination of genuine public and professional concern and of political opportunism) led to the establishment in 1972 of the Bullock Committee on literacy skills; in 1975 to the setting up within the DES of the Assessment of Performance Unit (APU); during 1976/7 to a national public debate on education (the 'Great Debate') culminating in the July 1977 Green Paper *Education in Schools: A Consultative Document*; from 1977 on, a series of discussion documents from HM Inspectorate on the work it was engaged in; and in September 1978, to the publication of a major national survey by HMIs of *Primary Education in England*. This provided a valuable benchmark for assessing what had happened in primary schools since Plowden.

This survey fulfilled one Plowden recommendation that the state of primary education should be assessed every ten years. Four other major Reports had their origins in a Plowden recommendation, although other factors dictated when

[1] *Primary Education in England: A Survey by HM Inspectors of Schools* (HMSO, 1978).

CHILDREN AND THEIR PRIMARY SCHOOLS

and why a particular Committee was set up to investigate an educational issue: the 1971 James Committee on teacher training, reporting in 1972; the 1973 Court Committee on child health services, reporting in 1976; the 1974 Warnock Committee on the education of handicapped children, reporting in 1978; and the 1975 Taylor Committee on school government, which reported in 1977.

Where to find out more

Books

The Home and the School: A Study of Ability and Attainment in the Primary School J. W. B. Douglas (Panther, 1964)

Children and Their Primary Schools The Plowden Report (HMSO, 1967; two volumes)

Primary Education in Wales The Gittins Report (HMSO, 1968)

Home and School Tyrrell Burgess (Penguin, 1973)

The Parent's Schoolbook Judith Stone and Felicity Taylor (Penguin, 1976)

The Pre-School Years Willem van der Eyken (Penguin, 1977)

The School Debate Adam Hopkins (Penguin, 1978)

Primary Education in England: A Survey by HM Inspectors of Schools (HMSO, 1978)

Mathematical Development (DES Assessment of Performance Unit, Primary Survey Report No. 1, HMSO, January 1980)

Children in Their Primary Schools Henry Pluckrose (Penguin, 1980)

Inside the Primary Classroom Maurice Galton, Brian Simon and Paul Croll (Routledge and Kegan Paul, 1980)

Under Five in Britain Jerome Bruner (Oxford Pre-school Research Project/Grant McIntyre, 1980)

Circulars

Circulars concerning pre-school and primary education include:
151 School Records of Individual Development (1947)
531(AM) School Registers and Records — Punishment Books (1956)
2/73 Nursery Education
14/77 Local Education Authority Arrangements for the School Curriculum
15/77 Information for Parents
S46/24/013 Coordination of Services for Children Under Five (jointly with the DHSS as HN 78/5, January 1978)
1/80 Education Act 1980.

7 The Age of Majority: The Latey Report (1967)

Why Latey was set up

Since the seventeenth century, 21 had been the age of majority in this country. There was no logical reason for this still to be the case — only historical and anachronistic ones. By the mid-twentieth century, young people were maturing earlier. Consequently many of the laws concerning the age of majority were becoming increasingly inconsistent and anomalous. In 1965 the then Lord Chancellor, Lord Gardiner, felt too that 21 was unnecessarily late for the age of majority and that there was a need to change the law. He believed it was time to 'bring adolescents into the body of society instead of keeping them on the sidelines'. But what should the age of majority be if not 21? And which laws should be changed? In July 1965, he appointed a Committee of Enquiry under Mr Justice Latey to consider these questions.

What Latey was asked to do

Consider whether any changes are desirable in the law relating to contracts made by persons under 21 and to their power to hold and dispose of property, and in the law relating to marriage by such persons and to the power to make them wards of court.

What Latey recommended and why

The Committee looked at two main issues: what should the law be for 'minors' (those who have not attained the legal age of majority) irrespective of the age at which they become legally adult; and what that age should be. The whole Committee agreed there should be some technical reforms in the law because there were 'exasperating and restrictive anomalies'. But the Committee was not unanimous on the need to reduce the age of majority from 21. Their conclusions depended 'to a very large extent on our assessment of the young today, how they live, what they need, what they are like and how mature they are'. The conclusions and recommendations listed below are those of the majority (all but two) of the Committee.

The Committee concluded that the historical causes for 21 being the age of majority were irrelevant to modern society today. Most young people were ready at eighteen for these responsibilities and rights. Not only would they themselves profit by them, but so too would the teaching authorities, the business community, the administration of justice and the community as a whole. The age of full legal capacity, i.e. becoming an adult, should therefore be lowered to eighteen for those areas covered by this Report.

Whatever the age of majority was finally fixed at, the law for those under it should still be reformed. Wherever possible, the law should be clear and simple. Some age distinctions were inevitable, but they should only exist if there were really strong reasons for them. Young people should stop being called 'infants' and be referred to as 'minors' until they became legally adult.

The Committee emphasized that decisions about what to do with young people who broke the law should not be affected by their findings. Such decisions should be related to each individual's circumstances, for it was the irresponsible, the disturbed and the inadequate who became involved in antisocial behaviour and law-breaking regardless of their age.

Marriage

On the whole, young people matured earlier, were able to earn high wages, were marrying younger, and were better able to cope as parents than their predecessors. They should

109

therefore be able to marry from eighteen on without needing their parents' or a Court's consent. The age of consent to sexual intercourse, together with the *minimum* age for marriage, should remain at sixteen for both young men and women. If someone's parents were dead or could not be traced, s/he should be able to apply to the Court for permission to marry. These applications should be heard in private.

Magistrates' courts tended to be too closely linked to the criminal business of court work. The two sides – domestic and criminal – should be separated. The proposed Family Court was a better forum for hearing applications for consent to marry. Statistics relating to domestic proceedings should be separate from those for criminal proceedings. The procedures for obtaining consent should be made the same for all modes of marriage and, to avoid false statements of consent being produced, there should be statutory authority for obtaining written evidence of consent.

Education at school in personal relationships and family life should be developed much more fully. The Government grants to the National Marriage Guidance Council and the Catholic Marriage Advisory Council were much too small and should be greatly increased.

Wardship and children's cases

Wardship gave the custody of a child to a Court which then decided who should be responsible for the child's care and control. This procedure was designed to ensure the child's welfare and could operate until a child was 21. The use of the wardship procedure had increased greatly and long delays could occur before cases were settled. Questions of wardship were dealt with in numerous courts – magistrates', divorce, Chancery (which dealt with issues of money and property). All this caused delay, anomalies, and procedural difficulties, to the obvious detriment of the children concerned.

Divorce courts had jurisdiction to make orders concerning

custody, access and education until children were 21, but orders were rarely made against a child's wishes once the age of sixteen had been reached. However, those dealing with these cases stated that they would prefer their jurisdiction to operate until a child was eighteen rather than sixteen or 21. The age limit for jurisdiction over children by magistrates' courts varied according to the kind of order being made — it could range between sixteen and 21. The age limits for dealing with these cases should be brought more into line in the various courts. Therefore, wardship and the power to make custody and access orders (together with care, protection and supervision orders in magistrates' courts) should end at eighteen.

Many children's cases were brought to courts which were inappropriate to the mainstream of their work. Much of the legal profession favoured the setting up of a Family Divison of the High Court to deal with *all* children's cases (usually arising from matrimonial or custody disputes) including wardship; with magistrates' courts having similar overall jurisdiction. The Law Commission should consider this proposal. In the meantime, the divorce courts should have the same powers as the chancery courts in cases concerning wardship, adoption and the guardianship of infants.

Maintenance for children could cause severe problems after sixteen, especially over the question of education and parental contributions to educational grants. The High Court and magistrates' courts should therefore be able to make maintenance orders beyond the age of eighteen. The Chancery Division should be able to make maintenance orders in wardship proceedings in the same way that the Divorce Division can now do so.

The Chancery Division should also have similar powers to the Divorce Division in being able to commit children to the care or supervision of a local authority or welfare officer.

It was difficult to decide in theory which cases concerning children were best heard in which courts. As such, the High Court and magistrates' courts should have wide powers to refer cases to each other's courts.

Different Acts gave different powers to magistrates' courts

in dealing with the custody and maintenance of children. The magistrates' courts should have power to order either or both parents to pay maintenance and to order a parent having legal custody of a child to make maintenance payments to the other parent who had been given the care and control of that child irrespective of the section of the law under which a case had come to court. (For example, the Guardianship Acts were more limiting than the Matrimonial Proceedings Act.)

Contracts

The law governing the contracts of young people below the current age of majority was unsatisfactory and needed reform. It was too complex, ambiguous and could be unfair to both sides of a contract. Many of the problems arose from treating nineteen- and twenty-year-olds as 'infants' or minors. Young people should therefore be able to enter into a full contract at eighteen instead of 21.

The law on contracts with young people under the proposed new age of majority (from birth to seventeen) should be tightened up. These contracts should not be enforceable against anyone under eighteen. But where the minor had received a benefit from a contract which s/he had failed to carry out, s/he should be liable to account to the other person for the benefit received. This might be tempered at the discretion of the court, which should have wide powers of discretion in making restitution against minors. A court should also have discretion over enforcing a minor's contract which it regarded as unreasonable, harsh or not in the minor's interest. A minor should receive back any money or property parted with under a contract which was not enforceable against her or him, minus any benefit the minor had received from the contract.

Normally, parents were not liable for contracts entered into by their children. But if an adult specifically made a contract to accept liability for a minor failing to carry out a contract, then the adult's contract *was* enforceable. Guaranteeing or indemnifying a minor's undertaking should only

112

be valid if the document made it clear what the adult's obligation was. The space for signing ought to be clearly marked, the wording short and designed to draw the signatory's attention to just what s/he was agreeing to.

A minor should be liable to be sued for fraud or deceit which was not connected to his or her age even if this meant indirectly enforcing a contract. However, if the fraud or deceit *was* connected with his or her age (e.g. falsely stating age) then s/he should be exempt from liability.

Servicemen

All boy entrants to the armed forces should be entitled to be released as of right on application anytime up to six months (instead of three) from the date of entry. After their eighteenth birthday, this period should be reduced to three months. Parental consent should always be required for someone enlisting who was under eighteen. All servicemen should be able to make wills, and be given an official reminder of any will that has been made when they leave the service.

At eighteen, young people should be free to give blood; make their own application for a passport; make a valid will; hold and dispose of a legal estate in land; hold the office of a trustee; have full powers to acquire, hold and dispose of personal property of any description; give valid receipts and discharges and otherwise deal with interests under trusts; act as a personal representative and make settlements; be liable for tax purposes; be able to acquire an independent domicile (i.e. the town or country where they live); take part in court proceedings without the intervention of a friend or guardian; be a member of a management committee of a branch of a friendly society.

At sixteen, young people were able to choose their own doctor, admit themselves to a mental hospital, have legal sexual intercourse. It should also be fully accepted that sixteen-year-olds could consent to medical or dental treatment without having to get the permission of parent or guardian.

Finally, the moment of reaching an age in law should be

the same for all legal purposes — the start of a person's birthday.

What happened to Latey

A flurry of legislation followed the publication of the Latey Committee's Report in July 1967. Not all of it was directly related to the Committee's recommendations. But much of it did significantly affect the status, rights and degrees of protection of children and young people.

The Family Law Reform Act 1969 dealt specifically with the Latey recommendations. It lowered the age of majority from 21 to eighteen, and tidied up some of the laws relating to young people still not legally adult. The 1969 Act enabled young people from eighteen to marry without parental or a court's consent, to make a valid will, give blood, make a legally binding contract, and obtain their own passport — indeed, all those activities listed by the Committee. The Act insisted on written evidence of parental consent to marriage for a minor being produced. It also accepted that sixteen-year-olds could consent on their own behalf to medical and dental treatment. Young people under the new age of majority were to be referred to officially as minors rather than infants, and the confusion over precisely when someone legally reached a particular age was resolved along the lines recommended by Latey.

Young people under eighteen who go into the armed services can now have up to six months to change their mind. A 1969 Tattooing of Minors Act made it an offence for someone to tattoo a young person under eighteen.

A Family Division of the High Court was set up following further proposals in 1969 by a combination of the Lord Chancellor, the Bar Council and the Law Society. The consequent Administration of Justice Act 1970 reorganized the Divisions of the High Court and introduced the new Family Division to handle divorce cases and the wardship, adoption and guardianship of children, including the work previously done by the Chancery Division. A 1971 Courts Act gave

THE AGE OF MAJORITY

more scope for transferring matrimonial cases between the
High Court and lower courts. The publication of separate
statistics on domestic proceedings rather than as part of the
criminal statistics was not done until after a further recommendation by the Finer Committee on one-parent families
in 1974.

Questions over custody, wardship, guardianship and
maintenance were dealt with in several of the Acts on marriage
and court reforms during the late sixties and early seventies.
Age limits for dealing with custody cases were gradually
made more uniform. The Family Law Reform Act 1969
though did allow maintenance payments to be extended until
a child reached 21. But the issue of one parent with care and
protection of a child (but not custody) having to pay maintenance to the other parent with custody was not cleared up
until the Domestic Proceedings and Magistrates' Courts Act
1978.

The Guardianship of Minors Act 1971 and, more important,
the Guardianship Act 1973 repealed the 1886 and 1925
Guardianship of Infants Acts. They reaffirmed that the welfare of the child (or young person) should always be the first
and paramount consideration. They gave equal rights to both
parents (the mother had been at a disadvantage) over the
custody or upbringing of a child and to the administration of
any property belonging to the child. They also extended a
court's power to put a child under the guardianship of a local
authority if that was considered to be in the child's best
interests. The later Matrimonial Causes Act in 1973 (a follow-
up piece of legislation to the Divorce Law Reform Act 1969
which liberalized the laws on divorce) also gave more protection to a child by extending a court's power in respect of
the supervision and protection of the child.

Eighteen-year-olds were given the vote by the 1969 Representation of the People Act. Ironically, the Latey Committee
had *not* recommended this reform. The proposal came
directly from the 1964-70 Labour Government through a
White Paper *Conclusions on the Review of the Law relating
to Parliamentary Elections*. Latey had avoided recommendations in this area of the law, adopting an uncharacteristically
reactionary line:

It does not seem to us that changes in the civic field are at all likely to follow changes in the private field even if we wished that they should. It is a very different thing to cope adequately with one's own personal and private affairs and to measure up to public and civic responsibilities.

One of the most significant pieces of legislation of that time was the Children and Young Persons Act 1969. This did not come out of the Latey recommendations (it was outside the terms of reference), but from another Government White Paper *Children in Trouble* (1968). This Act dealt specifically with children and young people in need of care and protection. It set up the administrative machinery for a comprehensive system of residential accommodation for these children — abolishing approved schools, remand homes, hostels and reception centres in favour of the single concept of the community home. It acknowledged the need for more flexibility in handling children who are brought before the courts, putting decisions about the most appropriate kind of care or treatment in the hands of the local authority or the child's supervisor rather than of the courts. The Act also set out the circumstances under which a child (up to fourteen) and a young person (fourteen to seventeen) could be brought before a court. There were six ways: if a child was ill-treated or neglected; living in a bad home; not attending school; reckoned to be in moral danger; beyond parental control; or had committed an offence.

As with the Children Act 1975 though, a substantial part of the 1969 Act has not been implemented. For example, the age of prosecution has not been raised from ten to fourteen; the minimum age of committal to borstal has not been raised from fifteen to seventeen (the number of fourteen- to sixteen-year-olds sent to borstal rose from 818 in 1969 to 2,117 in 1978); there is no compulsory consultation between the police and social services departments before proceeding (cautioning or prosecuting) against children in trouble. In December 1978 a joint circular was issued on *Juveniles: Cooperation Between the Police and Other Agencies* (DHSS LAC(78)26, DES 18/78, Home Office 211/1978, Welsh Office 169/78) suggesting ways in which collaboration between the police and other departments could be improved.

The use of supervision orders (brought in by the 1969 Act to replace probation orders) has declined, while children under seventeen (juveniles) are increasingly being committed to borstals and detention centres — which were to be phased out under the Act. Because of the incomplete implementation of the Act, more children are being committed to adult prison department establishments (2,947 in 1971 rising to 4,812 in 1976)[1]. Intermediate treatment schemes have been slow to develop.

In September 1975, the Social Services Sub-committee of the House of Commons Expenditure Committee published a report on developments since the 1969 Act and made 40 recommendations for reforming the law and practice on juvenile offenders. A Government response was published in May 1976[2].

Under Section 63 of the 1969 Act, the Social Services Secretary is required to report to Parliament on the working of the Act every three years. Two reports have so far been made — in December 1976 and November 1979[3].

The Act has been much criticized in its current state of implementation and the Government is committed to putting forward proposals for its reform. A NACRO report in January 1980 (*Some Facts about Juvenile Crime*) stated that there was no evidence that the 1969 Act had affected juvenile offending, with juveniles comprising a steady 30 per cent of all offenders in England and Wales since 1969.

Many of the reforms in this period of legislative zeal were long overdue — particularly those relating to the Latey Committee's recommendations. Apart from the fundamental issue of reducing the age of majority, the Family Law Reform Act 1969 had to repeal such laws as section 6 of the

[1] All figures supplied by NACRO from official sources — National Association for the Care and Resettlement of Offenders, 169 Clapham Road, London SW9 OPU (01-582 6500).
[2] *The Children and Young Persons Act 1969: Eleventh Report from the House of Commons Expenditure Sub-Committee* (H.C. 534, HMSO, 1975) and *Children and Young Persons Act 1969: Observations on the Eleventh Report from the Expenditure Committee* (Cmnd 6494, HMSO, 1976).
[3] *Social Services for Children in England and Wales 1973-75* (H.C.68, HMSO, 1976) and *Social Services for Children in England and Wales 1976-78* (H.C. 268, HMSO, 1979).

Employers and Workmen Act 1875, which allowed a judge to direct an apprentice to perform specific duties and to imprison any apprentice who failed to carry out such a direction.

But only some ten years after the Latey proposals became law, pressure is again building up for a further dismantling of 'anachronistic' age barriers for young people. New questions about the rights and responsibilities of young people (especially those between sixteen and eighteen) are being raised and demanding answers, in some cases as urgently as the earlier question of lowering the age of majority from 21. For example, the Latey Committee had touched on the question of *in loco parentis*, where educational bodies (schools, colleges) are empowered to assume parental responsibilities over pupils and students. The Latey Committee was concerned with those young people between eighteen and 21 — and the reduction in the age of majority solved that problem.

But two problems remain: the right of parents to withhold, if they so wish, their contribution of a grant to their student son or daughter who has in such cases no legal redress. Parents are not legally obliged to pay that contribution even though the size of a student's grant is calculated on the basis of the parents' income and in the expectation that the parents will contribute. The second problem was not considered by the Latey Committee (understandably becaue it was not in their terms of reference). How far should older pupils still at school — and particularly those between sixteen and eighteen — have a greater say in decision-making at school and also a greater control over their own lives, irrespective of the school's or their parents' views. The issue was raised to some extent by the Taylor Committee on school government (*A New Partnership for Our Schools*, September 1977) which wanted, and eventually got, an official 'ruling' that pupils could become governors from sixteen years on. It had been claimed that current law only allowed pupils from eighteen years of age to do so.

Young people in care are currently waging a vigorous campaign to win more control over their lives in institutions. Several groups have been set up, recently brought together under an umbrella organization called the National Association for Children in Care. Around 100,000 children are in care in this country — some eight out of every 1,000 children under seventeen years of age.

The laws regarding the employment of schoolchildren need reassessing[1]. While they make it clear that children under thirteen should not be employed in part-time work, once a child is beyond thirteen the various by-laws of different local authorities make a coherent, well-organized scheme of regulations difficult, to say the least. The laws concerning young people under eighteen and licensed premises require review and have been the subject of at least one official Government report.[2]

Minor changes canvassed in laws relating to the sixteen-to eighteen-year-old age group include the right to give blood and to see X certificate films. More serious issues have been raised concerning the sexual relationships of young people.

In June 1979, the Policy Advisory Committee on Sexual Offences, which had been set up by the Home Secretary in 1975, recommended that sexual relations between men should become legal at eighteen instead of, as at present, 21. It also recommended that the age of consent for girls should remain at sixteen.

The former recommendation would bring the law on homosexuality in line with the age of majority. The Committee based its proposal on the strong evidence that 'the sexual orientation of a large majority of young men is apparently fixed at sixteen — and of an overwhelming majority by eighteen'.

An even more contentious issue was highlighted in a report published in September 1979. A joint working party of the National Council for One-Parent Families and the Community Development Trust recommended in *Pregnant at School* that the law on the age of consent should be

---

[1] The Children Act 1972 provided for the minimum age at which school-age children could be employed out of school hours to remain at thirteen. The Employment of Children Act 1973 provided for local education authorities to supervise the employment of school-age children.

[2] Mainly in *The Erroll Report* (Cmnd 5154, December 1972).

abolished. The law had originally been introduced in 1885 to protect girls from prostitution and the working party believed that it was now irrelevant to modern society. Moreover it failed to deter sexual activity among young people; it unfairly punished the boy involved; it discouraged young couples from seeking contraceptive advice and, later, antenatal care. The working party found evidence that one in eight girls under sixteen had sexual intercourse before the age of sixteen (i.e. over 12 per cent). It also found that the level of sex education and lessons in personal development, social responsibility and preparation for family life at school was 'particularly poor'.

Government grants to both the National Marriage Guidance Council and the Catholic Marriage Advisory Council have been kept up — and in some years increased in real terms. In 1966, NMGC received £42,000; in 1980, £550,000. CMAC received 80 per cent of its income from Government sources — some £80,000 — in 1979.

None of these more recent issues dealt specifically with the general question of the age of majority. But taken together they indicate that when the law is out of sympathy or out of touch with the physical, emotional, sexual or intellectual maturity of young people, it needs to be set right. That can, of course, be done on an issue-by-issue basis. But from time to time the whole question of the age of majority has to be considered. In short, at some point, we shall be discussing whether to reduce the age of majority to seventeen, sixteen or even younger.

Where to find out more

Books

Report of the Committee on the Age of Majority The Latey Report (HMSO, 1967, Cmnd 3342)

Rights: A Handbook for People Under-age Nan Berger (Penguin, 1974)

Under Eighteen: A Guide to the Law as it Affects Young People (Citizens' Advice Bureaux, National Youth Bureau, 1977)

Civil Liberty: The NCCL Guide (Penguin, 1979)

First Rights: A Guide to Legal Rights for Young People Maggie Rae, Patricia Hewitt and Barry Hugill (NCCL, 1979)

Rights, Responsibilities and the Law: a Bibliography Judith Edmunds (Cobden Trust, 186 King's Cross Road, London WC1, 1979)

In Whose Best Interests?: The Unjust Treatment of Children in Courts and Institutions Laurie Taylor, Ron Lacey and Denis Bracken (Cobden Trust/ MIND, 1980)

Organizations

National Association of Citizens' Advice Bureaux, 110 Drury Lane, London WC2B 5SW (01-836 9231)

National Council for Civil Liberties (NCCL), 186 King's Cross Road, London WC1X 9DE (01-278 4575)

National Youth Bureau (NYB), 17-23 Albion Street, Leicester LE1 6GD (0533 554775)

Children's Legal Centre, c/o 61 Denman Drive South, London NW11 (01-458 2679)

8   Educational Priority:
The Halsey Report (1972)

Why Halsey was set up

The 1967 Plowden Report had recommended a policy of positive discrimination for schools in deprived areas which, said Plowden, should be designated 'educational priority areas' (EPAs). Schools in these areas were 'quite untypical of schools in the rest of the country'. They were housed in gaunt-looking buildings amid depressing surroundings. There was a high staff turnover; many teachers became 'dispirited by long journeys to decaying buildings to see each morning children among whom some seem to have learned only how not to learn'.[1]

The first major Governmental response to this part of the Plowden Committee's set of recommendations had come in August 1967. The Secretary of State for Education, Anthony Crosland, announced a special allocation of £16 million over the following two years for school-building projects in educational priority areas. A DES circular (11/67) was issued setting out the criteria for eligibility for funds, and asking LEAs to submit projects for approval. A further £18 million was added for 1971/2. The Urban Programme, under Home Office direction, also made allocations to increase the number of nursery places in deprived areas.

The second response had been a special flat-rate allowance for teachers in difficult schools. This was to operate from April 1968 and the annual allowance started at £75 (Plowden had wanted £120).

---

[1] From paragraph 134 of chapter 5 'Educational priority areas' of the Plowden Report.

122

The third major response was the establishment of five action-research projects in educational priority areas under the direction of A. H. Halsey. In October 1967, Education Secretary Patrick Gordon Walker[1] agreed to consider a proposal for the programme of projects. After lengthy discussions between the DES, the Social Science Research Council (SSRC), relevant LEAs and universities, an EPA programme was established. Four districts were chosen in England: Birmingham, Liverpool, London and the West Riding of Yorkshire. (A Scottish project was also agreed for Dundee.) In May 1968, a grant of £175,000 was allocated by the DES (£100,000) and the SSRC (£75,000) for a three-year programme in each of the four areas. The four projects started between September 1968 and January 1969; all were to end on the same day – 31 December 1971.

When the projects had been completed, the Government published the results in five volumes between 1972 and 1975. (In November 1972, Penguin Books also published a paperback *Priority Education* by Eric Midwinter, which dealt specifically with the Liverpool project.) The first volume was written by the EPA programme's national director A. H. Halsey, and considered the background, aims and conclusions of the programme. This volume (*Educational Priority: EPA Problems and Priorities*) became known as the Halsey Report. It differs from the other Reports covered in this book in that it describes a specific project, carried out as an experiment in applied social science. It is similar in that it covers in detail a particular, if narrower, issue – educational opportunity (or rather, the lack of it) in deprived areas.

What Halsey was asked to do

Pilot a policy of positive discrimination in favour of schools in areas of high social need; and to do so by the method of action-research. Four specific objectives were set out for the

[1] Patrick Gordon Walker took over from Anthony Crosland as Education Secretary in August 1967, after the £16 million allocation had been announced. Crosland became President of the Board of Trade.

EPA projects: to raise the children's educational performance; to improve the teachers' morale; to increase parental involvement in their children's education; and to increase people's sense of community responsibility.

What Halsey recommended and why

Halsey's Report was divided into three parts. The first part explained what was meant when people talked about EPAs; discussed the thinking behind the projects and described how successive Governments had responded to the recommendations of the Plowden Committee on EPAs. It also described similar projects on 'compensatory education' in America.

The second part looked at the four areas in England which had been chosen for the projects: the schools to be found there; the efforts to improve pre-school provision and the experiments tried out. The concept of the community school was explained and discussed, including the parts to be played by teachers, families and the local community generally in developing a successful community school. The third part discussed the conclusions drawn from the four English projects, together with the consequences for a future policy on EPAs.

The four EPA project teams expressed caution as to how far the education system could reform itself and were dubious about any strictly educational approach to the abolition of poverty. But they were optimistic — as Plowden was — in seeing the primary school and pre-schooling as 'points of entry' for creating changes in the relationship between the school and the community around it. The Halsey Report echoed the Plowden Committee's conclusion that for real equality of opportunity there had to be equality of conditions. Home circumstances, class and neighbourhood patterns were all important. The school could do little on its own to improve the life-chance of children: '. . . the decision to consider the EPA school in its communal setting was a wise one, and the Plowden Committee had been well advised to recommend that community schools should be developed in all areas but especially in EPAs'.

The Halsey Report drew seven major conclusions from the EPA projects, on which the teams based their recommendations.

The definition of the EPA

Despite difficulties of definition, the EPA was a socially and administratively viable unit through which to apply the principle of positive discrimination.

Criteria for designating EPAs had been set out in the DES circular 11/67 and included: what jobs local people did; the level of supplementary benefits distributed; the level of overcrowding in houses; lack of basic housing amenities; poor attendance at school; the proportion of handicapped and immigrant children; the turnover of pupils and of full-time teachers in the schools. But this set of criteria was not always very helpful because it was too imprecise. Applying the criteria often excluded areas which could legitimately be regarded as EPAs. Other criteria should be included, for example the language difficulties that children had (which should be monitored regularly and accurately). They should allow for the problems of small towns based on a single declining industry, of inner-city areas, of redevelopment housing estates, and of some rural areas. They should also be flexible enough to enable an EPA to operate as a smaller unit than an area — for example, a school, a class in a school, even families. In other words, while the concept of an area provided a convenient framework, closer and more detailed work had to be done within that framework with schools, classes, individuals and families so as to realize a fully effective policy of positive discrimination. Nevertheless, the focus on a *locality* remained essential to the general character of the policy of community schooling.

Pre-schooling

Pre-schooling was the outstandingly economical and effective way of applying the principle of positive discrimination and

125

of raising the educational standards in educational priority areas.

It was an excellent 'point of entry' into developing the community school for it linked the two networks of family and of formal education and helped to break down barriers between school and community.

Performing well in primary and secondary school had its roots in a child's experience during the pre-school years. Positive discrimination at that stage could create a range of other beneficial effects on a child's family and friends.

There was no unique blueprint of organization or content for pre-schooling which could be mechanically applied as a national policy. It was necessary to diagnose the needs of individual children and of particular local conditions. The provision of nursery education had therefore to be flexible.

A hybrid form of nursery centre should be developed — neither an expensive professionally-run nursery school nor a cheap, parent-run, amateur playgroup. It would inherit the vigour of both, would focus on learning (and would thus need professional guidance), have a carefully worked out curriculum and organized links with the local infant school. It would also need parental cooperation and the involvement of the local community.

Education for the under-fives had to be widely defined and linked to medical guidance and skilled attention to cases of social breakdown. At local level there should be a partnership between statutory and voluntary effort, with a coordinated format of pre-school provision under the guidance of LEA advisers and including a variety (in style, location and time) of playgroups linked with LEA nursery provision.

Experimental schemes tried out by the EPA projects included the industrial funding of a playgroup organizer, the use of a playmobile van, making use of primary school resources, setting up home-visiting schemes and a community education centre (the Red House in the West Riding). One experiment which tested children's oral language development through using an American-based structured language programme was sufficiently encouraging for the teams to recommend that British programmes be devised.

126

The project teams found that children responded enthusiastically to the systematic use of cognitive stimulations in a positive and benign environment. Gains made by the children during their pre-school years were maintained in the reception year at primary school. The vital task then was to extend pre-school provision in EPAs with additional state resources combined with voluntary activity.

The community school

The idea of the community school, as put forward in skeletal outline by Plowden, was shown to have greater substance and powerful implications for community regeneration.

The community school was originally conceived as a primary school, but the EPA projects had helped to broaden the concept. It could reflect the whole community and act as a focal point for the 'organization and process of learning through all of the social relationships into which an individual enters at any point in his lifetime'. The community school was the essential principle, along with that of positive discrimination, in any policy for educational priority areas.

A successfully-run community school was able to obliterate the boundary between school and community. All groups in the community would use it as a place both to learn from and to teach others. The whole social organization of the locality was seen from the view of its educational potential. The family, the school, the workplace, the WEA class, the pub, the street were all potentially both resources and barriers to a child's educational development.

There were difficulties in establishing a community school. Experience had shown that community schools in working-class areas had often failed because of the narrow, formal and traditional approach adopted by those in charge. The community side of such schools was frequently no more than the ordinary further education centre attached to the existing school building. Parents had little say in the running of such centres or in the activities offered for their benefit. The community school had to listen to parents, to advise and assist rather than tell them what to do.

The key to organizing a community school was 'linkage' — of school to family, school to teacher training, school to economy, and of school to school. The community school needed community management. A school would therefore have to reform the way it was governed, since it would need a community-based governing body: for example, a parent, head, a teacher representative, LEA officer, LEA elected member, an industrial or commercial representative, a college representative, with powers to coopt up to three others able to speak for interests particularly relevant to each school. Managers and governors should have obligatory training courses and their names widely publicized in the school's catchment area.

The partnership between school and family

There were practical ways of improving the partnership between families and schools in EPAs.

The first step was to improve the 'visibility' of school and education in the eyes of parents. Professionally-produced publications about education — newsletters, magazines, prospectuses, booklets — should be distributed among parents. Schools should advertise themselves more by, for example, exhibitions and live demonstrations in places such as shops, pubs, doctors' surgeries, churches, community centres and factory canteens. School sites and their local surroundings should also be improved, for example, reclaiming land for playcentres and gardens; upgrading interior decor; organizing litter campaigns. All these schemes were able to draw together what was taught in school and what was going on in the community. But the main aim was to show the community the content of the schooling and its relevance for community life.

A firm and constructive partnership between school and home should also be developed by designating a teacher to have special responsibility for home-school liaison. Such a teacher would explain and encourage participation and planning by all parents in a whole-range of school and school-linked activities. Arrangements for home-school liaison needed

128

to be flexible. Social workers and educational welfare officers should also help to develop home-school links, but they would be more concerned with families near or at the point of social breakdown — through being handicapped physically, socially or economically.

Parents should also be involved in what went on in the classroom — through pre-school or evening activities and in lessons. They should have the opportunity for mutual teaching and learning in parent-child projects at school.

The quality of teaching

There were practical ways of improving the quality of teaching in EPA schools.

In order to achieve the aims of the EPA programme, teachers needed to be adequately motivated, equipped and supported so as to be effective partners with parents and others in the community. This meant not just more money, but better conditions, smaller classes, adequate curriculum materials, teachers' aides, teachers' centres, effective links with colleges of education and with information about any successful EPA innovations.

The extra increment[1] awarded to teachers in schools of exceptional difficulty was found to have only a short-term effect. There had been a small initial impact on morale, but the long-term effect was limited. The amount given was too small and the scheme was badly administered. Nevertheless, the basic principle of a salary differential in EPA schools was generally approved of in schools and should be retained.

The curriculum of EPA schools should be aimed primarily

[1] The Government had implemented the Plowden Committee's recommendation that teachers in difficult schools should receive an additional allowance. The scheme began in April 1968 and the allowance was £75 a year. It rose first to £83 and then to £105 by October 1972. However, the funds made available for the scheme were limited so that the number of schools able to claim the allowance for their teachers accounted for only 2½ per cent of all primary school children. The Plowden Committee had estimated that 10 per cent of primary school children should be covered by such a scheme. Today the allowance is called the social priority allowance and amounts to £201 a year (£276 after three years' continuous service in a priority school).

129

at helping children to respond critically and constructively to the environment in which they lived. The balance of what they were taught may have to change from 'academic' to 'social', with work based more on the reality they encountered in their daily lives. Extensive language programmes should be used, but imbued with a high sense of social purpose. Reading and writing should involve socially relevant material. The emphasis in community studies should be on skills more than information. There had to be a change of attitude by teachers — from a defence of the *status quo* to an attempt radically to reform the area in which they taught, providing a compassionate, tolerant and critical examination of all social, political and moral issues.

Action-research

Action-research was an effective method of policy formation and practical innovation.

It brought together social scientists and administrators in a partnership forming public policy.

Within the context of planning for educational change, three functions had to be distinguished: discovery, innovation and dissemination. Action-research could serve the first two. More studies were needed (not always using the action-research method) on how the organization of EPA schools altered according to developments and population changes in their locality; on districts with new housing estates; and on the EPA secondary school. The DES should take the initiative and set up working parties to gauge the most urgent areas for research.

Both the successes and failures of research needed to be known by all LEAs and schools. There should be a central initiative to examine general arrangements for improving the dissemination of tested EPA practice. Teams of six or seven people could channel materials and funds; establish networks of action and communication; and create the essential impetus for change and innovation. These teams should be backed by LEA funding but be semi-independent, locally based and partly autonomous.

EPA and beyond

The EPA could be no more than a part, though an important one, of a comprehensive social movement towards community development and redevelopment in a modern urban industrial society.

Even with an EPA policy there were limits to an educational approach to poverty. But within those limits, there was a viable road to a higher standard of educational living for hundreds of thousands of children in the more disadvantaged districts. It was hoped that there was sufficient confidence in the results of the EPA projects for the Government and LEAs to create the framework of organization for pre-schooling and community schooling advocated here. If so there would be a new landmark in British educational progress.

What happened to Halsey

Successive Governments accepted the twin ideas of EPAs and of positive discrimination for deprived areas. The DES circular 11/67 declared unequivocally:

> The Government believe that better educational provision can, by compensating for the effects of social deprivation and the depressing physical environment in which many children grow up, make an important contribution to overcoming family poverty. Better education is the key to improved employment opportunities for young people in these districts and to enabling them to cope with the social stresses of a rapidly changing society.

Yet Government performance overall in ensuring that sufficient resources were made available, that opportunities were taken up locally, that there was adequate coordination between central departments and between central and local Government proved disappointing.

Pre-schooling was very much at the heart of the EPA approach to educational disadvantage. But, as described in the section on the Plowden Report, the aim of a full-scale pre-school network has yet to be achieved — even for priority areas. The initial response to the call for more provision

131

came through the urban programme. DES statistics show that between 1968 and 1973 nursery education, day nurseies and playgroups in England and Wales received over £13 million of the £31 million made available. By 1975, some 24,000 nursery places had been created by this method. But the first major initiative came in December 1972 with the publication of the White Paper *Education: A Framework for Expansion*. This began the ambitious programme recommended by the Plowden Committee. But it failed to keep to the structure and guidelines laid down by both Plowden and Halsey.[1] A subsequent DES circular (2/73) gave guidance to LEAs on the scale and nature of the nursery expansion outlined in the White Paper. It ignored the calls for greater flexibility in provision and for a shrewd assessment of local needs and pressured LEAs to provide pre-school places mainly through nursery classes attached to primary schools.

The programme turned out to be a disappointment. Government was not willing to be sufficiently directive towards local authorities in taking up the funding offered; local authorities were unwilling to commit themselves to long-term running costs of provision; the National Union of Teachers opposed any scheme that threatened a loss of teacher control; there were problems in matching the diverse 'approved of' elements in pre-schooling (for example, parental involvement, voluntary help, professional expertise and control, care that was appropriate for children of working mothers, the umbrella of a statutory framework). Moreover, the programme was not immune from financial cutbacks in the subsequent economic crises.

One essential element of the flexibility recommended by Halsey was the coordination between different departments — local and national. Any coordination between the two Government departments concerned with pre-school and day-care provision — the DES and the DHSS — took some time to develop.

A 'combined plan of action' did not begin to emerge until 1975, with talks between the DES, the local authorities

[1] See pages 96-9 of *The Pre-school Years* Willem van der Eyken (Penguin, fourth edition, 1977).

and interested organizations and the development of a permanent series of meetings between the DES and the DHSS. A joint DES/DHSS circular (S21(47)05) in March 1976 encouraged local authorities and health authorities to coordinate services and resources for under-fives. This dealt primarily with 'the machinery of coordination'. The July 1977 Green Paper *Education in Schools: A Consultative Document* (Cmnd 6869) further encouraged local authorities to 'improve the coordination of all available services for under-fives so as to make the maximum use of existing resources in the education, social services and health fields, as well as those which the community can provide through volunteers and voluntary bodies'.

But a joint report by the local authority associations[1] on *The Under-fives* in October 1977 criticized the failure of local and central Government to coordinate services for under-fives; the lack of liaison between the DES and the DHSS; the inadequate information available on finance and costs. The report called for local coordinating committees and joint budgeting between departments.

A second joint circular followed in January 1978 (HN(78) 5/S47-24-013) which was mainly a compendium of good practice in coordination of services. It claimed that there was 'an encouraging measure of cooperation between authorities and agencies providing services for the under-fives' and that 'the growing cooperation between education and social services departments is an especially satisfactory feature'. But this second circular was criticized for giving little practical help to local authorities and for failing to deal with the practical problems being experienced locally in trying to coordinate services, for example, the need for across-the-board local decision-making, the different pay and working conditions of the staffs being brought together, the need for training.[2]

A further move towards better local coordination came in the 1974/9 Labour Government's Education Bill 1978 and the subsequent Conservative Government's Education

---

[1] The Association of County Councils (ACC) and the Association of Metropolitan Authorities (AMA).

[2] Editorial in *The Times Educational Supplement* (3 February 1978).

Act 1980 where provision was made to enable LEAs to make the services of nursery education teachers available to children in local authority maintained day nurseries.

A more dramatic development occurred in November 1979 when Department of Education lawyers stated that clauses in the 1944 Education Act *could* be interpreted so as to put a statutory duty on LEAs to provide free nursery education for all children between two and five whose parents demand it. The duty was deliberately 'remade' discretionary by section 24 of the 1980 Education Act.

The effects of Government action and exhortation have been limited. In 1976, a study by the Thomas Coram Research Unit[1] concluded that:

> Registered private and public provision looks after 24 per cent of the nation's under-fives during some part of their day when they are not with their mothers. For these few it varies from childminder to local authority day nursery, from playgroup to nursery class, and less than half this provision is made by the public sector . . . For the very young child, up to three years of age, there is very little provision indeed, and the Government has no plans to increase the care for this group to any appreciable extent, despite the fact that they are the ones who cause most concern.

One year later in 1977, Willem van der Eyken[2] writing on the ten years since the publication of the Plowden Report concluded in similar vein: '. . . over the past decade, the pre-school child has been dependent, overwhelmingly, on private sector provision, while nursery schooling, though it has increased, remains an experience available to perhaps only one three-year-old in ten, and possibly one four-year-old in every three'. The latest research bears out the slow progress made overall not just in pre-school provision but in provision that best suits particular groups of parents and children.[3] However, a new study published in 1980, reveals that over the last five years there *has* been a marked increase in provision in some parts of the country, due primarily to the decline in the birthrate and

[1] *All Our Children: Pre-school Services in a Changing Society* Jack Tizard, Peter Moss and Jane Perry (Temple-Smith/New Society, 1976).

[2] *The Pre-School Years* Willem van der Eyken (Penguin, 1977).

[3] See section on the Finer Report and the Plowden Report.

only secondly to an increase in the number of pre-school places available.[1]

Halsey-style community schools have been developed on only a small scale. Figures from the DES indicate that some 200 primary and secondary schools in England and Wales are operating as community schools — fewer than one per cent of all maintained schools. In 1978, 3,444 primary and secondary schools were designated as social priority schools where 54,859 teachers received the priority allowance.

Statistics for 1977 show that around half of all primary schools and three-quarters of all secondary schools in England and Wales made some kind of provision for joint school/ community use.[2] But such provision varied considerably in scope, quality, intent, availability and access. A national survey carried out by the Advisory Centre for Education in 1976 documented the extent of the variations in the policies laid down by local authorities for the community use of school premises and equipment.[3] In March 1976, a joint local authorities' working party had recommended greater use of school facilities[4] — as did the Taylor Committee on the government of schools which reported in 1977.[5]

From 1968, a series of Government programmes had taken up the concept of positive discrimination and also incorporated educational projects into more general urban-aid schemes. A joint Home Office/DHSS/DES circular

[1] *Pre-schooling in Britain* Willem van der Eyken, Lynn Michelle, Neville Butler and Albert Osborn (Routledge & Kegan Paul, 1980) and *Nurseries Now* M. Hughes *et al* (Penguin, 1980). See also *Under Fives in Britain* Jerome Bruner (Oxford Pre-School Research Project/Grant McIntyre, 1980).

[2] *A Study of School Building* (DES/Welsh Office, HMSO, 1977).

[3] 'Who can use your school?' Judith Stone and Felicity Taylor (*Where* 118-20, July-September 1976, ACE).

[4] *Towards a Wider Use* Association of County Councils, Association of District Councils and the Association of Metropolitan Authorities (March 1976).

[5] One member of the Taylor Committee, Joan Sallis, wrote: 'On the question of the letting of premises and the community use of premises, I really felt that we needed another committee some time. We answered the questions about governors' responsibilities in the present framework adequately, and it would have been inappropriate in the context of the vast job we had to go any further, but I personally feel deep disquiet about the small extent to which school resources as a whole are available to their communities and the very high cost of using them in many cases.' (*School Managers and Governors: Taylor and After* Ward Lock Educational, October 1977).

19/68 announced the first phase of the urban-aid programmes (these projects have since been wound up). Between 1968 and 1973 over £13 million went into pre-school programmes from 'urban aid' funds. Following the 1972 White Paper *Education: A Framework for Expansion* specific extra funding for nursery education in urban programme funds were diverted into a wider range of educational projects including those concerned with the schooling of immigrant children.

In 1976, the country's economic problems were affecting the level of funding available for 'the needs of the disadvantaged'. While they were still to be given a high priority, 'current financial constraints have limited the Department's scope for positive intervention'.[1]

In June 1977, the White Paper *Policy for the Inner Cities* (Cmmd 6845) instigated a revised and more substantial commitment to disadvantaged areas. The funds for the urban programme as a whole were increased from £30 million to £125 million a year in 1979/80. Seven areas were designated as 'inner city partnerships' — Birmingham, Islington/Hackney, Lambeth, Liverpool, London docklands, Manchester/Salford, and Newcastle/Gateshead — where central and local Government would operate together to regenerate the area. These partnerships prepared schemes for 1978/9 costing £16 million.

Through the seventies, a series of reports dealt with the educational disadvantages experienced by the children of immigrant families. In September 1969, the Parliamentary Select Committee on Race Relations and Immigration had produced a report on the problems of coloured school-leavers, which recommended for example that teacher quotas be increased specifically to meet the needs of immigrant pupils. In 1971 and 1972, the HM Inspectorate produced three advisory documents on the educational needs of immigrant children. However, one of the most significant reports of this period came in July 1973 — again from the Race Relations Select Committee. Its *Report on Education* made some key recommendations which were duly taken

[1] Paragraph 16 *Education and Science in 1976*, annual report of the DES, July 1977 (HMSO).

up by the Government. A subsequent White Paper in August 1974 *Educational Disadvantage and the Educational Needs of Immigrants* (Cmnd 5720) established three new publicly-funded units to monitor and advise on ways of alleviating educational disadvantage: the Assessment of Performance Unit (APU), the Educational Disadvantage Unit (EDU) — both of which were attached to the Department of Education; and the Centre for Information and Advice on Educational Disadvantage, which was based in Manchester as a separate, relatively autonomous unit with its own governing body but funded[1] through the EDU. It has initially concentrated on issues such as cooperative care for the under-fives; the needs of West Indian communities; screening, diagnosis and remedial action for disadvantage; secondary schools in difficult social circumstances; and the disadvantaged school-leaver. It also began to collect and disseminate information on good practice in education. In November 1979, the Education Secretary Mark Carlisle announced that the DES grant would be withdrawn from the Centre, which would be closed at the end of the 1979/80 academic year, saving an estimated £310,000 a year.

The terms of reference[2] for the APU and the EDU were set out in the 1974 White Paper. Since 1975, the APU has conducted surveys on pupils' performance in mathematics at primary and secondary level and is in the process of carrying out similar surveys in language and science. The EDU's tasks include monitoring the work of the Manchester

---

[1] The Centre's grant for 1978/79 was £219,860.

[2] The APU was set up 'to promote the development of methods of assessing and monitoring the achievement of children at school, and to seek to identify the incidence of underachievement'.

The EDU was set up 'to serve as a focal point for consideration of matters, at all stages of education, connected with educational disadvantage and the education of immigrants; to influence the allocation of resources in the interests of immigrants and those identified, on the best currently available criteria as suffering educational disadvantage; to develop in association with the APU other relevant criteria to improve this identification; to establish suitable arrangements for promoting good practice by the educational system in its treatment of the disadvantaged and of immigrants'.

The Select Committee had recommended units specifically to concentrate on information, monitoring and advice about multi-racial education; the White Paper expanded the terms of reference to include 'educational disadvantage' generally.

Centre as well as contributing to the educational element of the urban-aid programmes.

The 1976/7 Select Committee on Race Relations and Immigration considered the West Indian community. Among the recommendations made in its February 1977 report was that an independent enquiry be set up to look at the under-achievement of children of West Indian origin in maintained schools[1]. The subsequent Home Office White Paper *The West Inidan Community* (April 1978, Cmnd 7186) endorsed the idea of an enquiry, but widened its brief after consultations through the Education Secretary with interested educational and ethnic groups. The general feeling was that such an enquiry should consider the achievements and needs of all ethnic minority groups and the needs of all pupils for education in a multi-racial society.

In March 1979, the Labour Education Secretary Shirley Williams announced the setting up of the Rampton Committee[2] to consider the educational attainments and needs of children from all ethnic minority groups and the educational preparation of all pupils for life in a multi-racial society.

Since the publication of the Halsey Report, the concept of the EPA has been criticized on the grounds, for example, that it has no direct effect on the disadvantaged home, thereby missing out a major influence on children's lives; there are more disadvantaged children outside EPAs than inside them; there are more advantaged children inside

[1] The Select Committee also recommended for education: special funds for racial minorities, especially West Indians; a programme to improve basic skills; an enquiry into why so many West Indian children were being directed to ESN schools and units; and a drive to recruit more black and coloured teachers.

[2] The members of the Committee and the full terms of reference were announced in July 1979. The Committee was asked to review in relation to schools the educational needs and attainments of children from ethnic minority groups taking account, as necessary, of factors outside the formal education system relevant to school performance, including influence in early childhood and prospects for school leavers; to consider the potential value of instituting arrangements for keeping under review the educational performance of different ethnic minority groups, and what those arrangements might be; to consider the most effective use of resources for these purposes; and to make recommendations. In carrying out its programme of work, the Committee was to give early and particular attention to the educational needs and attainments of pupils of West Indian origin and to make interim recommendations as soon as possible on action which might be taken in the interests of this group.

EPAs than disadvantaged ones. It became increasingly accepted that education on its own could not do enough for the disadvantaged child. Education had to be but one element in a more comprehensive and precise strategy taking in housing, employment, community resources and so on. The idea of the EPA was gradually absorbed into more general forms of aid programmes and concepts of priority action.

Unrealistically high and subsequently unrealized hopes for the success of positive discrimination created a powerful reaction during the mid-seventies. Evidence from work carried out in America in the late sixties and early seventies — notably a study by Christopher Jencks called *Inequality* (Penguin, 1975) — cast doubt on the value of schooling as any kind of useful instrument for altering for the better the life-chances of disadvantaged children. The pre-schooling programmes such as Headstart in America were criticized for not working except on a very short-term basis. However, subsequent work has shown that these criticisms were frequently misplaced and that the research used to support the criticisms was inadequate. Studies in Britain are now showing that schools can in fact make a substantial difference to children's lives both educationally and socially so long as they are organized and run in particular ways, for example, the comprehensive balance of the pupil intake, and the quality of the school's performance (what a school 'offered' the pupils; how well it treated them, and so on).[1]

The EPA strategy, on its own, delivered less than was hoped; the resources made available for helping disadvantaged children were less than was hoped. The concept was not quite right. But many of the current ideas for overcoming disadvantage still have their origin in the work done on the EPA projects — notably on the community school, the need for flexibility in curriculum and organization, the importance of pre-schooling, and the need for local diagnosis. At a DES-sponsored conference in April 1975 called *Educational Disadvantage: Perspectives and Policies*, A. H. Halsey acknowledged the limitations of the EPA approach, saying

[1] *Fifteen Thousand Hours: Secondary Schools and Their Effects on Children* Michael Rutter, Barbara Maughan, Peter Mortimore and Janet Ouston (Open Books, March 1979) is the key study.

there was no simple administrative or educational formula for tackling disadvantage since it appeared in so many different ways. More research and more resources were, once again, called for — plus a more wholesale social, political and economic approach to educational disadvantage.

Where to find out more

Books

Priority Education: An Account of the Liverpool Project Eric Midwinter (Penguin Education, 1972)

Educational Priority: EPA Problems and Policies The Halsey Report (HMSO, 1972) Other volumes have been published relating to the EPA projects: Vol. 2 *EPA Surveys and Statistics* (1974), Vol. 3 *Curriculum Innovation in London's EPAs* (1975), Vol. 4

The West Riding Project (1975)

Patterns of Community Education Eric Midwinter (Ward Lock Educational, 1973)

The School and the Community Cyril Poster (Macmillan, 1974)

Education and the Urban Crisis Frank Field (Routledge & Kegan Paul, 1977)

Education for the Inner City Michael Marland (Heinemann Educational, 1980)

Organizations

Advisory Centre for Education (ACE), 18 Victoria Park Square, London E2 9PB (01-980 4596)

Centre for Information and Advice on Educational Disadvantage, 11 Anson Road, Manchester M11 (061-225 8355)

Child Poverty Action Group (CPAG), 1 Macklin Street, London WC2B 5NH (01-242 3225)

9 The Adoption of Children: The Houghton Report (1972) The Children Act 1975

Why Houghton was set up

In 1968, some 27,000 children were adopted in England, Wales and Scotland — 24,831 in England and Wales; 2,155 in Scotland. That was a peak year for adoptions — the average number was around 25,000 a year. However, the laws on adoption and fostering were proving increasingly unsatisfactory. They had last been looked at in 1954 by the Government-sponsored Hurst Committee. Their recommendations had formed the basis of the 1958 Adoption Act. The question of fostering had not been considered since the Curtis Committee and subsequent Children Act of 1948.

Both Acts had some fundamental failings. The welfare of the child had not been made the paramount consideration, often coming a poor second when it conflicted with the rights of the parents. The timing and arrangements for the mother's consent to adoption, allowing her for example to change her mind up to the very last moment, often caused great anxiety and distress. The legal positions of a putative father and the guardian *ad litem* both needed to be re-examined. Many foster parents who wanted to adopt the children they were caring for were reluctant to do so because it was relatively easy for the natural parents to reclaim a child at any stage. Long-term fostering had a high level of failure, about half of all such fosterings. The patchiness in adoption resources across the country and the increasing pressures of work on voluntary adoption societies which undertook the bulk of adoption work were also causing concern.

A growing body of social workers, local authorities, adoption groups and MPs called for a review of the law to see if the adoption process could be improved and long-term foster children given greater protection. A series of 'tug-of-love' cases where the natural parents had, after many years, reclaimed their children from foster homes helped to build up a head of steam for reforming the law.

The Home Office and the Social Work Services Group in Scotland had already been collecting information on adoption work, together with views on how the laws could be improved. Two research projects had just been completed: one provided up-to-date statistics on adoption; the other studied the progress of a group of adopted children from the National Child Development Study (made up of children born in 1958).

In July 1969, the Home Secretary and the Secretary of State for Scotland established the Houghton Committee to consider all the material acquired so far, and to take further evidence on adoption and fostering. Even as the Houghton Committee proceeded, significant social changes were altering the adoption landscape. Fewer children were becoming available for adoption[1], partly through the effect of the 1967 Abortion Act (which made it easier for more women to have an abortion), partly through more universally available and free family-planning services, and partly through a growing social acceptance of illegitimacy. (There is now pressure to end the legal term of illegitimacy.) More children, originally born illegitimate, were being adopted by mother and step-father. Many children were being adopted by a parent and a second marriage partner. Indeed, over half of all adoptions were by one or both of the natural parents. Although the number of couples wanting to adopt outstripped the number of babies and young children available for adoption, other children remained unadopted. These groups were identified as 'hard to place' because, for example, they had physical or mental handicaps, were of black or mixed parentage, or were one of several brothers or sisters all available for adoption.

[1] In 1975, the number of adoptions in England and Wales was 21,299; by 1979, the number had dropped to 10,870.

142

In 1970, the Committee published a working paper of
provisional proposals so as to 'trawl' for advance comments
and criticisms which could be incorporated into the final
recommendations of the Report proper, which was published in October 1972.

What Houghton was asked to do

Consider the law, policy and procedure on the adoption
of children and what changes are desirable. The Committee
was asked to interpret these terms of reference fairly broadly
and to consider such issues as whether relatives should be
able to apply for guardianship instead of adoption; the relation between adoption law and that part of guardianship
law which gives the natural father of an illegitimate child the
right to apply for guardianship; and in particular the position
of long-term foster parents who wish to keep a child perma-
nently, by adoption or otherwise, against the will of the
natural parent.

What happened to Houghton

The Committee made 92 recommendations relating to the
provision and operation of a statutory Adoption Service,
the approval of voluntary adoption societies by the DHSS,
the procedures and criteria for adoption, court procedures,
guardianship, improving the system of fostering, and the
rights of adopted children to know their origins and background.

But the Houghton Report is unique among the Reports
looked at here for it is the only one (apart from some aspects
of the Latey Report) which has been specifically legislated
for not just comprehensively, but quickly. Out of it came
the Children Act 1975, only three years after the Houghton
Report was published. How did this come about?

Initially, the 1970-4 Tory Government was slow to respond to the Report — it was not debated in the Commons
until 9 November 1973, a year after publication. (In that

143

time, responsibility for adoption had been transferred from the Home Office to the Department of Health and Social Security.) The debate produced no promise of any early Government-inspired moves to legislate on the Houghton recommendations. The Government claimed only to be 'hastening slowly with legislation'.

A week after that debate, the Association of British Adoption Agencies (ABAA)[1] criticized the Government 'for apparent lack of enthusiasm for initiating new adoption legislation'. The whole issue of the rights of the child in adoption, fostering and care proceedings was then given fresh impetus by a series of tragic and fatal child batterings, notably the death of Maria Colwell. Calls for a new and comprehensive Children Act increased, although a more modest adoption-oriented Act seemed the most likely outcome.

In the meantime, Dr David Owen, then a backbench Labour MP, took up as a private member's bill an adoption bill drafted by a small group of committed lawyers and designed to implement most of the Houghton recommendations. The ABAA took on the job of lobbying and public relations for the bill and, along with the PPIAS (the Parent to Parent Information on Adoption Services) became part of a campaigning group called AGRO — the Adoption and Guardianship Reform Organization.

The Bill had a first reading in the Commons on 28 November 1973, but was lost when the February 1974 General Election was called. A new bill — this time a Government bill — was introduced after the Election and debated first in the House of Lords in January 1975. Primarily responsible was Dr Owen (now a minister of state at the DHSS) who had persisted with a new bill after the private member's bill was lost. Aimed at protecting the rights of adopted and fostered children, the new bill again followed closely the Houghton recommendations.

There were two other major influences on the bill, and the subsequent Act, apart from the Houghton Report. There

---

[1] ABAA became ABAFA in 1975 — the Association of British Adoption and Fostering Agencies.

was growing concern about children in long-term care and in private fostering arrangements, which had as its focus the 1973 study of children in long-term care, *Children who Wait* by Jane Rowe and Lydia Lambert (ABAFA). Secondly, the 1974 report of the enquiry into the death of Maria Colwell helped to create the demand for immediate and stringent measures to reduce the powers of natural parents over children considered at risk from severe mental or physical abuse.

Moved to the Commons, the bill had a second reading in June 1975 and received the royal assent (became an Act) on 12 November 1975. The Children Act took in three major elements: improving the law on adoption; introducing custodianship as a legal status between adoption and fostering so as to create security for those children for whom adoption or fostering is inappropriate; and extending local authority powers over children in care and in private fosterings.

The Children Act

Adoption

Every local authority must set up and maintain a comprehensive Adoption Service for its area as part of its general child-care provision. This Service should meet the needs of the children to be adopted, their parents or guardians, and those who adopt. It should include provision for counselling, assessment and accommodation where required. (Not implemented.)

All adoption societies must be officially approved by the Secretary of State. Criteria for approval include the society's adoption programme, record and reputation, financial and staff resources, and quality of organization. Approval is renewable every three years and can be withdrawn if the society proves unsatisfactory. Societies would work in conjunction with local authorities to provide the area's Adoption Service and can be helped with finance and other resources, where appropriate. (Not implemented.)

A new 'welfare test' (section 3) must guide the courts

and adoption agencies in reaching a decision about a child's future. Although all circumstances must be taken into account, first consideration must go to the need to safeguard and promote the welfare of the child throughout childhood. So far as possible, the wishes and feelings of the child about a decision must be given due consideration in relation to the child's age and level of understanding.

An adoption order can only be made if a child is free for adoption or each parent or guardian agrees to adoption. It is open to a court to dispense with this argument on certain grounds, i.e. if a parent is failing to fulfil parental duties, cannot be found or is incapable of giving agreement or is withholding agreement unreasonably; if the child has been abandoned, neglected, persistently or seriously ill-treated, or has little likelihood of being rehabilitated back into the family. An adoption order vests all the rights and duties which by law the mother and father have in relation to a legitimate child and his property in the adopters. An adopted child receives the legal status of a child born into the adopting family and so, for example, no adopted child can thereafter be illegitimate.

An adoption agency should as far as practicable when placing a child take into account the wishes of parent or guardian over the child's religious upbringing.

A new procedure called 'freeing a child for adoption' enables parents to consent to a child being adopted at an earlier stage than an adoption hearing. So parental consent can be given before an application for a child to be adopted has actually been made. The interests of the putative father would be considered at this stage. The parents' rights and duties are then vested in the adoption agency until the child is adopted. Such rights can be transferred to another agency if this is considered in the child's interests and it would enable an adoption to take place more easily. If after twelve months the child has not been adopted or there is no adoption order pending, the natural parents may apply to the court to have the 'freeing for adoption' order revoked and, if successful, resume their parental rights and duties over the child. (Not implemented.)

At eighteen, an adopted child should have the right to

know his/her origin and background, and therefore is entitled to a copy of his/her original birth certificate. The Registrar General, local authorities and adoption societies have a duty to offer a counselling service to anyone who applies for an original birth certificate.

The basic legal conditions for eligibility for adopting a child cover the domicile (must be the UK), minimum age (must be 21) and marital status of the adopters. Only a married couple may adopt jointly. Since adoption by a parent and a step-parent extinguishes the rights of the other natural parent, it should only be agreed to in special circumstances. The matter should rather be dealt with through an application to vary the terms of the custody order made at the time of divorce.

The section of the 1958 Adoption Act which prohibited a sole male applicant from adopting a female is repealed, and single adopters of either sex can now apply.

Pilot schemes to enable adoption agencies to pay allowances to adopters can be carried out with the specific approval of the Secretary of State. (Not implemented.)

The existing procedure for adoption was criticized by Houghton for the number of social workers likely to be involved with the adoptive parents: the adoption agency worker, the guardian *ad litem*, the welfare supervisor and the health visitor.

To reduce this waste of resources, the Act has provided that: the agency placing the child — be it a voluntary society or the local authority — should alone be responsible for presenting a welfare report to the court on the suitability of the prospective adopters. The appointment of a guardian *ad litem* would be at the court's discretion. The court may also appoint a reporting officer to witness agreements to adoptions. In non-agency adoptions, the local authority retains the duty to present a report to the court. (Not implemented.)

Most adoption applications take place in magistrates' courts and county courts. Most guardianship applications are heard in magistrates' courts. However, the latter are heard as domestic proceedings; adoption applications are heard in the juvenile court. Houghton recommended that both should be heard in the same court. The Act duly transfers adoption application hearings to the domestic court to be presided over by suitably qualified magistrates. (Not implemented.)[1]

The Act strengthened the security of a child who is the subject of an adoption application by placing extra restrictions on the natural parents from removing the child from his current home while the adoption order is pending, in particular when foster parents apply to adopt a child they have looked after for five years.

The Act also made amending provision for adoption between different countries; for the procedure for a court's refusal to make a final order for adoption, including rights of appeal; and improved the procedure for provisional and interim orders.

Custody

A new order called a 'custodianship order' has been introduced by the Act. This follows the Houghton recommendation that adoption by a child's relatives, say grandparents or parent and step-parent, was not always appropriate as it could cut off completely links with other members of a child's direct natural family and could create confusing inter-family relationships. Long-term foster parents, who wanted a more secure legal relationship with a child but did not want to go all the way to adoption, would also benefit from a custodianship order.

Under current law, parents may apply for custody in matrimonial proceedings or guardianship proceedings (a putative father, i.e. the father of an illegitimate child, may also apply). When implemented, this part of the Children Act will allow others to apply for custody through custodian-

[1] The 1978 Domestic Proceedings and Magistrates' Courts Act brings matrimonial law administered by magistrates' courts more in line with divorce proceedings in the High Court. Eventually, only magistrates with specialist training on a domestic panel will be able to hear domestic proceedings. Once these panels are operating, it is then hoped to transfer adoption proceedings from the juvenile court to the domestic proceedings court.

ship proceedings. Basically, the thinking behind the 1975 legislation is that where there is already machinery for applying for custody (e.g. for divorced parents, step-parents, a putative father), they cannot use the new custodianship order provisions because they have existing paths to court. Where there is no parent-child relationship, the new custodianship path may be used.

A relative or fosterparent then can apply to the court (after first notifying the local authority) for legal custody of a child. If this is agreed, the successful applicant becomes the 'custodian' of the child. It falls short of adoption in that the order is revocable on application by the natural parents, a local authority or the custodian; it does not wholly cut off the child's link with the natural family, who may apply for access to the child and may be obliged to pay maintenance to the custodian; the custodian in turn cannot change the child's name, receive a new birth certificate for the child, consent to the child's adoption, or arrange the child's emigration. (Not implemented.)

Children in care

The Act made several amendments to the laws relating to children in the care of a local authority or voluntary organization — specifically under the Children Act 1948 and the Children and Young Persons Act 1969. The intention is to give greater protection to the child.

A local authority must abide by the new 'welfare test' introduced by the 1975 Act when reaching any decision about a child in its care.

Parents who wish to remove their child from the care of the local authority or voluntary organization (for example, a child in long-term foster care) must give twenty-eight days' notice to the local authority if the child has been in such care for six months or more. It is an offence not to give such notice.

The Act sets out additional grounds on which a local

authority may assume parental rights over a child — for example, when a child has been in its care for a continuous period of three years. Where it already has such rights because of one parent's actions, the local authority may refuse the other parent's request for the return of the child if the 'offending' parent remains in the household.

Where a child is in the care of a voluntary organization, a local authority can also assume parental rights on behalf of that organization or vest those rights in the organization itself, whichever is felt to be in the child's best interests. (Not implemented.)

Parents have a right of appeal to the High Court if a juvenile court awards parental rights to a local authority or refuses to terminate the transfer arrangement.

In any proceedings under section 2 of the Children Act 1948 (the assumption of parental rights), the High Court and the juvenile court can appoint a guardian *ad litem* to safeguard the interests of the child. (Not implemented.)

Additional powers are given to magistrates to recover children in the care of a local authority who have run away or been taken away from the accommodation provided by the local authority. A magistrate may act on reliable information to issue a summons directing a person to return the child or a search warrant to recover the child from specific premises.

The 1975 Act also amended specific parts of the Children and Young Persons Act 1969. For example, a new measure was brought in whereby the child could, in certain circumstances, be represented separately (by a guardian *ad litem*, usually a social worker) from the parents. This could happen in care proceedings under section 1 of the 1969 Act relating to the child, in any application to discharge a supervision or care order, or in any appeal relating to these actions. Previously, the child had no right to independent representation and had to rely on the parent acting on his behalf.

A new ground for initiating care proceedings was introduced — where someone who has been convicted of murder, manslaughter, infanticide, or physical or sexual assault against a child, is likely to become a member of the same household as the child and that consequently the child is

150

likely to be ill-treated, or neglected, or in some other way disadvantaged.

Where a court orders that a child be separately represented, the parent or guardian can apply for legal aid so as to be able to take part in the proceedings. (Not implemented.)

The Act also tightened up the arrangements which govern the making and operating of supervision orders on children. These changes were a direct consequence of the report of the enquiry into the death of Maria Colwell. The courts and the police are given more powers to apprehend and return a child missing from any 'place of safety' where the child has been required to stay — community home, hospital, police station.

Many children, regarded as 'unruly', are committed to prison rather than to a community home because of a lack of secure places and adequately trained staff in community homes. In an attempt to tackle this problem, the Act gives power to the Secretary of State to award grants to local authorities to set up secure accommodation in community homes, and also makes it more difficult for courts to issue certificates declaring a child to be unruly.

The Act also attempts to improve the quality of private fostering by giving power to the Secretary of State to make regulations about local authority visiting of private foster homes, about the duty of parents to provide a local authority with information about any private fostering arrangements, and about the placing of any advertisements relating to private fostering. (Not implemented.)

The Secretary of State was given power to hold an enquiry on any matter concerning the work of a local authority social services committee as it related to children; the operation of an adoption agency, a voluntary home run by a voluntary organization, a community home; and the detention or imprisonment of children.

The future of the Act

The irony is then that although the Act is on the statute book, it has largely still to be brought into force, including some fundamental aspects designed to improve or ensure the well-being of children in care or who are to be fostered or adopted. The reason is familiar: a lack of resources to carry the measures through adequately. The Government specifically stated that no provisions would be implemented until the necessary resources were available. For example, one estimate puts the cost of administering the new-style comprehensive Adoption Service at £5 million more than the current arrangements. The DHSS is now costing out the 1975 Act to get a more detailed figure.

In January 1976, the 'welfare principle' provision (section 3) came into force — that in decisions on the adoption of a child, both courts and adoption agencies should give first consideration to the child's needs and pay due regard to his or her wishes. (Some technical and other provisions were also implemented.) In November 1976, three major provisions were introduced — adopted people's right of access to their original birth certificates (section 26); the time-limit provisions restricting the right of a parent to remove a child from care if the period of care has lasted six months (section 56), making three years in care a ground for assuming parental rights and duties (section 57), and guaranteeing an adoption hearing to foster parents who have cared for a child for five years or more (section 29). Some of the provisions on the separate representation of children in care proceedings were also implemented (section 64).

The Domestic Proceedings and Magistrates' Courts Act 1978 has added to and amended some sections of the Children Act 1975 — mainly to bring as much similarity as possible between custody proceedings under the Children Act and those under matrimonial and guardianship proceedings. As yet, none of the Act's sections on custody (sections 33 to 46) have been implemented. Much of part one of the Act on adoption and part three on children in care have still to be brought into effect.

It is currently an Act that has yet to get off the ground as at present there is no comprehensive Adoption Service, no central approval of voluntary societies, no freeing for adoption option, no payment of allowances to adopters, no separate representation of children's interests in adoption and care proceedings, no custodianship orders, no measures to improve private fostering. What are the consequences of this lack of action?

Many children grow up without experience of family life and without security because plans cannot be made for their future. More voluntary adoption societies are closing through lack of finance, a decline in the number of referrals, or an inability to adapt to the changing needs in adoption. But underlying these reasons is the uncertainty about the future implementation of the Houghton-style Adoption Service and the central approval scheme.

The Act, as it stands, remains controversial. There are two basic reasons for this: the amount of additional resources (money, staff, time) required to carry out the terms and intentions of the Act; and the reapportioning of the powers in relation to children, to natural parents and to foster parents. In turn, the British Association of Social Workers (BASW) maintains that resources and time allocated to setting up such a Service could damage further what is provided for preventive work with natural parents.

The attempts to extend the rights of children through separate representation and the welfare test have been generally welcomed — so far as they go. For the main criticism here is that — for some — they don't go far enough. The reduction in the rights of natural parents — done in part to improve the protection afforded to children in care, and in part to enhance the security of foster parents — is the most contentious issue. For example, it is feared that the reduction in rights (the new time limits, the reasons for taking a child into care) will act specifically against working-class parents and one-parent families. Children are frequently taken into care because of inadequate day-care provision. Those most in need of such provision are children from working-class or one-parent families. The more stringent clauses can put such families at greater risk. Moreover the additional powers of the local authority may discourage such parents from going to the authority for help. The generally low level of help available for rehabilitating families where children have been ill-treated may also stack the odds against the natural parents.

The potentially greater security given to foster parents links in with a growing interest in seeing fostering as a valuable option in providing for children in care. In 1976, over 50,000 children were fostered or 'boarded out' through the local authorities. Little detailed national information is available, but it is clear that long-term fostering has a high rate of breakdown. Greater legal security (through the custodianship order) may be part of the answer to that. But it also needs more good quality social-work support and more research in defining the nature and quality of fostering.

The other key outstanding issue is the need to integrate adoption more into the overall child-care service (part of the Act's intention) along with fostering and residential care. What links all these issues though is that the potential effectiveness of the Act in achieving these aims (a better adoption service, more protection for children, a just balance of rights) can only be judged in the context of a coherent and integrated social and education policy. It would be a policy aimed at preventing family breakdown, ensuring adequate day care and educational opportunities, preventing and treating illness. The Houghton Committee and the Finer Committee were originally seen as complementary elements in a drive to ease two related social problems. They were later joined by the Select Committees on violence in the family. All produced detailed analyses of the problems and made practical (and for the most part realistic) recommendations. Little of what they recommended has been acted on.

In November 1979, the Secretaries of State for Social Services and for Wales presented a report to Parliament on how the Children Act was operating[1]. It also noted some of the major changes going on in adoption. For example, there are fewer placings of 'healthy white infants with childless couples' and an increasing concentration on children with

[1] Section 105 of the Children Act placed an obligation on the Secretaries of State to do this within 3 years of the Act coming into force. Thereafter reports are to be made every five years. This report was combined with a similar appraisal of the operation of the Children and Young Persons Act 1969 (required under section 63/5 of that Act). The two reports are available in a single publication from HMSO as House of Commons Paper 268 *Social Services for Children in England and Wales 1976-79/ChildrenAct 1975: First Report to Parliament* (November 1979).

special needs and traditionally regarded as 'hard to place'. More such children are being considered suitable for adoption and there is more cooperation between statutory and voluntary agencies to find suitable homes for them. In turn, prospective adopters previously considered unsuitable — people who are disabled, single or of a more mature age than is usual for adopters — are now accepted. Adoption is more integrated in local authority child care services, with 'an ever increasing over-lap between long-term fostering and adoption'. A wider range of children are being considered for adoption although only a small proportion of children in care would find adoption appropriate since 'many children in care remain only for short periods, and others in long-term care are in close contact with their families'.

The report also listed the research commissioned by the DHSS into various aspects of the Act — from the National Children's Bureau on how courts and adoption agencies are interpreting the welfare of children principle (section 3); Newcastle University on the effect of section 26 giving adopted people right of access to their original birth certificate[1]; ABAFA on long-term fostering, including adoption by foster parents; and Keele University on the implications of section 56 (requiring parents or guardian of a child in care for more than six months to give at least 28 days' notice of an intention to remove the child from care) and its effects on policy and social work practice.

With the current reduction in the level of resources available to health, welfare and educational services, it is unlikely that much more of the Act will have been implemented by the time the next report is due in 1984.

---

[1] Between November 1976 and the end of 1978, 7,669 people had applied to see their original birth certificates under section 26. That was just over one per cent of those eligible. Since the first Adoption Act came into force in 1926, a total of 711,506 adoption orders had been registered in England and Wales.

Where to find out more
Books

Growing Up Adopted Jean Seglow, Mia Kellmer Pringle and Peter Wedge (NFER, 1972)

Report of the Departmental Committee on the Adoption of Children The Houghton Report (HMSO, 1972)

The Children Act 1975 (HMSO, 1975)

Adoption in the '70s (ABAFA, 1976)

A Guide to the Children Act 1975 Jennifer Terry (Sweet and Maxwell, 1976)

Fostering in the '70s and Beyond (ABAFA, 1977)

Social Services for Children in England and Wales 1976-78/ Children Act 1975: First Report to Parliament (House of Commons Paper 268, HMSO, 1979).

Organizations

Association of British Adoption and Fostering Agencies (ABAFA), 11 Southwark Street, London SE1 1SM (01-407-8800)

British Association of Social Workers (BASW), 16 Kent Street, Birmingham 5 (021-622 3911)

National Foster Care Association, Francis House, Francis Street, London SW1P 1DE (01-828 6266/7)

Parent to Parent Information on Adoption Services (PPIAS), 26 Belsize Grove, London NW3 4TR (01-722 5328)

Parents for Children, 222 Camden High Street, London NW1 8QR (01-485 7526)

Circulars

Key DHSS circulars on the adoption, fostering and care of children include:

LAC(75)21   Children Act: Main Provisions and Arrangements for Implementation

LAC(76)15   Children Act 1975: Programme for Implementation in 1976/77

LAC(76)20   Children Act 1975: Implementation Separate Representation in Certain Care and Related Proceedings (Sections 64/part/ and 65)

LAC(76)21   Children Act 1975: Implementation of Section 26 Access by Adopted People to Birth Records

LAC(76)22   Children Act 1975: Commencement No 1 Order

LAC(76)23   Children Act 1975: Implementation Adoption Agencies Regulations 1976/Adoption Court Rules 1976

LAC(77)18 Payments by Adoption Agencies: Amendments to the
Adoption Act 1958 (Criminal Law Act 1977)
LAC(78)19 Hague Convention on Adoption: Adoption Act 1968 and
Children Act 1975

10 One-parent Families: The Finer Report (1974)

Why Finer was set up

Up to the 1960s, it was popularly assumed that the development of the welfare state was well on the way to making poverty in British society a thing of the past. This assumption was eventually shown to be cruelly false, largely through the investigative work of Professor Richard Titmuss ('the promise of welfare through widening social services had been more impressive than its performance'). Many groups of people, including several million children, were found to be living in poverty or were close to it.

The late 1950s and early 1960s was a period of near full employment and rising living standards. One consequence was even greater contrasts between what became known as the 'affluent society' and those groups struggling to make ends meet. One of those groups was the one-parent family.

Pressure groups were set up or revitalized to publicize the problems and needs of groups in poverty and to press for changes in the law across the social spectrum — housing, welfare benefits, taxation, education and employment. In 1962, the National Council for the Unmarried Mother and Her Child set about redefining its aims, and subsequently changed its name to the more relevant National Council for One-parent Families. Self-help groups like Mothers in Action, Gingerbread and Families need Fathers were started up by lone parents themselves. In 1965, the Child Poverty Action Group was established.

By 1971, one family in ten with children had only one

parent. The dramatic rise in the divorce rate which followed the liberalizing of the divorce laws in 1969 helped to increase their number. Official estimates, from the information obtained through the 1971 national census, concluded that two-thirds of a million parents were looking after one million children single-handed. (Today, that figure has risen to over 1½ million children.)

Government was becoming increasingly aware of the kind of problems being faced by one-parent families. They were a well-defined group making specific and growing demands on welfare resources. The Finer Committee's Report made the point that 'by 1969 one-parent families had been forced upon the attention of politicians and administrators of the social services as a special group having exceptionally low standards of living'. In November 1969, the Secretary of State for Social Services, Richard Crossman, appointed a Government Committee under Sir Morris Finer to consider the problems of one-parent families.

What Finer was asked to do

Consider the problems of one-parent families in our society. Examine the nature of any special difficulties which the parents of the various kinds of one-parent families may encounter; the extent to which they can obtain financial support when they need it; and the ways in which other provisions and facilities are of help to them.

Consider in what respects and to what extent it would be appropriate to give one-parent families further assistance, having regard to the preservation of the discretion vested in local authorities by section 1 of the Children Act 1948, section 1 of the Children and Young Persons Act 1963, and sections 12 and 15 of the Social Work (Scotland) Act 1968 as to the exercise of their duties under those provisions; the need to maintain equity as between one-parent families and other families; and practical and economic limitations.

What Finer recommended and why

Family law, social security and one-parent families

One-parent families were subject to three systems of administering family law — the divorce courts, the magistrates' courts and the Supplementary Benefits Commission, which runs the scheme for paying out through local social security offices supplementary benefits to people who haven't enough to live on. The Committee considered this triple system to be irrational, inefficient and discriminatory. They called for a reform of the law concerning family breakdown and how it was administered.

Moreover, since the Divorce Reform Act 1969 and the Matrimonial Proceedings and Property Act 1970 had widened the gap beween how the law on maintenance operated in divorce courts and how it operated in magistrates' courts (the latter being more restrictive), the Committee also called for the procedures in magistrates' courts to be brought more in line with the other courts.

They recommended further:

Maintenance The Supplementary Benefits Commission should itself be able to assess and collect maintenance by an administrative order against the liable relative. What a relative had to pay would normally be by reference to published standards. But the Commission would be free to exercise its discretion. Any order would be binding on the relative and enforceable by the Commission.

Family courts A family court should be established to operate a single and uniform system of family law. It should be organized to provide the best possible facilities for conciliation in a matrimonial dispute. It should work closely with social security authorities in assessing need and liability in cases involving financial provision. The Family Division of the High Court should be the top tier of the family court and be the link with the rest of the higher judicial system. The family court should be organized to be as comfortable and convenient as possible for the people who appear before

160

it. It should be locally accessible, and operate quickly and cheaply. Local branches of the court should use county court judges, stipendiary magistrates and lay magistrates (an indispensable source of lay experience). Magistrates should be trained in the needs of family courts. No proceedings which may involve criminal investigations should go before a family court.

The family court would provide financial relief for parents and their children (except in connection with the termination of a marriage). Any maintenance or administrative orders in an existing marriage should be reviewed after two years at a special conference which all interested parties would attend. The conference would check that these orders were adequate for the parties' needs, and would allow a couple to consider their future.

Official statistics Information about family proceedings in magistrates' courts should no longer be part of the annual *Criminal Statistics*. Regular data should be published about the working of the family court and about one-parent families generally, with an annual volume of family statistics (legal, social and demographic). The DHSS should provide improved statistics about the work of the Supplementary Benefits Commission and of those who receive benefits.

Income

Even before the Finer Committee was set up, there was already general official agreement that widespread financial hardship existed among one-parent families. Indeed, it was one of the reasons for establishing the Committee in the first place.

The financial circumstances of one-parent families were, in general, much worse than two-parent families. Part-time work was discouraged by the way the existing supplementary benefits scheme treated part-time earnings. Full-time work often created problems of child-care. A lack of part-time work could reduce morale, create social isolation and prevent single parents from making a gradual transition back into full-time work when the children were older.

The Committee concluded that there was a need for a flexible benefit to fit in with the idea of varying the amount of work done according to family circumstances: full-time, part-time or none at all. They recommended there should be a special non-contributory social security benefit for one-parent families called the Guaranteed Maintenance Allowance (GMA). It should be available on proof of status as a one-parent family rather than of need. There should be no minimum age of eligibility. Claims should be dealt with by post and the allowance reviewed every three months. GMA should act as a qualifying source of income for the proposed tax-credit scheme and be set at a level linked to supplementary benefit, which with tax credits, or other family benefits, would bring income above supplementary benefit level for most one-parent families.

Someone's entitlement to GMA should be assessed without regard to maintenance payments. Means-tested benefits should be adjusted to take account of GMA, and not the other way round. GMA should be reviewed annually, kept in line with supplementary benefit and account taken of changes in housing costs, tax credits and tax rates. The child portion of GMA should be paid to all one-parent families regardless of income. The adult portion should be reduced proportionately according to a single parent's level of earnings.

The possibility of making families of long-term prisoners eligible for GMA should be looked at by the Home Office.

GMA should replace maintenance and not be additional to it. Any maintenance should be assessed and collected by the authority which would adminster GMA. Any maintenance received by a lone mother direct would have to be declared and deducted from her GMA.

The Committee recognized that until GMA was introduced, the mainstay of many families would be supplementary benefit. They therefore suggested the following changes.

Lone parents under eighteen who received supplementary benefit in their own right and who were not householders should automatically receive the full non-householder scale rate. Lone parents should get a special addition to the normal benefit. The long-term addition qualifying period should be reduced from two to one year for families with children. The increase in disregards[1] should keep pace with cost of living increases. The requirement for lone fathers to register for work should be waived.

A claimant who risked losing benefit on the ground of cohabitation should get a written statement of the alleged facts and be able to go before an appeals tribunal. Where benefit was withdrawn, the exceptional needs payment for children should be increased for a period of three months rather than for just four weeks.

The proposed tax credits scheme included a system of child credits, and the Committee regarded this as a priority. They recommended that if the scheme was not introduced, tax-free family allowances at an equivalent rate should be provided; maternity grants should be paid without any contribution conditions; educational maintenance allowances should be put on a national basis with a standard scale of allowances and qualifying parental income, the scales to be the same whether there is one parent or two.

Housing

In November 1972, half the unmarried mothers and one-fifth of separated wives on supplementary benefit were not householders. Many were forced into the rapidly shrinking privately-rented sector, paying high rents for poor conditions. They tended to move frequently and were likely to become homeless.

The Committee endorsed the principle stated in the Housing White Papers of April 1973 that housing authorities should have a comprehensive responsibility for *all* housing needs in their areas. They felt this offered the best hope for decent housing for one-parent families. They recommended:

Matrimonial home A wife's legal rights of occupation of the matrimonial home should be increased. Social security departments and advice centres should make sure that expert

[1] Those parts of earnings and other income not taken into account when supplementary benefit is being assessed.

163

housing advice was freely available. The legal profession should ensure its members were trained to deal with problems of ownership and occupation of a home when a marriage breaks down.

Homeless families Neither husband nor children should be separated from their families when in temporary accommodation. Help for a homeless family should never be lacking because authorities could not agree on which authority was responsible. Potential homelessness should be monitored more closely. There should be no eviction for rent arrears alone.

Local authority tenancies Lone parents should not be discriminated against in council house allocations because they were reckoned to be less deserving than others. Where a points system existed, a lone parent should be regarded as a married couple with a comparable family. Once families with children were on a housing list, they should be considered solely in terms of need and the avoidance of separating parents and children. When a marriage broke up, a local authority should provide for both husband and wife where necessary. Local authority tenancies should, like other tenancies, be transferable from one spouse to the other, and should have the same security of tenure as other tenancies under existing Rent Acts.

Rents There should be more safeguards against rent increases in any change of tenancy through marital breakdown. The Supplementary Benefits Commission (SBC) and housing authorities should be more aware of and involved with the problems of one-parent families over the fixing of rent, the payment of rent and rent arrears.

Owner-occupiers Local authorities should do more to help a family under threat of foreclosure by a building society. A wife should be told of any foreclosure proceedings against her husband, and given the right to apply to the court. The SBC and local authorities should obtain agreements with building societies for paying only mortgage interest for a time if necessary. The SBC should also consider meeting capital repayments.

Furnishing a home When considering applications for exceptional needs grants, the SBC should take account of the problems faced by one-parent families in furnishing a home. Local authorities should be able to provide furniture free of charge and ensure a home was adequately furnished.

Employment

The Committee held to the principle that lone parents should not be obliged by financial pressure to go out to work when they felt it was in their children's interests that they stay at home. But a lone parent who wanted to work should be free to do so. Financial, employment and child-care arrangements should make this possible. The Committee recognized though there were some fundamental problems. A lone parent had to cope with the dual responsibility of earning a wage and making a home. Most lone parents were women; many endured the additional disadvantages of low pay, lack of skill and poor training. They recommended:

The pay and status of women had to be raised and their work opportunities widened. (The Committee recognized that a start had been made with the 1970 Equal Pay Act, but felt that anti-discrimination legislation was also needed.) Employers should adopt a more flexible attitude to working hours and conditions along the lines already accepted for civil servants. Women too though must change their attitudes and take a more active part in their own interests.

Employees working less than 21 hours a week should receive the same rights as other employees to a minimum period of notice, to a remedy for unfair dismissal, and to redundancy payment. As a minimum, those working eighteen hours a week should be covered. Opportunities for part-time work should be expanded. Conditions of part-time work should be improved and 'best practice' spread more widely. Unions and employers should negotiate agreements for a minimum standard of maternity leave of three months' paid and three months' unpaid leave.

Radical changes were needed in the secondary school curriculum and the careers guidance offered to girls. Training advice and opportunities should be the same for men and women, including day release and the courses of industrial training boards, the Manpower Services Commission and the Training Opportunities Programme. Women with family commitments should not be excluded from these opportunities.

Parents and children

The Committee were also concerned with what it was like for one-parent families in terms of living from day to day, rearing children and coping with the repetitive small problems as well as the pervasive great ones. For example, a parent may have a sense of loss and social isolation with the added burden of having to cope alone with the emotional and material needs of children. In turn, a child may have to cope with a lonely and depressed parent, grief at the loss of the other parent, and a feeling of being different from other children. Some children performed badly at school or displayed disturbed or delinquent behaviour. The Committee recommended:

Social and education services The personal, social and education services should play a greater role in the lives of one-parent families, helping to improve their quality of life and preventing waste and suffering. However, it had to be accepted that these services could not solve every problem encountered. There was no need to set up special services for one-parent families, but it was vital that resources were available on a sufficient scale to ensure that groups in need were not neglected.

Day care Local authority day-care services for children under five should be greatly expanded, with suitable arrangements made for the children of lone working parents. Part-time day care, nursery schooling and playgroups were usually more suitable than full-time care. Children under three should not normally be parted from their mothers for long periods, and there should always be skilled substitute care to compensate for the absence of the mother.

166

Central and local Government should encourage more playgroups in deprived areas, and there should be more coordination over policy and services for day care generally. Charges for day care should be rationalized on a national basis. Employers should be encouraged to provide day nurseries, including joint provision with local authorities.

Childminders should be helped to improve their standards of care by local authorities providing training courses and loaning equipment.

Day-care services for children of school age should be the responsibility of local social services departments. Educational facilities should be used with additional financial backing to provide more effective day care for these children. Local authorities, in consultation with social services departments, should look sympathetically at the needs of one-parent family children for boarding education. They should provide more help in the home, especially for motherless families.

Legislation on fostering should ensure that private placements are of the same standard of supervision as local authority fosterings. Day-fostering schemes should be developed. Local authorities should require and monitor specific standards for mother and baby homes and ensure there were enough places to meet demand.

Education There should be greater home-school contacts through a child's schooling, with more support from guidance staff for one-parent family children. Parents should be kept informed of school welfare benefits. There should be closer liaison between schools and health and social services agencies. More male staff should be recruited to infant and nursery schools and day nurseries. Schools should help pupils become aware of the realities of family life and of practical home economics.

Schools should do as much as possible to help girls who become pregnant and who wanted to continue their education, including the provision of home tuition.

Special groups The difficulties of particular groups — children of women prisoners, families of long-term hospital

167

patients and immigrant families — should be studied to make a proper assessment of what needed to be done for them. In particular, accommodation to enable children up to the age of five to stay with their mothers in prison should be expanded as soon as possible.

Advice and research Local authorities should make sure both statutory and voluntary advice and counselling services were readily accessible and could give an efficient, sympathetic and expert service for lone parents, both at the time of death or marital breakdown, and for more long-term problems. Advice on birth control and family planning should be more deliberately accessible and geared to young people and to those groups who were most likely, statistically, to produce illegitimate children or suffer marital breakdown. Further research should be done into the effects on children of living in a one-parent family.

What happened to Finer

The Finer Committee reported in July 1974. The Government did not initiate any debate in Parliament on the Report until October 1975. Then it merely asked MPs to 'take note' of Finer's recommendations. The motion failed.

In the five years since Finer reported, over half of its recommendations were rejected by the 1974-9 Labour Government, including those two major planks of the Finer plan to help one-parent families — the Guaranteed Maintenance Allowance (GMA) and the Family Court. Only 48 (a fifth) have been implemented — and many of those were fairly minor recommendations. A further 23 were officially endorsed by the Government, which urged local authorities to take them up as and when they were able. A few were still being considered when the May 1979 General Election intervened.

Only one recommendation on maintenance and administrative orders was acted on — that the Supplementary Benefits Commission (SBC) no longer seeks to involve lone mothers in extracting maintenance assessment or contributions from the liable relative. The proposal for a Family Court was rejected for the time being (mainly on grounds of cost). Some changes have been made to matrimonial proceedings in magistrates' courts. The new Domestic Proceedings and Magistrates' Courts Act (which came into effect in autumn 1979) brings these courts more in line with the High Court and the divorce county courts on how they settle financial relief for families.

Statistical data on the family (and more specifically the one-parent family) has been improved along Finer lines, including an end to the publication of family proceedings with criminal statistics.

The Finer Committee set out alternative proposals alongside their plan for the Guaranteed Maintenance Allowance. The Government duly turned down the GMA proposal. It was, in any case, subsequently regarded generally as a flawed scheme; the proposal has since been improved by the National Council for One-parent Families, though with no greater chance of being accepted. However, few of the alternatives have been implemented either. Lone parents under eighteen who get supplementary benefit can now also automatically get the full adult non-householder scale rate and 'disregards' were increased once but without any commitment to keep them in line with the cost of living. The full-time work qualification for one-parent families to go onto the Family Income Supplements Scheme has been reduced from 30 hours to the recommended 24 hours a week. Lone fathers no longer have to register for work. The personal tax allowance for lone parents has been made the same as for a married man, and more information about tax has been made available to lone parents through a special Government leaflet. But lone parents still do not get priority in claims for tax repayments.

One-parent families continue to rely on the *discretionary* powers of the SBC for any additional benefit rather than be entitled to the Finer-recommended special addition. Nor has the qualifying period for a long-term additional rate for families with children been reduced from two years to one. Educational maintenance allowances for children at school remain in the discretionary hands of the LEAs.

169

In 1978, a £100 million scheme for a national allowance was proposed by the Education Secretary Shirley Williams. This was reduced in Cabinet to a £10 million pilot scheme and abandoned after the May 1979 General Election.

New guidelines on the rules and procedures concerning cohabitation were established for social security offices in 1976 following a report by the Supplementary Benefits Commission (*Living Together as Husband and Wife* Supplementary Benefit Administrative Paper no. 5, HMSO). But many couples still claim to find them largely inflexible and unfair, particularly with the exceptional needs payment for children still being paid for only four weeks instead of the recommended three months. A non-contributory maternity grant proposal was also turned down.

The most positive Government response to this part of Finer was the eventual introduction of the Child Benefit Scheme in April 1977, which combined child tax allowances with family allowances (including a new allowance for the first child) into a new tax-free cash allowance payable to the mother as of right. This has since been supplemented by the introduction of the Child Benefit Increase payable to a single parent looking after a child on his/her own.[1]

The most comprehensive Government statement on housing policy for one-parent families came in a Circular from the Department of the Environment in August 1977 (*Housing for One-parent Families*). This endorsed much of what Finer had to say about housing, and urged local authorities to carry out the recommended policy as and when they were able. The Circular pressed local authorities to consider one-parent families on the basis of need alone when allocating council houses and to regard them as equivalent to a married couple with children on any points system. It recommended the abolition of residential qualifications for entry to a housing waiting-list and an easier system of tenancy transfer from one parent to the other. Local authorities and the SBC were both urged to be more helpful towards families in difficulties over rent, underscoring Finer's specific suggestions. However, the Government claimed that the existing

[1] Child benefit is £4 a week (£4.75 from Nov. 1980); child benefit increase is £2.50 for the first child only (£3 from Nov. 1980).

powers for help with furnishing a home were adequate and no changes were necessary. The Circular also endorsed many of the recommendations on owner-occupiers and the need to ease those problems that can occur with mortgage repayments when a marriage breaks up. But an investigation of the idea that the SBC should be able to meet capital as well as interest repayments was turned down.

The 1976 Domestic Violence and Matrimonial Proceedings Act (which came into force in June 1977) increased a wife's legal rights to remain in the family home once a marriage had broken down and also allowed a court to evict the husband if considered necessary. Other aspects concerning the transfer of a tenancy from one partner to the other (either on marital breakdown or on the subsequent death of the owner-partner) are still being considered following a Law Commission report on family law in 1978.

Finer's recommendations on homelessness were taken up by the 1977 Housing (Homeless Persons) Act which transferred (and greatly extended) the duty to provide accommodation for homeless people from the local authority social services to the local housing authority. The Act also emphasized the need to keep families together, for local authorities to be more alert to those circumstances that are likely to lead to a family becoming homeless, and for priority to be given to families with dependent children, including one-parent families. This Act has unquestionably been of help to many one-parent families. In the first half of 1978 figures showed that nearly 10,000 one-parent families, who represent 51 per cent of homeless families with children, were housed under the Act by English local authorities. More recent official figures are yet to be made available. However, there are problems. Some local authorities have successfully found loopholes in the Act and consequently fail to fulfil their statutory obligations. Many families are finding difficulty in satisfying local authorities that their homelessness is 'unintentional'. The quality of housing offered to one-parent famlies is sometimes poor and substandard.

More training opportunities for women are gradually being opened up and more widely publicized through the work of the Manpower Services Commission and the Training

Services Agency, which have also been encouraging the industrial training boards to review their policy for women employees. However, progress is slow. For example, the opportunities for day and block release from work have remained fairly constant. The proportion of girls and boys signing on for these courses has slightly declined — 8.4 per cent of all sixteen- to eighteen-year-old girls not in full-time education or registered unemployed in 1974/5; 7.1 per cent in 1976/7. The comparable figures for boys are 33 per cent and 28.6 per cent.

The Sex Discrimination Act 1975 and the Equal Opportunities Commission have provided a basic legal, advisory and research framework for developing better provision for girls over curriculum choice and careers guidance in schools. It is too early to see any of the 'radical changes' urged by the Finer Committee. Many more schools though are aware of the need to provide equal opportunities and choices. However, in July 1977 the House of Commons Expenditure Committee looking into the attainment of the school leaver was obliged to report that 'in spite of the establishment of the Equal Opportunities Commission there is still general concern, which we share, that girls are not receiving appropriate guidance or encouragement to pursue certain areas of study and work traditionally reserved for boys and men'. In October 1979, the Equal Opportunities Commission (EOC) published a special booklet for schools setting out guidelines for good practice by schools and LEAs (*Do You Provide Equal Educational Opportunities?*).

The recent HM school inspectors' survey of 384 maintained secondary schools (*Aspects of Secondary Education in England*, HMSO, December 1979) noted some minor improvement in equality of subject opportunity. But this still meant that two thirds of the schools surveyed insisted on or acquiesced in the traditional divisions in craft subjects — woodwork and metalwork for boys, home economics and needlework for girls — especially after the first year at school. Only a third of the schools claimed to offer a wholly open choice of subjects — and even they admitted that the numbers crossing the traditional boundaries were few. While many schools provide equal opportunities in the first year

172

of a child's secondary schooling, the opportunities drastically reduce after that.

A greater measure of protection for part-time workers (those now who work more than sixteen hours a week) has been given by the 1975 Employment Protection Act, which also lays down a statutory minimum period of paid maternity leave plus reinstatement in the same or a similar job. Statistics about women's employment are now regularly and readily made available in Government publications. More efforts have gone into ensuring that job centres are better able to cater for women and especially for lone parents who have special problems in getting work (for example, having to combine a job with caring for children).

The Government endorsed the need for a variety of day-care services and nursery provision for children under five, and set out to improve coordination between the two departments responsible — the DES and the DHSS. A letter was also issued to local authorities in March 1976 on the need for coordinating local services. This was followed by a joint DES/DHSS circular letter on *Coordination of Services for Children under Five* in January 1978. This specifically referred to the need to combine educational and day-care provision.

However, day-care and nursery provision remain unable to meet the demand. In February 1979, Margaret Jackson (then an under-secretary of state at the Department of Education) wrote that 'there is still a great unmet need for educational and other facilities for the children of working women'. Demand is growing as more mothers want or have to go out to work, usually to make ends meet. Even two-parent families find they need two incomes for a satisfactory standard of living.

One Government survey[1] found that in 1974 some 64 per cent of mothers in England and Wales wanted some form of day care for their under-fives. (In three inner-city areas, the figure was 90 per cent for three- and four-year-olds, and 73 per cent for two-year-olds.) A more recent survey published

[1] *Pre-School Children and the Need for Day Care* Margaret Bone (HMSO, 1977).

in *Woman's Own* (February 17 and 24, 1979) indicated that this proportion has risen considerably.

The recent booklet from the Equal Opportunities Commission *I Want To Work . . . But What About the Kids?* (September 1978) sets out the nub of the problem:

> In Great Britain there is no coherent or systematic provision for the day-care needs of families with pre-school children. The limited provision which does exist is essentially a by product of policy commitments in other areas — by the Department of Education and Science, which provides nursery education for three to five-year-olds, and by the Department of Health and Social Security, whose 542 local authority day nurseries provide care for those under-fives who meet its definition of priority children.

The booklet went on to say that the division of responsibilities between the two Government departments was a major factor in there not being a systematic policy. But there are two further difficulties: the amount of money that Government feels able to make available for day-care and nursery provision; and whether and how the local authorities take up that money to provide for the needs of working mothers.

Since 1974, some £60 million has been made available by the Government for nursery education building programmes. For the year 1979/80, the 1974-9 Labour Government allocated £5.9 million to English local authorities for this purpose — and planned for £14.3 million between 1979 and 1982. (The future pattern under the new Conservative Government has yet to become clear. But its policy of reducing public expenditure means in some areas a slowing down of new provision and in others an actual reduction in existing provision.)

All this has meant that between 1974 and 1979, there has been a marked improvement in provision. But it has been patchy and much of it unsuitable for many working parents. Local authorities vary enormously in what they provide, whom they cater for and how much they charge for care. Some — Avon, Bromley, Croydon, Hampshire, Isle of Scilly, Sutton and Wiltshire — have consistently failed to take up the offer of central Government funds for nursery building programmes between 1974 and 1979. The autonomy of local authorities means they can opt for one particular form of provision (say, playgroups) or initiate a policy of allowing a large number of four-year-olds into primary school (known as 'the rising-fives'). Unfortunately, some forms of provision are clearly less appropriate for working mothers and lone parents than other forms; part-time places may be plentiful in an area when the real demand is for full-time places. Two revealing figures are that in 1977 the national average for the proportion of nursery-age children actually being provided with a nursery place expressed as a *full-time* equivalent was only 9.1 per cent; and in 1978, the Inner London Education Authority could not fill all its part-time places, but was over-subscribed for its full-time places.

What then are the statistics to support the marked improvement? In 1979, there were some three million children in England and Wales under five: two-fifths of whom were aged three or four, i.e. some 1,200,000 children of nursery age. Between 1974 and 1979, the proportion of three- and four-year-olds receiving some kind of state nursery provision grew from 28 per cent to 39 per cent. Some 17 per cent were in nursery schools or classes (the comparable figure for 1974 was 8.5 per cent). The most recent figures available reveal that a further 36 per cent of four-year-olds were going into primary school early.

In numbers, there are places for over 200,000 three- and four-year-olds in nursery classes; 230,000 in reception classes in infant schools. Local authority social services departments currently have full-time day-care places for 30,500 under-fives, most of which go to children in special need. But in September 1978, a report from the Central Policy Review Staff — the Government's 'think tank' — stated that 'at any one time there may be 12,000 children in England on waiting lists, many of whom will never get a place, but many children are not put down on waiting lists because their chances of getting a place are so slight'.

As for playgroups, the Pre-school Playgroups Association estimates that some 46 per cent of three- and four-year-olds in England and Wales can be catered for through playgroup sessions. The latest Government figures available (as at

175

31 March 1977) showed that there were 366,000 places in premises registered in *England* to provide sessional care (i.e. mainly playgroups). This represented 119.6 places for every 1,000 children under five, although this did not account for the number of children who would actually use a single place in a week since few children go every day to a playgroup.

In fact, many working parents use the services of a child-minder. In 1976, there were 63,000 full-time and 20,000 part-time *registered* places with childminders in England. But the latest estimates reveal that up to 100,000 children are placed with childminders every day. In most cases parents use childminders as a last resort. A survey published by the Office of Population Censuses and Surveys (OPCS) in 1977 found that only 3 per cent of mothers wanted childminding for their children and 73 per cent of the mothers who did use a childminder would have preferred some other kind of care. Some progress has been made to improve the quality of care given by childminders both through local authority and voluntary agency involvement in training and provision of equipment. But the childminder, both registered and unregistered, will be a major figure in day care for many years to come.

Care for school-age children outside school hours and during the holidays has been given little official attention[1]. Holiday playschemes have increased in number, catering mainly for secondary-age children — the larger problem is with primary-age children who are less able to look after themselves. Few schools are used to provide an alternative service. In September 1978, the Equal Opportunities Commission estimated, through official Government surveys, that about 20 per cent of five- to ten-year-olds are left alone during the school holidays and about 15 per cent after school, i.e. 300,000 and 225,000 children respectively out of a total age group of 1½ million. For the eleven to fifteen age group, the figures are 25 per cent (375,000) and 20 per cent (300,000) respectively — out of 1½ million children.

The problem is not new — as far back as 1948 an official Government Report from the Central Advisory Council for

[1] *Day Care for School-Age Children* Robin Simpson (EOC, 1978).

England called *Out of School* recommended that 'the Minister should make an urgent appeal to LEAs to apply their powers under the Education Acts so as to increase and improve by every possible means, facilities for the play and recreation of children out of school hours'.

The recommendations on private fostering were dealt with in the 1975 Children Act, although the relevant sections (95 and 96) have yet to be implemented.

As with all the above areas of welfare, public spending cuts on top of already limited resources have eaten into intentions and attempts to come to grips with the problems documented by the Finer Committee. These restrictions have also affected action on additional help in the home for one-parent families, the provision of mother and baby homes for unmarried mothers, and of adequate advice and counselling services for lone parents. Since the Finer Report, family planning services have been brought under the National Health Service so as to provide a free and comprehensive service.

Little has been done specifically to help those groups marked out as special by Finer — families of long-term patients in hospital, immigrant families, the children of women prisoners. In 1974 there were 29 places for mothers with babies or heavily pregnant women in three prisons in England (two open, one closed). Two catered only for children up to twelve months old; the third up to three years. Six years later there are 63 places. One new purpose-built unit has opened and a second will open in the mid-1980s at Holloway to provide an additional fourteen places. The Home Office states that the places currently available are oversubscribed.

Various studies have been and are being made of the special needs of ethnic minority groups: in 1977, for example, there was the Report by the House of Commons Select Committee on *Race Relations and Immigration: the West Indian Community*, which included a call for a high-level enquiry into the causes of underachievement among West Indian pupils. The Commission for Racial Equality and the Association of Directors of Social Services, and the Community Relations Commission have all produced recent

177

studies on the needs of ethnic groups. In October 1979, the Rampton Committee of Enquiry, set up the previous March by the Education Secretary, started to look at the education of children from ethnic minority groups.

Little information is available as to the extent to which schools are providing the appropriate kind of detailed and sensitive help for children from one-parent families. Incidents that reflect a lack of help or sensitivity tend to get more publicity than the successes. A detailed study, funded by the Department of Health and Social Security, into the effects on children of living in a one-parent family was carried out by the National Children's Bureau and published in 1976.

The difficulties faced by one-parent families — parent and child — are now more widely recognized and appreciated. One of the most helpful developments has been the more accepting and more supportive prevailing social attitude to the one-parent family. For some those problems are still formidable.

For the fifth anniversary of the publication of the Finer Committee's Report, the self-help group Gingerbread produced a *Social Policy Document*. It listed many of the original — unfulfilled — recommendations made by the Finer Committee. There remain key areas of life where little fundamental progress has been made on behalf of the one-parent family.

Where to find out more

Books

Fatherless Families Margaret Wynn (Michael Joseph, 1964)

Motherless Families Victor George and Paul Wilding (Routledge & Kegan Paul, 1972)

Mothers Alone: Poverty and the Fatherless Family Dennis Marsden (Penguin, 1973)

Report of the Committee on One-parent Families The Finer Report (HMSO, 1974)

Growing Up in a One-parent Family Elsa Ferri (NFER, 1976)

Finer Report: Action and Inaction (One-parent Families, 1978)

Organizations

Equal Opportunities Commission (EOC), Overseas House, Quay Street, Manchester M3 3HN (061-833 9244) and at 20 Grosvenor House, London W1X 0HX (01-629 8233)

Gingerbread, 35 Wellington Street, London WC2 (01-240 0953)

National Council for One-parent Families, 255 Kentish Town Road, London NW5 2LX (01-267 1361)

Families Need Fathers, 97c Shakespeare Walk, London N16 (01-254 6680)

Circulars

DES 2/76 Sex Discrimination Act 1975
DES 4/77 Race Relations Act 1976
DoE 78/77 Housing for One-Parent Families
DHSS HN(78)5 Coordination of Services for Children Under Five

11   A Language for Life:
The Bullock Report (1975)

Why Bullock was set up

The early 1970s were marked by a long and virulent controversy over how well schools were doing their job. Were they providing children with those essential basic skills of literacy and numeracy which they needed to develop and progress at school and through life?

The arguments most often centred on how children were taught — by 'traditional' or by 'progressive' methods. It became, in the way it was conducted, a stale and self-defeating exercise. The main protagonists grouped under the title of the Black Paper movement (after a series of critical pamphlets about state education) seemed more concerned to preserve a highly-selective system of schooling than to guarantee a good schooling for all children. But leaving aside the fact that much of the argument was fuelled for party political advantage, the controversy did indicate a heightened level of genuine public concern about just what children were taught in school. In short, were they all getting a fair deal?

No reliable national evidence was available to back up the various claims of either side; indeed so little worthwhile information was around at the time that when a small-scale study on standards of reading comprehension was published by the National Foundation for Educational Research (NFER) in March 1972, it created a major row.

It also created more confusion than ever. For it suggested — albeit cautiously — that after a rapid and steady period of improvement in children's reading standards between 1948 and 1964, there had been no significant change in standards for about the ten years since 1960. There might, it hinted, have been a marginal decline in standards for some age groups.

Throwing the NFER's caution to the wind, many right-wing educationists and politicians declared that standards were quite definitely falling. In turn, the research itself was criticized mainly for being on too small a scale to make the results in any way significant and for relying on out-dated and unfamiliar tests. Indeed, precisely because standards had risen, the abilities of more able children were now bumping against the ceiling; the tests did not have headroom for higher standards.

Whatever the quality of this single piece of research and whatever the motives of many of the critics of the current educational standards (whatever those standards might be), the NFER survey acted as a spur for finding out just what was happening to the quality of children's schooling in literacy skills. Within a month of the NFER survey being published, the Secretary of State for Education, Margaret Thatcher, had announced a DES Committee of Enquiry into reading and the use of English in schools. It was to be chaired by Sir Alan Bullock.

What Bullock was asked to do

Consider in relation to schools all aspects of teaching the use of English, including reading, writing, and speech; how present practice might be improved and the role that initial in-service training might play; to what extent arrangements for monitoring the general level of attainment in these skills can be introduced or improved; and to make recommendations.

What Bullock recommended and why

In all the Committee made some 332 recommendations and conclusions, which they summed up in seventeen. Again no real evidence was found that reading standards had fallen. They *may* have dropped marginally since 1960 — notably for seven-year-olds; they *may* not be rising as fast as they had previously done so. Certainly, said the Committee, new method of teaching (for example, vertical grouping, the integrated day) had not had any detrimental effect on standards. The Committee also found that while standards at the lower end of the ability range had improved in most socio-economic groups, poor readers among children of unskilled and semi-skilled workers had not improved in line with most children. The result was that the lower end of the ability range contained an increased proportion of these children. (The critics of education had been so concerned with the concept of the average, that they seemed to have missed this very dramatic finding completely.)

The Committee concluded that no matter how current standards compared with those in the past, they *had* to be improved to meet the demands of a more complex and literacy-oriented society. The skills required had to be taught. There was no simple way to improve reading and the use of English. The solution did not lie in a few neat administrative strokes, nor in the adoption of one set of teaching methods rather than another. Action was needed on a broad front with a full appreciation of the many complexities in teaching these skills. There was nothing to equal in importance the quality and achievement of the individual teacher, and consequently most of the Committee's recommendations were aimed at teachers — how they were trained and what they did in school.

Language in the early years

Home background, and what goes on there, was vital to a child's language development. Positive steps should therefore be taken to develop the language ability of children in the pre-school, nursery and infant years. Parents should be involved in this development; staffing ratios in infant schools improved; and teachers' aides, trained in language development, employed.

Health and education authorities should cooperate to provide expectant parents with advice and information on the language needs of young children. They should introduce home-visiting schemes to help parents of pre-school children play an active part in the children's language growth. Antenatal clinics should regard a child's language development to be as important as physical and emotional growth. The existing language element in the training of nursery nurses and assistants should be extended.

Schools should encourage parents to spend plenty of time talking with their young children. In areas of social disadvantage, every school should have enough teachers to enable one or two of them to maintan close contact with the home. Older pupils in secondary schools should learn to understand the adult's role in young children's linguistic and cognitive development.

Language in the middle and secondary years

Each school should have an organized policy for 'language across the curriculum' with every teacher (whatever his or her subject) involved in language and reading development throughout the years of schooling. They should adopt a policy of 'planned intervention'. For example, in large and small discussion groups, pupils should have the chance to investigate and illuminate a topic rather than to advance inflexible points of view. There should be a conscious attempt by the teacher to improve children's listening ability, not through formal exercises but by creating opportunities in the normal work of the classroom. These talking and listening sessions should be supported by audio-visual resources. Drama could also play a valuable part in developing children's language.

The teacher could extend writing ability by encouraging work based on children's own experiences and then by working on the techniques appropriate to them. Progress should be marked by a growing differentiation in the kinds of writing a child could successfully tackle.

Spelling needed to be taught according to a carefully worked-out policy, based on the needs of children's own writing and not upon lists of unrelated words. The ability to spell should be regarded as a responsibility shared by all teachers. Children should be taught handwriting and encouraged to develop a concern for how their written work looks.

English required a wide and flexible range of assessment, a need which was better met by school-based assessment than by rigid syllabuses. English should be assessed at sixteen-plus and post-GCE O-level English syllabuses should also contain a language element.

Reading

Every school should devise a systematic policy for developing reading competence in pupils of all ages and levels of ability. There was no one method, medium, approach, device or philosophy that held the key to the progress of learning to read. But a detailed understanding of how children learn to read should be the basis of all decisions about the organization of teaching, the initial and in-service training of teachers, and the use of resources.

The reading process The accurate perception of individual letters and groups of letters was an important factor in learning to read. Young children should be helped to learn the characteristics of letters through a variety of games and activities, not through formal exercises. The matching of sounds and symbols was of critical importance in learning to read, and a child should steadily gain phonic knowledge within the context of whole-word recognition and reading for meaning. Children should be introduced early on to the relationship between spellings and meaning. Most children needed a lot of help to develop the various skills in comprehension to a high level. An important aspect of reading behaviour was the ability to use different kinds of reading strategy according to the reader's purpose and the nature of the material, and children should acquire those skills which would free them from dependence on single-speed reading.

Reading in the early years Children should be introduced to books in their pre-school years and parents should be helped to recognize the value of reading to their children — children's librarians, LEA advisers, nursery and infant schools, voluntary bodies, and radio and television were all vital sources of guidance and initiative. Schools should be able to lend books to parents of pre-school children and provide book-buying facilities for them.

Every child should spend part of each day in reading or pre-reading activities. The teacher should give each child individual attention several times a week, helping with the child's reading and keeping a meticulous check on progress. Children showing signs of visual or hearing problems should be referred for testing and appropriate treatment. A reading scheme should be only a part of a school's reading programme, which should draw on a wide range of sources. A good reading scheme was one which provided a sound basis for the development of all the reading skills in an integrated way.

The later stages In the middle years, there should be an emphasis on reading for pleasure and personal development, and on extending pupils' reading from the general to the more specialized. For example, there were specific reading techniques for helping pupils to improve efficiency in mastering more complex material across a range of subjects. Pupils also needed to acquire what were called flexible reading strategies such as the ability to skim, scan or read intensively as the occasion demanded. A school should agree a common approach to teaching reading as part of its policy for helping pupils use language across all subjects.

Literature Teachers should have a wide knowledge of fiction geared to the various needs and levels of their pupils' reading ability. Early reading material for young children needed to be relevant to their own experience. However, fantasy, fairy tale and folk tale were just as important. The experience of literature for many older secondary school pupils was too often distorted by the demands of examinations and confined to summaries, model answers, and stereotyped commentaries. All pupils should have the opportunity to experience and to enjoy poetry which was relevant to their lives and their interests.

185

Organization

Every LEA should appoint a specialist English adviser and should establish an advisory team with a specific responsibility for supporting schools in all aspects of language in education. Every school should have a suitably-qualified teacher with the responsibility for advising and supporting colleagues in language and the teaching of reading.

English in the secondary schools should have improved staffing, accommodation and ancillary help. Improving the staffing ratio in schools should mean not just reducing average class size, but creating (when needed) very small groups. LEAs should take account of the need for additional help in schools which involved parents and secondary school pupils in work with young children. Extra staff should be made available to schools in inner-city and other areas where marked social disadvantage affected reading and language development. There should be close consultation between schools, and between schools and parents. Effective pupil records should be maintained to ensure continuity in the teaching of reading and language development of every pupil.

Most of the Committee had reservations about streaming or setting pupils for English according to ability. Mixed-ability grouping (where practicable) offered most hope for English teaching, provided it received a great deal of thought and planning.

The current substantial turnover among secondary school English teachers and the use of a large proportion of teachers whose main specialism and loyalty was to another subject, worked against the continuity that was vital to English teaching and against collective planning. Moreover, one third of teachers who taught English had no discernible qualification for doing so. English should therefore be given a high priority in the school timetable and in staffing policy – it was too often sacrificed to the interests of other subjects. The role of the head in the teaching of English was of the greatest importance, and s/he was uniquely placed to encourage a policy of language across the curriculum.

Reading and language difficulties

LEAs and schools should introduce early screening procedures to stop cumulative language and reading failure and to guarantee every pupil received the right treatment.

The infant school should be given, in confidence, relevant details of a child's medical and developmental history. Close liaison was vital between school, school doctor, health visitor, social worker, educational welfare officer and speech therapist. A detailed profile of a child's strengths and weaknesses in language development should first be compiled by the teacher. This should be used to plan an appropriate learning programme and should accompany the child when transferring to another school. As pupils grew older, they should be encouraged to make self-appraisals, recording their achievements and difficulties.

More diagnostic tests should be devised which were easy to administer and capable of revealing the maximum practical information. Teacher, doctor and educational psychologist should act as a team. The teacher should be able to decide when a dificulty needed further investigation. Educational psychologists could help teachers in their training, particularly over diagnostic techniques.

Children with reading difficulties Additional help should go to children retarded in reading. Schools which withdrew pupils from their classes for special help should continue that support when they returned to their class. In many secondary schools, work with slow learners attracted less than its fair share of resources. A senior member of staff should take responsibility for them and coordinate all the school's resources on their behalf.

Every LEA should appoint an adviser to be responsible for children with learning difficulties. There should be a reading clinic or remedial centre in every LEA, giving access to a comprehensive diagnostic service plus expert medical, psychological and teaching help. It should provide for children with severe reading difficulties and it should also offer an advisory service to schools.

Adult literacy Provision for helping adult illiterates and semi-literates should be greatly increased, with a national reference point for coordinating information and support.

School leavers with reading difficulties should have guidance on where to go for continued tuition. LEAs should provide an information and counselling service on what provision was available and the best kind of tuition for an individual's needs.

Employers, social services departments, probation officers, youth leaders, and careers and employment services should also give advice to young adults on where to get help. LEAs should help to expand provision of literacy schemes, make generous financial grants to voluntary schemes, and provide in-service training for tutors in adult literacy work. There should be a wider range of reading material geared to the needs and interests of adult students.

Children from families of overseas origin These children should have more substantial and sustained tuition in English. Advisers and specialist teachers were wanted in greater strength in areas of need.

Children should not be expected to cast off the language and culture of their home once they got into school, and the curriculum should reflect the different cultures. All teachers should be aware of how books and pictures shaped children's attitudes to one another and to society, and of the ethnic and cultural bias of many school books.

Teachers and librarians should select books which again reflected the different cultures of their pupils. There was a general shortage of such books and publishers could make a valuable contribution by filling this gap.

Teaching English as a second language should be continued until pupils had gained a fluency in speaking, reading and writing. The early language development of immigrant children was enhanced by attendance at nursery classes geared to their specific needs and providing extra help with language.

Resources

A standing working party should be formed, made up of representatives from the DES and LEAs, to consider capitation allowances and the resources of schools. A satisfactory level of book provision should be its first subject of enquiry. There was great variation in spending on books between LEAs. Provision was inadequate. The disparity between schools in terms of resources was also disturbing. There should be a detailed examination of allowances to schools and how they were distributed. The working party should recommend a minimal figure for book provision to be reviewed annually.

The printed word would remain of the highest importance in education. Every primary school should have a 'book policy', with every classroom having its own collection of books, backed up a central school collection which contains print and non-print material. Every secondary school should have library accommodation and appropriate ancillary help. School library services should be able to supply on demand a wider range of resources other than books, cooperating with the museum service and local archives. There should be more training for library work in schools and, as a long term aim, all school librarians should be doubly qualified in teaching and librarianship.

Teachers should be trained to use audio-visual and other technological aids. Authorities should provide technical advice, prompt maintenance of equipment and help in preparing material. Educational radio and television was a valuable source of stimulus for talking, reading and writing. Every school should have facilities for recording programmes and storing tapes. The needs of nursery and infant schools in particular called for urgent consideration.

Educational broadcasting for children in the pre-school and early schooling stages and for older children with learning difficulties should be urgently expanded. This would need help from public funds and charitable foundations. Programmes should also be made to help parents develop their children's language skills.

189

Teacher education and training

A substantial course on language in education (including reading) should be part of *every* primary and secondary school teacher's initial training. There should be more in-service education opportunities in reading and other aspects of teaching English (including courses at diploma and higher degree level). Teachers in every LEA should have access to a language/reading centre. There should be a national centre for language in education, concerned with the teaching of English in all its aspects, from language and reading in the early years to advanced studies with sixth forms.

Attitudes and standards

We needed an improved system of monitoring reading and writing in schools, which used new instruments to assess a wider range of attainments. We should redefine what we mean by 'literacy'.

A national research organization should be responsible for the monitoring of standards. The monitoring procedure should be given to children at eleven and at fifteen. Test material should be drawn from a large pool stocked with carefully developed items representing all the skills to be assessed. A system of 'light sampling' should be introduced, testing children on a termly basis so as to produce an ongoing estimate of standards. This new scheme should begin in 1977.

What happened to Bullock

The Bullock Report was published in February 1975 and got a poor launching from the 1974-9 Labour Government. The introduction to the Report by the Education Secretary Reg Prentice declared that no additional funds would be made available to implement the Report's recommendations.

The Committee had been aware of the current financial restraints and had geared their recommendations accordingly. Many needed little or no extra funds at all; only eight of the

190

seventeen key recommendations were reckoned to need 'significant sums of money'. But even the 'low-cost' and 'no-cost' recommendations for central Government action were ignored or rejected. At a national conference one year after the Report was published, Alan Bullock (by then a lord) said that 'the present Government are not interested in the Report and never have been'. The Report was one of the numerous official Government reports on children never to have been debated in Parliament.

Bullock wanted a national system of monitoring achievement in reading and writing; a national working party on capitation allowances and resources in schools; and a national centre for language in education. All required Government action – none has been set up.

The DES's own Assessment of Performance Unit is the only example of some sort of Governmental response to those three key recommendations – and that was established in 1974, before Bullock reported. The APU is working to devise and carry out tests and to monitor standards in schools. One of its teams is concentrating on English and will be carrying out a national 'light sampling' exercise in 1980. Bullock's target date for a new monitoring system was 1977.

More generally, the Bullock Report can be seen to have had some influence on Governmental statements over curriculum needs and the renewed official emphasis over ensuring that children are able to acquire basic literacy skills. But responding to Bullock merely by compiling policy and consulation documents of such generality as the 1977 Green Paper *Education in Schools* provided an absurdly inadequate lead to central Government departments and LEAs to spend money and time, establish practical schemes of training, review and recommit resources, and develop greater coordination between services, staff, and parents.

A survey carried out by the *Times Educational Supplement* in 1976 revealed that only a quarter of LEAs were energetically trying to set up Bullock-inspired policies in their schools. Only two-thirds had a specialist English adviser and only just over half had a formal system for screening all primary children for reading and language difficulties.

191

Few home-visiting schemes have been set up; the supply of books and other aids to schools remains pitifully low; in-service training courses for teachers readily fall victim to public expenditure cuts. No public funds have been allocated to develop more educational broadcasting.

One successful development has been the adult literacy campaign which was already being prepared for as Bullock reported. Between 1975 and 1978, a vigorous, imaginative, but not always well-financed programme of action and tuition was organized by the Adult Literacy Resources Agency through LEAs and the BBC. Even here though, Government has been reluctant to ensure that this programme continued with adequate, let alone 'generous', funding.

Four years after Bullock, its overall effect is still difficult to gauge at school level. There was no machinery set up for checking just how well schools were progressing. However, a national survey[1] of secondary schools carried out between 1975 and 1978 by HM Inspectorate and published in December 1979 revealed a disappointing response to Bullock. The survey report declared that the Bullock recommendations had had little effect on secondary schools during the period of the survey. The suggested policy of 'language across the curriculum' had been difficult to achieve. There was still too much emphasis placed on writing and not enough on reading and talking. The report said: 'In a great majority of schools throughout the three years of the survey, no moves of any significance towards language policies have taken place. Sometimes there was no one in a senior position who had been convinced of the importance of language or no appropriate forum for the necessary professional discussion had been created . . . By the last term (of the survey) some schools were developing or maintaining an interest but many had scarcely considered the subject'. Other indications suggest that more schools and teachers have taken up the Bullock philosophy than this HMI survey concludes have done so. But one reason for the evidently disappointing lack of 'take-up' was also documented by the

[1] *Aspects of Secondary Education in England*, a survey by HM Inspectors of Schools (HMSO, December 1979).

survey — many schools lack sufficient and appropriate books and library resources. Bullock himself said that the Report needed five years before any real assessment could be made. Another member of the Committee put the time-scale at 25 years. Certainly much of what the Committee wanted could only be carried out by the actions and energies of LEAs, schools and individual teachers rather than by any Government action. But where central Government could have acted, it has failed to do so, either at all or with any positive commitment. Many schools remain desperately hard up for essential resources — teachers, ancillary help, books and equipment. Indeed, many heads are now asking parents to pay or help to pay directly for the books and equipment their children use in school.

The Schools Council is about to report on a special project on *Language Across the Curriculum: Case Studies* which has surveyed what has happened in six schools since the Bullock Committee reported. Significantly, the Schools Council last year announced a major policy shift. In future, it will move away from a narrow concentration on subject areas, which tended to exclude any issue that did not fall neatly into an established category, and will adopt a wider approach spanning the whole curriculum. This will allow not only for the concept of language teaching across the curriculum, but will enable the Bullock 'message' to be spread into other subject areas such as numeracy, health education and graphicacy.

A working party from the National Book League has recently made a study of the provision of books to schools. This group was made up of teachers, local authority representatives, librarians and publishers. In their report *Books for Schools* (May 1979), the working party found it necessary to repeat several of the major recommendations made four years earlier in the Bullock Report. Political parties seem to find it easier to criticise children's literacy skills than to attempt to do something to help them.

Where to find out more
Books

The Trend of Reading Standards K. B. Start and B. K. Wells (NFER, 1972)

A Language for Life The Bullock Report (HMSO, 1975)

Language Across the Curriculum: Guidelines for Schools Mike Torbe (Ward Lock Educational/NATE, 1977)

Language Across the Curriculum Michael Marland (Ed.) (Heinemann Educational, 1977)

Books for Schools (NBL, 1979)

Organizations

National Book League (NBL), Book House, 45 East Hill, London SW18 2HZ (01-870-9055)
The NBL has an exhibition on language across the curriculum which may be hired for a small fee.
Schools Council for the Curriculum and Examinations, 160 Great Portland Street, London W1N 6LL (01-580 0352)

Circulars

14/77 Local Education Authority Arrangements for the School Curriculum

12 Violence in the Family: The Parliamentary Select Committee Reports (1975 and 1977)

Why the Select Committees were set up

It was the death of Maria Colwell in 1973 that really brought the problem of child battering to public and political attention. But professional concern had been growing for some time before that. The National Society for the Prevention of Cruelty to Children (NSPCC) had for years been compiling evidence and experience of young children found to have serious physical injuries for which there seemed to be no satisfactory explanation. In 1968, the NSPCC set up a special battered child research department (later to become the National Advisory Centre on the Battered Child).

The term 'battered child syndrome' had been coined in 1962 by an American, Dr Henry Kempe. He defined it as 'clinical condition in young children who have received serious physical abuse, generally from a parent or foster-parent'. Other terms used are 'non-accidental injury' (nai) and the more general term 'child abuse'. The NSPCC has defined child battering in this way: 'All physically injured children under the age of sixteen years, where the nature of the injury is not consistent with the account of how it occurred or where other factors indicate that there is a reasonable suspicion that the injury was inflicted or not prevented by any person having custody, charge or care of the child.' Such physical abuse may be intentional and conscious, or unintentional and unconscious. There is no one cause of abuse; few injuries though are due to pre-meditated sadistic acts. Many are the result of a sudden loss of control by a desperate parent or guardian — often, for example, through drunkenness, stress from living on a

195

low income or in bad housing, or an inability to cope with family pressures. Some parents have a low point of tolerance because of poor mothering or constant denigration in their own childhood.

The NSPCC produced two key reports based on the experiences of its local inspectors which provided crucial information about child abuse. *Seventy-eight Battered Children* (1969) and *A Study of Suspected Child Abuse* (1972) highlighted how early in their lives were children at risk from a battering parent (under four was the danger period, and especially up to the age of one), and how inadequate was the help for both child and parent in terms of treatment and prevention. They found that for those children who stayed at home or were sent back home after being battered, there was a 60 per cent chance of them being battered again. Ten out of every 10,000 children under four years of age in England and Wales were seriously battered; one out of each ten died from their injuries. By the mid-seventies, child battering had become the fourth most common cause of death for children up to five years of age. Between 40 and 60 out of every 10,000 under-fours would suffer moderate or slight injury or neglect[1].

Concern for battered children became part of a more general concern about violence in the family — between husband and wife as well as by parents on their children. The practical and campaigning work of Erin Pizzey at the Women's Aid Centre in Chiswick, West London did much to publicize the need for official action. Once again, the NSPCC produced a timely survey on the effects on children of violent marriages called *Yo-yo Children* (1974).

In February 1975, after a series of widely-publicized incidents of children dying after being severely battered at home had added weight to the pressure for an enquiry, a Select Committee of MPs was appointed to look at the problem of violence in the family.

These Select Committees spanned three Parliamentary sessions and produced two Reports. The first, in September

[1] No official statistics are kept on child abuse. One NSPCC estimate suggested that in 1975 some 7,500 children in England and Wales suffered abuse, with 110 deaths.

196

1975, mainly concerned battered women and was called *Violence in Marriage*. But the Committee recognized the seriousness of the violence being done to children and felt there was a desperate need to break into what was regarded as a cycle of violence which in some families persisted from generation to generation. Its second Report in June 1977 therefore concentrated more on the needs of children (*Violence to Children*).

What the Select Committees were asked to do

Consider the extent, nature and causes of the problems of families where there is violence between the partners or where children suffer non-accidental injury; and make recommendations.

What the Select Committees recommended and why

Violence in Marriage (September 1975)

The Committee found the ignorance and apparent apathy of some Government departments and individual Ministers towards the extent of marital violence alarming. Hardly any worthwhile research into either causes or remedies had been financed by the Government. Responsibility was divided between seven Government departments: the Home Office, Department of Health and Social Security, Department of Education and Science, Department of the Environment, Lord Chancellor's Office, Scottish Office and the Welsh Office. Few of these gave the problem any priority either in terms of manpower or financial resources.

The Committee considered violence in marriage a wide and difficult subject involving a range of issues: the general attitudes that men and women had about one another, housing problems, psychiatric problems, alcohol, the social and emergency services, the police, the law and legal services, the basic causes of violence in general, and many more.

There were, they declared, no easy solutions. They recommended:

Children As much as possible ought to be done to break the 'cycle of violence' — whereby children of a violent father or mother were themselves likely to become violent as they grew up — by looking to the welfare and special needs of these vulnerable children. Their education should not be allowed to suffer and more thought should be given to providing special nursery and other educational help. Schools should give more serious attention to discussions about family life and the conflicts (sometimes violent) that could arise.

Refuges Round-the-clock family crisis centres should be set up in every large urban area. A few should operate as action-research projects. Specialized refuges should be made rapidly and readily available by local authorities and voluntary organizations, with an initial target of one family place per 10,000 of the population. There should be legislation to clarify the duty of local authorities over providing temporary accommodation for battered women and their children.

The Courts Magistrates' courts should be given more power to help in cases of battering and marital breakdown. Where an injunction had been served on a battering husband, a judge should be able to grant a power of arrest if the wife was likely to be in continuing danger of assault. Magistrates should be able to make an injunction restraining a husband from assaulting his wife and also temporarily excluding him from the matrimonial home. The grounds for obtaining a matrimonial order in the magistrates' court should be brought in line with the grounds for obtaining a divorce. A wife should be able to apply for an order excluding her husband from the matrimonial home. When a wife was in danger, decisions should be reached quickly to prevent her and her children from being homeless.

Police The police should review their policy to see how much more they could do to help battered wives. The police regarded this as a sensitive area and were reluctant to intervene in cases of domestic violence. More training should be given to police on how to handle such incidents. Both the police and the Home Office should keep statistics specifically on incidents of domestic violence.

Alcohol The Government should introduce a vigorous publicity campaign against the excessive use of alcohol, and should agree on a positive policy on alcohol advertising.

The Finer Report Government and local authorities should consider how far the Finer Committee's recommendations could be implemented in the short term without an unacceptably high demand on financial resources, particularly those recommendations about advice services and the attitudes of the Supplementary Benefits Commission. The Finer Committee's proposals on local authority and private tenancies of homes should be implemented at an early date.

Advice All the agencies involved should be able to offer expert advice to battered women, and should hold a referral list of solicitors. Law centres should be able to deal with emergencies caused by domestic violence. Violent husbands should also be able to get help for the causes of their violence, such as alcoholism or mental illness.

Government action The Government should decide quickly whether to provide the money for the Committee's recommendations and for closely monitoring the effects of any action taken. It should also plan for further action that might be necessary.

Violence to Children (June 1977)

The Committee felt it was important to prevent parents from abusing their children rather than to try and 'pick up the pieces' afterwards. They did not believe that child battering could be wholly eradicated but wanted to make sure preventive measures work efficiently. Physical violence was not the only form of violence children had to contend with. Great harm could also be done by psychological punishment, by emotional violence and by passive forms of neglect.

199

The community should be more alive to its duty towards families with young children. In turn, the Government should respond to greater community awareness and to local initiatives on child battering, for example with help through the rate-support grant and with grants to organizations like the NSPCC. More funds should be made available for research into specific aspects of violence in the family.

Education There should be adequate care facilities for the under-fives throughout the country, including pre-school playgroups, childminders and mother and toddler clubs. Along with financial aid and advice, local authorities could provide accommodation in existing 'spare capacity' buildings such as schools, church halls and clinics. More official help should go on education for parenthood courses and materials for both children and adults. Self-help groups for anxious parents and good neighbour schemes should also be encouraged.

Social services Social workers — and the police — needed more training in how to handle child battering and how to care for injured children. Only qualified and experienced social workers should supervise children at risk. Social services departments should be well-known, accessible and welcoming, providing an 'open door' for worried parents. Local authorities should eventually have a legal duty to provide a 24-hour standby service for families at risk.

The police should be fully involved in managing non-accidental injury; be invited to all case conferences; and liaise closely with the social services departments.

At risk registers Area Review Committees[1] should ensure they work efficiently, speedily and humanely — notably with their at risk registers. Children reckoned to be at risk

[1] Area Review Committees were set up after the death of Maria Colwell. They are local policy-making bodies run jointly by the local authority and the Area Health Authority, and staffed by senior representatives of those professions concerned with child abuse — social services, housing, education, police, probation, medical, dental, nursing, and usually, the NSPCC. They are intended to check and strengthen measures to prevent, diagnose and manage cases of non-accidental injury and to set out policy guidelines.

and those who had already been injured should be recorded as two separate groups on the register. Parents should always be told their child was on the register. Local registers should be amalgamated and kept either by the social services department, the area health atuhority, or the NSPCC, with round-the-clock access to them. Registers should be reviewed regularly and there should be clear guidelines on removing children's names from a register when the danger was passed. The DHSS should give more guidance on the compilation, use of and access to information held in at risk registers.

Health services The health services should be more aware of the importance of 'early bonding' between mother and newborn baby and should make sure the whole birth experience was handled sensitively and sympathetically. There should be more contact between obstetric units, health visitors and midwives. Health visitors should be closely involved with mother and baby immediately after leaving hospital. Serious consideration should be given to making the option of home confinement more widely available. Despite cuts in public spending, the Government's target of increasing the number of health visitors by 6 per cent a year should be kept to.

All children under school age should have the right to regular medical examinations. Social workers should be involved in the work of health clinics. Doctors should be given more advice about the effects of drugs, particularly on the level of aggression they created. Medical students and GPs should get detailed training in diagnosing and handling cases of non-accidental injury and in taking part in case conferences. When a case of nai was diagnosed, paents should be given a full explanation by a senior consultant pediatrician and be told of any arrangements for bringing in community agencies. Extra resources should go to children who had suffered abuse and were in care, and to those who care for them, such as foster parents. The Goverment should 'take on board' the thinking behind the Court Report's recommendations.

Housing Local authority housing policy should enable young people to be housed in the area they were brought up in and near to close relatives, should they wish it, and cater for families in acute housing need but with no residential qualifications. It should not discriminate against lone parents.

Legal issues A person's right to safeguard his home ought to be limited when it conflicted with a child's right not to suffer abuse[1]. So where a supervision order had been made on a child because of a case of non-accidental injury, the child's supervisor should be given *legal* authority to visit the child or obtain a medical examination.

To make sure that all relevant facts were brought before a court in a case of non-accidental injury, the rules on what evidence was admissible should be made clearer. The Criminal Law Revision Committee should consider whether a husband or wife should be compelled to be a witness for the prosecution in criminal cases concerning their child. When a parent was prosecuted on a criminal charge where care proceedings were also involved, the trial should be as soon after the committal as possible.

A draft Bill should be published as a Green Paper outlining the new system of family courts recommended by the Finer Committee.

What happened to the Select Committees' recommendations

The Government responded to both Reports with its own written reports to Parliament, as requested by the Committees. Both reports, one in December 1976, the other in March 1978, set out what Government thought of the recommendations and what had been achieved thus far.

Government action on violence in the family has been primarily concerned with producing discussion papers and

[1] A number of legal provisions enable a child to be taken away from the charge and control of parents and kept in a place of safety. The one most commonly used is section 28 of the Children and Young Persons Act 1969. A magistrate may order the removal of a child if satisfied that the child is being illtreated, neglected and so on. In 1977/8, 5,872 children in England and Wales were removed to places of safety — 2,271 under five, 3,321 between five and fifteen, and 280 over fifteen.

guidelines for local and health authorities and for the relevant voluntary organizations. Initially, the Select Committee's first Report was sent out by the Government to all local and health authorities in December 1975 for consultation. Since 1976, a series of Government publications — discussion papers, circulars and white papers — have been produced which detail and expand on the Government's main theme: prevention. Basically this means the need to establish preventive programmes to safeguard people's health and well-being, and particularly children's.

In April 1976, the DHSS consultative document *Prevention and Health: Everybody's Business: A Reassessment of Public and Personal Health* had been issued. This was followed by a joint DHSS/DES White Paper *Prevention and Health* (Cmnd 7047). Both stressed the need to give priority to preventive programmes for children. They emphasized that the key to prevention in non-accidental injury was the setting up of effective means of 'identifying and treating cases at the earliest possible stage'. Following another consultative document *Priorities for Health and Personal Social Services in England* (March 1976), the Government set down its national strategy for the country's health and personal social services plus guidelines for local and health authorities in two key documents — *The Way Forward* (September 1977) and *All-Wales Policies and Priorities for the Planning and Provision of Health and Personal Social Services from 1976 to 1981*.

Any official response to violence in the family would have to be compatible with that national strategy. Briefly, the boundary of the strategy was this: although some small increases in real terms were allowed for in health and welfare programmes, limited resources would restrict the scope of any developments. Providing extras for priorities would have to come mainly from making the best use of existing resources and expertise. Official policy was based on three elements: prevention, encouraging self-help and community care, and protecting local Government autonomy in deciding priorities and spending. In many respects, the Select Committee's recommendations could be seen to fit in well with this policy.

As the Committee had expected, little official funding was forthcoming, even though they had pointed out the long-term savings in costs that would most likely come from carrying out their recommendations. Government's reply was:

> Whether or not this would prove to be so, a similar case could be made for many other proposals for increased spending by central or local Government across the whole public expenditure field . . . Increased expenditure on services for the victims of violence in marriage can in practice only take place by a redeployment by the bodies concerned of resources already available to them.[1]

Although the general principle of preventing ill health rather than waiting to cure it is a sound one (as is any official policy based on that general principle), there is a catch. It is assumed that such a policy needs little (as opposed to less) funding to back it. For example, of some £5,000 million currently spent every year on the National Health Service, less than £100 million (under 2 per cent) is spent on preventive work.

All this then is the context within which Government-inspired efforts to combat violence in the family has to be seen — and judged.

Government has accepted that refuges should be provided for battered women and made some funds available through the urban aid and job creation programmes. These have helped a few refuges for battered women and children: there are now in all some 160. But many more are needed. Only a handful receive official funding. Modest grants for research (for example, a NWAF/DoE joint project) and for the Chiswick Women's Aid and National Women's Aid Federation (£75,000) have also been provided. The self-help group Parents Anonymous has just received a one-year grant of £10,000 from the DHSS to fund full-time staff, permanent premises, a 24-hour aid service and the setting up of new groups. This group (providing for parents who feel they are near to, or have already become batterers) had used the publication of the Select Committee's first

[1] *Violence to Children* (HMSO, Cmnd 7123).

Report to launch itself. There are now between 40 and 50 groups. The Government felt unable to commit itself to setting up a network of family crisis centres — leaving it to the work of voluntary groups and the priorities of local authorities.

The NSPCC's National Advisory Centre on the Battered Child and its seven special units (which provide both care and aid to parents and children as well as producing case-work and research findings[1] and acting as a local educational agency on child abuse) has also received modest central Government funding. But this has always been regarded as 'pump-priming' with Government expecting local authorities to take over the long-term financing of these units. For this reason, no new unit has been set up since the Select Committee reported. The NSPCC is unable to fund them itself, relying as it does on voluntary donations of almost half a million pounds over the last two years. An additional problem is that there has been a gradual shift of emphasis from concentrating on non-accidental injury to catering for the more general problem of child abuse, which puts more pressure on its financial and staff resources.

Such financial help then has been meagre and the Government specifically rejected the suggestion that it should make funds available through the rate-support grant. The emphasis has been firmly on self-help. For example, the Government's Good Neighbour Scheme, which encourages community help for the elderly, has been extended to include families with young children.

The Government's rejection of the Finer Committee's proposal for family courts has meant that many of the problems the Finer Committee (and subsequently the Select Committee) hoped would be solved by these new courts still remain. No Green Paper was forthcoming. Government also felt unable to support the recommendation that cases of child abuse brought before the courts should be given preference, since this would only delay other cases. The question of whether a husband or wife should be a com-

[1] In November 1978, the DHSS's Children's Research Liaison Group set up a sub-group to define specific priorities into non-accidental injury to children.

pellable witness for the prosecution in criminal cases concerning the abuse of their child remains under discussion. Rules of evidence (what is admissible) are gradually being clarified.

The Government considered that in a case of child abuse a child's supervisor already had sufficient legal authority to visit that child in the parent's or guardian's home against the wishes of the parent or guardian. (The right is given under rule 28 of the Magistrates' Courts [Children and Young Persons] Rules 1970, as amended by the Magistrates' Courts [Children and Young Persons] [Amendment] Rules 1976.) The right to order a medical examination was ambiguous and would be tightened up when the opportunity to legislate occurred.

However, three major pieces of legislation have directly affected the well-being of victims of family violence: the Children Act 1975, the Domestic Violence and Matrimonial Proceedings Act 1976 and the Housing (Homeless Persons) Act 1977.

The Children Act provided for a guardian *ad litem* to represent children's interests in court hearings for care or supervision orders — a direct response to the concern expressed over cases of battered children where the rights of parents to keep a child tended to be the deciding factor in any judgment rather than the more urgent right of the child to be protected. This provision though has yet to be fully implemented.

The Domestic Violence and Matrimonial Proceedings Act increased the powers of courts in matrimonial proceedings and gave effect to some of the Committee's recommendations. A judge can now grant a power of arrest where an injunction has been served on a battering husband and the wife continues to be in danger of assault. A court's power to regulate the occupation of the matrimonial home has been extended. Magistrates have been given the power in matrimonial proceedings to make an injunction restraining a husband from assaulting his wife and when necessary can exclude him from the matrimonial home. The procedure for obtaining matrimonial injunctions in county courts has been simplified.

A Law Commission Report in 1976 also made recommendations in this field and the Government accepted that there was a need to change the law in certain respects with regard to magistrates' matrimonial jurisdiction, providing a form of relief for battered women in the lower courts similar to the injunction available in the higher courts.

The Housing (Homeless Persons) Act has given some relief to families in housing difficulties with the new obligation on local housing authorities to provide accommodation for families made homeless. A 1977 Department of the Environment circular *Housing for One-Parent Families* gave detailed guidance to local authorities on treating as a priority the housing needs of one-parent families, and the Government expressed the view that where a woman left home with her children because of serious violence they should be treated as a homeless family. Another circular *Better Use of Vacant and Under-occupied Housing* urged local housing authorities to make adequate provision in their housing allocation schemes for young people. Several Government publications have recommended local authorities to review their housing policy in the light of the urgent needs of particular groups in society. But the response and the level of subsequent provision varies greatly across the country.

Despite the advances that these Acts surely represent, they have not given families as much protection as was originally hoped. For example, some local authorities, unwilling to honour the intention of the Act, have sought — and found — loopholes which enable them to refuse accommodation to homeless families. Victims of family violence can still find the Domestic Violence Act less than reliable in providing protection from a battering partner or parent.

Additional educational and care provision for children has been a victim of the numerous public spending cuts since 1975. The under-fives have suffered disproportionately, despite attempts by central Government to make some additional funds available. Although the day-care places that are available do go firstly, and rightly, to those in greatest need, there are still not enough places even for these children. In January 1978, a joint DES/DHSS circular[1] was issued on the need for greater central and local coordination of services

[1] Listed as LASSL(78)1, HN(78)5, DES S47/24/013. It was a follow-up to a previous joint circular issued in 1976.

for children under five.

Many schools have, to some extent, responded to the need for a greater emphasis on bringing the problems of domestic violence and, more generally, married life into the school curriculum. The DES Green Paper *Education in Schools: A Consultative Document* issued in July 1977 recommended that children should learn at school how to cope with domestic tasks and with parenthood. It noted that health visitors, doctors, nurses and other allied professions can make a valuable contribution to the design and content of courses concerned with health education and preparation for parenthood. It also recommended that links between schools and local playgroups and nursery classes should be strengthened to enable young people to have some practical experience with young children. The above would also apply to further education colleges. The Open University has also produced a valuable set of teaching materials on child abuse and offers courses on conflict in the family and the first years of life.

Nevertheless, such school programmes remain patchy and not always effective because of limited resources, an already crowded curriculum, the pressure to concentrate on 'core' subjects concerned with literacy and numeracy, and of course the continuing spending cuts. A report published by the National Children's Bureau (NCB) in January 1980 (*Preparation for Parenthood*) found that although such courses had grown rapidly over the last ten years (notably through publicity of child-abuse cases), their development has been patchy. Adolescent boys had less opportunity than girls to take part in such courses.

The provision of more training for education and social work professionals on how to recognize and handle child abuse and family violence has been left up to the professions themselves with little active financial encouragement from Government. Area Review Committees have been encouraged to ensure there are sufficient joint training programmes in their area. Although there has been some improvement, training remains a worrying gap in the efforts to secure a better deal for battered children.

The Government endorsed the recommendation that case conferences should be carried out quickly, efficiently and with as few members as is necessary for a conference to be conducted properly. Two research studies by the NSPCC and Keele University's Social Work Research Project have provided additional information on how conferences do, and should, work. Government has asked local authorities to consider all the suggestions made. Another official response was the earlier DHSS/Home Office/Welsh Office circular[1] issued in November 1976 on case conferences and the police. Subsequent police involvement in case conferences has in fact been regarded by many social work professionals as a significant advance in handling child abuse in a sympathetic and efficient manner. Previously the police had been largely excluded from conferences mainly at the instigation of social workers and doctors fearful that a rigid police attitude to battering would make matters worse and jeopardize any successful resolution for the family concerned. Nevertheless, police involvement in case conferences remains a controversial issue.

The codes of practice on alcohol advertising for both the Independent Broadcasting Authority and the Advertising Standards Authority were tightened up in 1975 and again in 1979. Following the allocation of an extra £1 million of Government money for 1977/8, the Health Education Council launched a campaign on alcoholism in Scotland and the north of England. Nevertheless the amount we spend on alcohol continues to increase in real terms and in relation to other forms of spending. The incidence of drunkenness and alcoholism also rises. Excessive drinking accounts for over half of all cases of wife battering. More women are drinking excessively with consequent detrimental results on the lives of their children. In 1976, consumer expenditure on alcohol in the UK came to £5,912 million — about the same amount spent by local authorities on education. In 1978, alcohol expenditure had gone up to £7,484 million. Of that, the Government received £2,585 million in customs and excise duty and VAT. One further statistic illustrates the unequal nature of the battle to control alcoholism and the need for more vigorous Government action: in 1978, the amount

[1] LASSL(76)26, HC(76)59.

spent on alcohol and tobacco advertising was, according to the Advertising Association, some £121 million. Of that, the National Council on Alcoholism has estimated, around £50 million went on advertising alcohol. The total campaigns budget of the Health Education Council for 1978 was £2½ million.

The Government has repeated its commitment to a 6 per cent increase in expenditure on district nurse and health visitor services. Progress varies according to the health authority area involved and the Government admitted that 'with the present wide variations in staffing levels, it will be some time before shortages of health visitors can be eliminated in all areas' (*Violence to Children*, March 1978). Official statements, in speeches and in publications, endorse the need for greater cooperation in the health and social services so that the chances of successful 'bonding' at birth between mother and baby are as high as possible and that any signs of rejection by the mother or of actual baby battering are picked up quickly. Home confinement remains a rarely offered option. In 1977, the DHSS published a discussion paper on *Reducing the Risk: Safer Pregnancy and Childbirth* which advised on this, along with other spects of childbirth. In the main, the document endorsed the recommendations made by the Select Committee on closer liaison between mother and professional, and between professionals. The idea of regular medical examinations for pre-school children received little support from Government or from health authorities and many professional bodies. A more 'informal' approach prevails, although Government has asked health authorities to ensure that 'a basic programme of health surveillance' is offered to all children. A statutory duty to do so is unlikely to be imposed. Perhaps the real litmus test of Government action in this area is its response to the recommendations of the Court Committee on child health services — and that has not been impressive.

The Government accepted the recommendations of the Select Committee about the need for a greater standardization in registers of children at risk. It had previously recommended that authorities set up central registers: in April 1974 and again in February 1976 (see DHSS circulars

LASS L(74)13 *Non-accidental Injury to Children* and LASS L(76)2 *Non-accidental Injury to Children: Area Review Committees*). Government also noted in its reply to the Select Committee that there were areas of disagreement in the social work profession over how best to administer the registers. A promised set of Government guidelines based on the evidence produced by the Select Committee plus additional consultations by the DHSS has yet to emerge, and it is increasingly likely that they will not be published. Until they do, the registers will continue to differ in the way they are compiled, in what goes on them and how they are used. The question of whether parents should always be told their child is on a register has been put in abeyance for 'further consultations'. So the decision still remains 'a matter for professional judgment, where appropriate in a case conference' (*Violence to Children* March 1978).

There is, as yet, little detailed information about the accessibility, extent and quality of service available to victims of domestic violence through law centres and other advice agencies. Where they do exist they perform invaluable service, although several law centres are currently threatened with closure because some local authorities are reluctant to fund such ventures. Referral lists of solicitors prepared to deal with matrimonial work are now more widely available.

The final, official word on violence to children remains slightly ambiguous:

> . . . doubts have been expressed, both in the evidence the Select Committee received and in the comments which have been made on its Report, about the extent to which attention has been concentrated on this subject at the expense of other pressing demands which are made on social work, health, voluntary and other services. Such doubts must be set against the suffering experienced by each non-accidentally injured child and the costs to him and to the community over long periods. It is encouraging that the results of research and the developments in services are identifying ways of predicting — and preventing — cases before they arise. We can, however, never hope to eliminate all these cases and must, therefore, ensure that all concerned are alert to recognize the risks that remain and prompt to take action. (*Violence to Children* paragraph 104, Cmnd 7123)

Where to find out more
Books

Scream Quietly or the Neighbours Will Hear Erin Pizzey (Penguin, 1974)

Children in Danger Jean Renvoize (Penguin, 1975)

Report from the Select Committee on Violence in Marriage Volume 1 (HMSO, 1975)

First Report from the Select Committee on Violence in the Family: Violence to Children (HMSO, 1977)

Women's Rights: A Practical Guide Anna Coote and Tess Gill (Penguin, 1977)

Observations on the Report from the Select Committee on Violence in Marriage (HMSO, 1978, Cmnd 6690)

Violence to Children: A Response to the First Report from the Select Committee on Violence in the Family (HMSO, 1978, Cmnd 7123)

Child Abuse C. and R. S. Kempe (Fontana Open Books, 1978)

Violence in the Home M.D.A. Freeman (Saxon House, 1979)

Violence against Wives R. E. and R. Dobash (Open Books, 1979)

Organizations

National Society for the Prevention of Cruelty to Children (NSPCC), 1 Riding House Street, London W1P 8AA (01-580 8812)

NSPCC National Advisory Centre on the Battered Child, Denver House, The Drive, Bounds Green Road, London N11 (01-261 1181)

National Women's Aid Federation, 374 Gray's Inn Road, London WC1 (01-837 9316)

Parents Anonymous 29 Newmarket Way, Hornchurch, Essex; *London branch:* 6/9 Manor Gardens, London N1 (01-669 8900)

Circulars

Key circulars concerning children and violence include:

LASSL(74)13 Non-accidental Injury to Children.

LASSL(76)2 Non-accidental Injury to Children: Area Review Committees.

LASSL(76)26/HC(76)50 Non-accidental Injury to Children: The Police and Case Conferences.

LASSL(78)5/HC(78)15 Violence to children — A Response to the First Report from the Select Committee on Violence in the Family.

LASSL(76)5/DES S21(47)05 Coordination of Local Authority Services for Children Under Five.

LASSL(78)1/HN(78)5/DES S47(24)013 Coordination of Services for Children Under Five.

13 Fit for the Future —
Child Health Services:
The Court Report (1976)

Why Court was set up

The Court Committee themselves documented just why an enquiry into the state of health services for children was long overdue. There had, they said, been great improvements in children's health this century. Much of this was due to a reduction in overcrowded living conditions, better nutrition, smaller and better spaced families, immunization, better treatments, higher standards of medical and nursing care and the growing educational role these services provided in the care of mother and child.

But the present state of child health remained a cause of deep concern. Britain had not kept pace with many other countries to reduce the infant mortality rate. In England and Wales, eleven out of every 1,000 births were stillborn. Eleven out of every 1,000 babies died in the first four weeks and a further sixteen did not survive their first year. Many others suffered handicap; one in seven had a moderate or severe handicap causing educational concern.

There were wide variations in the life-chances of children according to where they lived and which social class they were born into. The perinatal mortality rate for social class V was twice that of class I, and was 50 per cent higher than the lowest national rate. Children in classes IV and V were twice as likely to die in infancy as those from classes I and II. These gaps had been widening for 25 years. Children still died for nineteenth-century reasons.

Improvements in mental health and in people's ability to cope with day-to-day living had been poor. Accidents were the main cause of death and disability of children aged between one and fifteen; for the under-fives, the home was more dangerous than the roads. Less than a third of five-year-olds had decay-free teeth; by seven half had some kind of gum disease.

Disadvantaged children were more likely to be born to young mothers who did not use antenatal services and had smoked heavily during pregnancy. Children who lived in urban areas suffered more ill health than those who did not. Inner-London children were twice as likely to be psychologically disturbed as children in rural areas. Even so, more money was spent on health services in areas with more well-off people. The variations in provision were much the same as in 1948.

An official enquiry into child health was finally agreed to, but more for 'administrative' reasons. When the National Health Service was reorganized in 1973, responsibility for all local authority health services was transferred to the NHS's Area Health Authorities. This meant that, for the first time, the NHS was taking on preventive services, such as school health and other community services. It also meant that several professional groups in health care were put into a state of limbo. For example, medical officers of health employed by local authorities to carry out community health work in child health clinics and the school health service were transferred to direct NHS control and renamed clinical medical officers. But there was no new career structure for them and a dilemma existed over whether they should operate within community health services or within hospital services. A committee of enquiry was thought officially to be a useful vehicle for finding answers to these sorts of reorganization problems.

Such an enquiry would also chime in well with the need to consider child health services as a whole following the new reorganization policy of integrating the three services which provided care – the hospital, the general practitioner (GP), and community services. Moreover, since 1972, the DHSS was viewing health care in terms of the specific group or 'clients' served (children, the elderly, and so on) rather than of the service providing the care (the hospital, the GP, the community services, and so on). No one had yet looked at

214

child health in a detailed client-oriented way. At the end of 1973, the Committee of Enquiry, appointed by the Secretary of State for Health and Social Services, Sir Keith Joseph, and headed by Professor Donald Court got under way. The Committee sat for almost three years and included representatives from education and the social services, plus three parents representing those who used the services involved.

What Court was asked to do

Review the existing health services for children, judge how effective they are for the child and his parents, and propose what the new, integrated child health service should try to achieve and how it should, therefore, be organized and staffed.

What Court recommended and why

The Committee set out to provide information and guidance for developing a child- and family-centred service. They saw it as an integrated service, in that it would view the child as a whole and as a continuously developing person. They also saw the child as different from the adult and needing different services. They recommended:

This service should provide readily available and accessible skilled help, ensure that paediatric skill and knowledge were given to all children whatever their age or disability or wherever they lived, and be oriented towards prevention.

In the long run, only a combined approach by housing, health, education and social services could even begin to eradicate the causes of disadvantage. A society that wanted to remove differences in the health chances of children would not only provide remedial health services but concentrate on preventive health services and on environmental improvements.

There was no better way to raise children than to reinforce the ability of their parents, whether natural or substitute, to do so. Almost all parents wanted the best for their children.

215

But too many still set low expectations and assumed that their children would somehow automatically achieve their mental, physical and emotional potential. Parents needed to be made more aware of the learning (in the widest sense) that went on day after day through experience, and of their own part in that process. Future improvements in the health of children would depend as much on the beliefs and behaviour of parents as on the services provided.

Those professionally concerned with children should ensure they had a detailed understanding of a child's emotional, educational, social, psychological and physical needs — and of the essence of being a child.

Child health services: today and tomorrow

The major health problem affecting children was no longer acute episodic illness but malformations, chronic illness, physical and mental handicap, psychiatric disorder, and ill health arising out of family stress and breakdown. These called for a different and multi-disciplinary approach by professional staff with a greater willingness to work together and to recognize the wider implications of chronic ill health and handicap.

Parents should therefore have more chance to learn about the care of sick and handicapped children and develop a close relationship with professionals. They had to be sure that professional help, specialist skill and judgment would be readily and consistently available to them and have confidence in the ability of the doctor or nurse to deal with the child as well as treat the illness. Services needed therefore to be more accessible and professionals had to improve their level of paediatric knowledge and training.

Adverse social conditions would continue for years to come. Special efforts were required to identify those children and families whose health was most at risk, and to provide comprehensive help and advice geared to meet their particular needs — social as well as medical. With all their shortcomings, the present services at least provided the foundations on which to build a new service.

216

An integrated child health service

When the NHS was set up in 1948, child health services were divided into three separate units: the community health services provided by local authorities for children in school, for children under five and for expectant mothers; the general medical services provided by GPs; and the specialist services provided in hospitals. Despite changes under NHS reorganization in 1974, services remained divided. There was an unreal distinction between acute and preventive medicine. For example, clinical medical officers were not allowed to *treat* children. The belief in the child as a whole and developing person implied the integration of acute and preventive medicine. Preventive services (clinics and the school health service) and treatment (GPs and hospitals) needed to be brought together as a two-tier system based on comprehensive primary care, firmly linked with supporting consultant and hospital care. The primary health care team should continue to be the service unit providing 24-hour first contact and continuing therapeutic and preventive health care for children of all ages.

Because children were different from adults, they should be cared for by doctors, nurses and other professionals who were trained specifically to care for children. Therefore in any group of general practitioners, one or more GPs should be specially trained in paediatrics.

A general practitioner with a special interest in paediatrics should be eligible (with additional training leading to a qualification) to practise as a general practitioner paediatrician (GPP). A GPP would ensure full developmental surveillance, preventive and treatment services for all children (including handicapped children) registered with his general practice. He would act as a link between the health services in the community and the local hospital, and as the doctor for one or more local schools.

There should be a special group of nurses in the community services called child health visitors (CHV) working with the GPP. CHVs would have a 'patch' in the community and be responsible for preventive and curative work with children, advise parents and make sure a child was registered

217

with a GPP. They should be helped by a child health nurse with paediatric training, and in schools by a specially-trained school nurse.

Supporting care for children should continue to be a district service based on children's departments in district general hospitals. Consultant paediatricians and other specialists in the hospital should provide continuing support for the primary care teams in their district.

There should also be a new type of consultant pediatrician — a consultant community pediatrician (CCP) — with special skills in developmental social and educational paediatrics. He would support GPPs in some of their work, particularly in normal schools. He would also act as the school doctor for special schools.

A special district handicap team (DHT) should be set up, based on each district general hospital to provide more help for handicapped and chronically-ill children. It would be similar to a primary care team and work from a 'child development centre'. It would provide a special diagnostic assessment and treatment service for handicapped children, advise and support parents, and provide some training for other professionals working locally. The CCP would be a key member of the team. The DHT would draw together the different services currently provided in schools and hospitals, and create a single district supporting service made up of staff from health, education and social services — to which parents could have direct access.[1]

Similarly, there should be an integrated child and adolescent psychiatric service combining the work of the present child guidance services and the hospital-based psychiatric services.

Particular needs and remedies

The unborn and newborn baby More should be done to ensure the right sort of advice was readily available to parents during the antenatal period. Methods of prenatal diagnosis

[1] See also section on *Handicap*, p. 222.

and on monitoring the well-being of the foetus should be developed which were easy to apply and caused no distress to the mother. Mothers should take more part in the care of newborn babies, and hospital staff should be more sensitive to their social and psychological needs. Every newborn baby should be medically checked immediately after delivery and have a full postnatal examination between six and ten days old. This should be the basis of the child's health record.

The child health visitor should visit the expectant mother during pregnancy and the first days of a baby's life. Nursing staff and midwives should have more training in the care of the newborn, particularly on the social and emotional aspects of childbirth. High priority should go to research on what caused handicapping conditions, and on the regional and social class variations of perinatal deaths.

There should be better and more extensive education on family planning, especially for needy groups, with greater awareness and involvement by and cooperation between professional workers other than doctors.

Health and development in the early years All children should be offered a basic programme of health surveillance shared between the CHV and the GPP. There were five principal professional activities required of health care staff who worked in child health preventive services, which would make up the programme of health surveillance: oversight of health and physical growth of all children; monitoring the developmental progress of all children; providing advice and support to parents, and when necessary arranging treatment of referral of a child; providing a programme of effective vaccination and immunization against infectious disease; participation in health education and training in parenthood. Any programme that was established should enable both health care staff and parents to be involved in the health surveillance. Incidentally, parents should be fully informed of the risks as well as the benefits associated with immunization of their child prior to any request for their consent, which should immediately precede immunization. The additional surveillance of children with special needs should be one of the most important aspects of the concept of health surveillance.

219

Home-visiting should play an indispensable and increasing role in the future child health services. There should be a national study to find out the reasons why many mothers did not attend clinics regularly. Clinics should have a social and a health element and be run with the parents' convenience in mind. Parents who moved from a neighbourhood should be more closely monitored to ensure a child continued to receive health surveillance; it would help if parents had to register a change of address when applying for family allowances. CHVs should have wider legal powers to make sure children were medically examined, when thought necessary for the child. The use of risk and observation registers should end. Schemes to encourage a better take-up of immunization should be devised and a standard health record system (possibly computer-managed) for children up to fifteen should be considered.

Health surveillance was in practice essentially a function of primary health care. One of the objects of integrating the former local authority pre-school and school health services with the general medical services provided by GPs would be to make sure that one and the same health care team had clinical responsibility for both the promotion of a child's health and the treatment of any ill-health or developmental disorder or handicap, no matter under what circumstances the contact between child and professional staff was first made.

Health for education There should be a statutory medical examination of all children when they start school. Subsequent examinations should be made on individual children only when needed. Every child should have an annual health care interview, including a vision test, with the school nurse; and at thirteen with the school doctor. Every school should have both a nominated doctor and nurse. Every special school should have a consultant community paediatrician (CCP) as a nominated school doctor with appropriately trained nurses. Headteachers should have the right (on reasonable grounds for concern) to request the examination of a child in their charge, if necessary without the consent of the parents. At present a medical examination of a child without parental consent could only be made by removing a child from home under a Place of Safety Order.

Health records should be kept on every child and relevant information made available to the education services. The views of parents and pupils should always be taken into account by health care staff. The present restriction on LEAs providing special education for children under two should be removed.

Self-referral and walk-in counselling services should be available in school and elsewhere for adolescents. They should be able to get advice on contraception, VD, psychological problems, developmental disorders, drug and alcohol abuse. Health education programmes should be aimed particularly towards 'at risk' groups. Accidental injury was the commonest cause of death among adolescents; the Government proposal for the compulsory wearing of seatbelts and a more rigorous driving test (which should be extended to mopeds) was welcome.

Skilled counselling on abortion should be available to girls and, when appropriate, to boyfriend and family in advance of any decision. Girls in care should be able to discuss abortion with someone not administratively concerned with their care.

Handicapped adolescents should have more access to psychiatric, genetic and psychosexual counselling, be encouraged to seek help on their own initiative, and have direct access to the professionals treating them.

Illness Detailed local studies should be carried out on illness to find how health facilities were used, where people went for what illness, and how far accident and emergency departments were used as primary care services. District services for all acutely ill children should be centralized in one department, which would provide paediatric and specialty services. The majority of out-patient departments attended by children paid scant attention to their personal needs; a study should be undertaken to document conditions and ensure improvements. All sick children admitted to hospital should be nursed together in children's wards in

district hospitals and cared for by nurses with special knowledge of their needs and special training to meet them.

Dental health Dental decay was the most prevalent disease
in our society. Immediate steps should be taken to fluoridate
water supplies nationally. A satisfactory national dental
service should be established with children as its priority.
Practitioners should be attracted into understaffed areas by
incentives. Training facilities for postgraduates in children's
dentistry and for dental auxiliaries should be improved.
Dental care for mentally- and physically-handicapped children
should be brought up to the level of the service for other
children. There should be a more vigorous campaign of
dental health education. A model should be set up to investigate a service for children based on the General Dental
Service with payment based on a capitation fee.

Handicap Services for handicapped children were characterized by overlap and by poor coverage. The deployment of
the scarce resources of staff and facilities left much to be
desired: highly qualified staff spent much of their time
doing work which could be done by others with less training.
There was a serious lack of communication between the
various professional staff who provided help to handicapped
children and their parents. Nor was it always clear where or
with whom responsibility for the continuing surveillance of
handicapped children lay.
    The special needs of handicapped children should be met
within the structure of an integrated child health service
rather than through a separate special service. Area Health
Authorities should carry out their own surveys of handicapped
children to obtain appropriate data on which to base services
to meet their local needs.
    The most important and practicable contribution to the
prevention of handicap was early identification with subsequent treatment of a potentially handicapping disorder.
The programme of health surveillance already outlined would
play a key part in fulfilling this aim. Difficulties at school
could indicate a handicapping condition. The proposed
medical examination prior to children starting school should

be part of an exercise to discover learning and behaviour disorder as well as of physical and sensory disorder. Health staff, teachers, social workers and psychologists should meet frequently to encourage early and informal requests for a medical opinion of children about whom teachers felt concern.

Parents of handicapped children needed a local rather than a district-based service, linked with educational medicine. The primary health care team should provide the main health service contribution in quantitative terms to the diagnosis, assessment and treatment of handicapped children. The GPP and the CHV pattern of staffing, with allied services, would provide a more adequate services for handicapped children than was currently available.

(The Committee endorsed the guidance set down in the DES circular 2/75 issued in 1975 — *The Discovery of Children requiring Special Education and the Assessment of their Needs*.)

As a support to the local primary care service, a special handicap team should be established in each health district and based in the district general hospital (DGH). This would be known as the District Handicap Team (DHT) and the section it occupied in the hospital would become the Child Development Centre. The DHT would have a clinical and an operational function and be a specialized hospital-based, multi-professional comprehensive assessment unit. The basic staff should comprise a consultant community paediatrician, a nursing officer for handicapped children, a specialist social worker, a principal psychologist, a teacher with wide experience of handicapped children of nursery and infant school age, together with supporting administrative staff. Regional multi-professional centres for handicapped children with disorders needing highly specialized personnel and investigation should be set up in university hospitals.

Parents should have the right of direct access to the district handicap team and others concerned in the treatment of their child. Each health, education and social service authority should assume responsibility for ensuring that transport, if necessary, was provided for handicapped children and their parents when attending their services.

The number of speech therapists should be expanded (as

recommended by the Quirk Committee on speech therapy services in 1972) and one senior experienced therapist attached to every child developmental centre. An area-based audiology service, linked with each child development centre, should be established. The same recommendations should apply to ophthalmological clinics.

There was evidence of shortcomings in the supply and quality of aids and appliances to handicapped children. The DES and DHSS should look at the complaints about the service as a matter of urgency. Aids for children should aways be supplied promptly and each DHT should keep a watching brief over the service locally. Physiotherapists, occupational therapists and remedial gymnasts who worked with children should be specially trained to do so.

The health and social services required by mildly mentally handicapped children should be met by the general services provided for the child population as a whole. Consultant paediatric and child psychiatric services should take on responsibility for providing supporting health services for severely handicapped children.

District handicap teams should make sure that help for parents in dealing with problems of managing severely retarded children at home was provided through visits of individual team members to the family as well as through clinic attendance. This would need a considerable expansion in community services for this group of children. Local authorities should increase their provision of both short- and long-stay residential accommodation for severely retarded children. Long-stay hospital accommodation should generally be in units forming part of the children's department of the district general hospital.[1] Wider publicity should be given to the paper issued by the DHSS in 1974 following a conference on long-stay children in hospital which contained proposals for hospitals to provide 'home-care' for long-stay children.

Psychiatric disorder Innovation, research and more training were all needed in the areas of preventive services, treatment

[1] Considered in detail in *Better Services for the Mentally Handicapped* (Cmnd 4683, HMSO, 1971).

224

and therapeutic techniques. Services were fragmented and lacked coordination. Professionals from a wide range of disciplines were required to treat psychiatric disorder and collaboration and communication were vital. All who work with children with psychiatric disorders should have some knowledge of normal and abnormal child development, family pathology and interaction, the effect of parental personal problems and a range of treatment techniques. Training involving therapeutic skills should include supervised clinical work.

Child guidance clinics and psychiatric hospital services should be integrated into a child and adolescent psychiatry service. Consultative staff from psychiatric clinics should provide support and advice to children and staff in community homes and special schools. More attention should go on providing services to pre-school children. Specially-trained child psychiatrists should give the psychiatric care needed by mentally handicapped children.

Local education authorities should support the provision of counselling in schools, and teachers should have greater access to the consultative services of psychologists and child psychiatrists. The services in schools should have good functional links with other services, and especially with child psychiatric clinics, the school psychological service and social services.

There should be long-stay residential provision for just over a third of all severely mentally handicapped children, of whom at least half could be cared for in local authority hostels.

A voice for children The needs of children and the services provided to meet them should be under continuous review. The Child and Family Life Group of the Personal Social Services Council (PSSC) should be reorganized as a Joint Committee for Children working as a sub-committee to both the PSSC and the Central Health Services Council but also having direct access to the Secretaries of State for Health and Social Security and for Wales. Joint Consultative Committees should be responsible at local level for ensuring the needs of children received due priority. Every three years, the Social Services Secretary, the Secretary of State for Wales (and where relevant, the DES and Home Office) should present a report to Parliament on all aspects of their responsibilities for children. This should begin in 1979.

The existing practice of permitting children under sixteen to receive medical advice and treatment without parental knowledge in sensitive cases, such as for sexually-transmitted diseases or contraception, should continue. No research investigations involving children should be undertaken without approval from the appropriate ethical committee.

Consideration should be given to how best to ensure that the well-being and needs of children in long-stay hospitals were adequately reviewed at appropriate intervals, with particular attention given to the possibility of loss of parental contact.

The way forward: the machinery for change

The Committee set out proposals for the transition towards the new child health service — the staffing, training arrangements and administration. These included a formal review by AHAs of how things were going after five years.

Training of new and existing staff, particularly with regard to the needs of children, would be a major element in this transition. Initial emphasis should be on supplementary training for those doing the work already, plus part-time training schemes for women doctors in paediatrics. Social work training should also include the opportunity to specialize in children's needs, notably those of handicapped and hospitalized children.

On administration, district planning teams for children's services should be established by Area Health Authorities in consulation with Joint Consultative Committees.[1]

The Committee also described how the 1974 NHS reorganization would affect the child health services; in par-

---

[1] The NHS planning system recommended by the DHSS is set out, in part, in the DHSS consultative circular *Joint Care Planning: Health and Local Authorities* (HC(76)18).

ticular, the new roles of the Specialist in Community Medicine (Child Health)[1], the area and district nursing personnel and the work and membership of community health councils[2].

The Committee concluded their Report by recognizing that they were reporting against a background of mounting inflation, severe restraints on public expenditure and a limit on human resources. Consultation was needed with a wide range of professional interests on the new kinds of staff envisaged and their training programmes. Many recommendations had long-term objectives to be achieved over fifteen to twenty years. But there were also some immediate priorities.

Of utmost importance was the need for Government to reach a quick decision about the recommendations for re-organizing and staffing the primary care services for children. Other urgent recommendations which needed extra resources were establishing child health visitors, general practitioner paediatricians, consultant community paediatricians, and children's nurses in hospitals. Other priorities were increasing the number of child psychiatrists, improving services for the newborn and for mentally retarded children in community services, in the provision of local authority hostels and children's homes, and in short-term residential care. A trained school nursing service was also a priority; as was the fluoridation of the nation's water supplies. Key recommendations which did not need large-scale resources included the setting up of district handicap teams, of a Joint Committee for Children, and of children's departments in hospitals.

[1] These are community physicians with special knowledge of the epidemiology of child health and of the health and related services for children – see DHSS circular HRC(74)5.

[2] Community health councils (CHCs) were established under the NHS reorganization of 1974 to represent the consumer in the health service and to monitor and evaluate local health services on behalf of the consumer. The Royal Commission on the NHS (July 1979, Cmnd 7615) had recommended that the powers and resources of CHCs be expanded. A consultative paper issued by the Social Services Secretary, Patrick Jenkin, in December 1979 considered the structure and management of the NHS in England and Wales (*Patients first*, HMSO). It questioned the value of CHCs in relation to the proposed changes in NHS administration. The Government called for 'views on whether community health councils should be retained when the new district health authority structure has been implemented'.

What happened to Court

The Court Report, published in December 1976, provoked considerable discussion among the medical and caring professions; many of them were firmly opposed to some of the specific proposals, especially over staffing, if not to Court's basic principles. *The Lancet* described the Report as a 'splendid statement of the needs of children and of policy goals, but an unsatisfactory practical guide to the organization of health services and to the improvement of child health'. For example, many GPs opposed the idea of general practitioner paediatricians as they feared their 'traditional role of caring for the whole family' would be undermined.

The Report also provided a considerable silence from Government. It was not — and never has been — debated in the House of Commons. It was, in fact, over a year before the 1974-9 Labour Government made any response to the Court recommendations. Admittedly, in that time, it gathered comments from the professions on six of the key recommendations (the district handicap team, the integration of child guidance and child psychiatry, the Joint Committee on Children, the GPP, the child health visitor, and the consultant community paediatrician). In January 1978, a DHSS circular HC(78)5 was published in which the Government accepted the 'overall philosophy of the Court Report' — in other words, an integrated child health service. In more detail, the key points of that philosophy were taken to be that professional staff who deal with children should be adequately trained and experienced in the special needs of children; that the children's health services should be integrated, as should community and hospital services; that an integrated child health service should follow the child's development from the pre-school years through school and adolescence; that health cover should exist for all children and families who need help; that the family dimension in child health was paramount; that there should be close cooperation between professionals and between parents and professionals.

These principles were not challenged, either by the professions or by the Government. But accepting principles and taking action are two different matters, and many of the fundamental recommendations for action have not been followed up.

The suggested new posts of general practitioner paediatrician, child health visitor, consultant community paediatrician and child health nurs were all rejected on the grounds that there was not at present sufficient support from the professions for them. Many doctors and health visitors though consider that they are already working along the lines recommended by the Court Committee and claim the structure of the services will eventually catch up with what is happening in much of the field. (In effect, the professional opposition comes much more from the professional *organizations* than from the grass roots.) The school health service would remain much the same — without the involvement of GPs — but with a few improvements, and eventually, with a national training scheme for school nurses.

Three recommendations were accepted. The idea of the district handicap team was taken up in principle, although much of the detail worked on by the Committee was left out of the Government's guidelines for the future development of these teams. For example, only severely handicapped children should come under their care rather than all handicapped or chronically ill children; there would be no child development centres. Teams have certainly been growing in number around the country, but their quality and comprehensiveness vary considerably because of the lack of specific guidelines; and it is difficult to know how widely they have spread because it is not clear where there is and where there is not a Court-type district handicap team.

In February 1978, the Government agreed to Court's recommendation for a Joint Committee for Children, to be called the Children's Committee. This has been established as a joint committee of the PSSC and the Central Health Services Council (CHSC) to advise the Government on the coordination and development of health and personal social services as they relate to children and families with children. It also has a direct access to the two Secretaries of State.

229

So far, it has helped to persuade Government to initiate a major campaign for rubella vaccination and has produced a report on perinatal and mortality morbidity. This has come from one of its four working parties — on antenatal and perinatal care. The others are on inner-urban areas and effects on children; out-of-hours medical and social care for children; the needs of the under-fives in the family.[1]

The recommendation of a formal report to Parliament from the Social Services Secretary every three years has so far come to nothing, despite a recent revival of interest and persistent pressure from the Children's Committee.[2]

The dental service continues to become less accessible and more expensive as more dentists leave the National Health Service. Some 17,000 fifteen-year-olds in Britain have false teeth; three out of ten people over sixteen have no teeth. By the age of 60 almost half the population is toothless. There is still no national programme to fluoridate the public water supply.[3]

Ironically, the specific problem for which the Court Committee was originally set up remains unsolved — the future of clinical medical officers. This is primarily because the recommendations on restructuring the preventive medical services were not fully adopted. Discussions are still in progress on their training and career structures.

As an alternative to Court's recommendations, the Government proposed an extension of the specialist hospital-based paediatric services into the community; an increase in the

[1] On 5 December 1979, the Social Services Secretary, Patrick Jenkins, announced that the PSSC and the CHSC would be abolished. He indicated that the Children's Committee would be allowed to complete its three-year term originally laid down. Thus its long-term future remains in doubt. During 1980, the Children's Committee hopes to look at residential care, the school health service and services for children.

[2] The current Government policy is that 'the publication of yet another regular Government report could not be justified bearing in mind the cost and staff time involved'. The two reports required to be presented to Parliament on the operation of the Children and Young Persons Act 1969 (under section 63/5) and of the Children Act 1975 (under section 105) were published as a joint report in November 1979. The Criminal Justice Act 1961 also carries an obligation for the Social Services Secretary to provide a report to Parliament.

[3] Less than 12 per cent of the population in England and Wales receives fluoridated water (see *Which?* April 1980).

number of health visitors, with children as their top priority (the trend has been for them to concentrate on the elderly); better training for GPs to undertake more preventive work, especially with the under-fives; and an enhanced role for the clinical medical officer in the work of the child health service, which Court had earmarked for the GPPs and GPs.

The Government also urged health authorities to discuss on a local basis how best to accommodate the Court Committee's views on primary care; set out to encourage more specialized training on the needs of children; begin to issue guidance on good practice and to recommend that any additional resources which might become available be used in areas of greatest need. Its views on timing were set out in more detail in the DHSS Planning Guidelines for 1978/9.

The plan to increase the number of health visitors goes back to 1956 when the James Committee on health visiting recommended an increase of 8,000 on the existing number. This was promised by the 1955-9 Conservative Government, and the promise repeated in 1972 by the 1970-4 Conservative Government. The 1974-9 Labour Government maintained a commitment to a 6 per cent increase in expenditure on district nurse and health visitor services. But quality of services varies from area to area and it remains unclear just how much of any increase actually goes on work with children.

The training scheme for school nurses has yet to be announced. The plan to produce guidelines on good practice in child guidance and child psychiatric services, also promised in the January 1978 DHSS circular HC(78)5, have still to be published.

In April 1978, a day conference organized jointly by the DHSS and the Child Poverty Action Group discussed the low take-up of antenatal services. A promised follow-up conference has yet to take place.

The needs of handicapped children have been particularly ill-served by the Government's piecemeal response to the Court Report. Their educational needs have had to wait for the Warnock Committee's Report published in May 1978, and have now to wait for eventual official action on Warnock's recommendations.

The Government acknowledged the 'importance of the

231

family dimension in all child health care and the need to develop a closer partnership between parents and professional staff', but it has so far failed to implement the Court proposal that parents have direct access to district handicap teams and to other specialist staff. A joint draft circular on *Prevention in the Child Health Services* was produced for discussion, but the final version has yet to be issued.

Counselling services for adolescents remain inadequate both in schools and outside, according to the recent study *Pregnant at School* (September 1979), despite this being a recommendation of numerous reports in the past, from Crowther through to Warnock. Court also called for greater research into the needs of children. In 1980, the Wing Report was published on *Behavioural and Emotional Disturbance in Children and Adolescents*, which dealt with many of the research issues raised by the Court Report. The Morris working party report on research priorities in the child health services was also published in 1980. It noted two priorities as being 'the development and evaluation of formal collaboration of local district hospital and primary health care teams in providing full cover for the children of a defined local population, particularly in places of multiple social deprivation' and 'assessment of the standards of care provided'. In other words, research which led to an improvement in the quality of care, particularly where it related to training, was to be encouraged. However, the Morris report did not cover two key aspects of child health: how parents can and do learn to look after their child's health; and the dental health of children.

David Ennals, the Secretary of State for Health and Social Services at the time that the Court Committee reported, referred to the Morris working party (still at work at the time) in a speech[1] in January 1978 to coincide with the DHSS circular on Court. He said: 'There undoubtedly is a need for further research and experiment in the child health services to ensure that changes we make do really have the expected impact on the health of children'.

[1] Eleanor Rathbone memorial lecture, Bristol, 27 January 1978; extract available as annex A of DHSS circular HC(78)5 *Health Services Development: Court Report on Child Health Services.*

Particular areas of the Court Report that Government has yet to make any response to include the need to improve genetic counselling services; the removal of the legal restriction on local education authorities to make a contribution to the assessment and management of handicapped children under two years of age; the integration of the clinical and educational sectors of the psychological profession; the assumption of parental rights by local authorities where children in long-stay hospitals have been abandoned; and the need to provide better transport services for handicapped children and their families.

The disappointing response by Government has been put down to the lack of resources and the powerful opposition from sections of the medical profession to many of the key recommendations. What the Government did was to commit itself, in principle, to an integrated child health service without having control of the administrative means to begin to create – even over a fifteen to twenty year time scale – the service that Court at least intended. Nor did it commit the resources, however modest or long-term, to implement the key recommendations for the service. One further example will suffice. The Government said nothing about the number of paediatricians and child psychiatrists needed to improve paediatric primary care. Court recommended modest increases of 353 and 180. Criticizing this silence, Professor Court himself has written: 'It is difficult to see how specialist pediatric services can extend increasingly into the community or the promised training of general practitioners, health visitors, school nurses, child therapists and social workers in child development and child health become a reality.' (*The Lancet* 25 March 1978).

Government then has put the onus on hard-pressed health authorities and reluctant professional bodies to do what they can to help to integrate child health services in whatever way they care to – Court-style or not. So, for example, GPPs will only exist where local GPs decide it is a good idea. Professional bodies will only introduce new training if it suits – and that means some GPs will have new training courses available to them, but they will not be compulsory.

In short, the scope is there – in theory. The resources, the support of a substantial part of the medical establishment, and the firm commitment and leadership by Government (both by the previous 1974-9 Labour Government and the current Conservative one) are not.

The Personal Social Services Council put it this way:

> It is not clear to us how authorities are to achieve the aim of an integrated service without more detailed guidance on the creation of an adequate substitute for the recommendations of the Court Report and without the additional resources such action will entail. As it stands the Government's response could be construed as willing the end without the means. We understand the difficulties faced by the Government, particularly those created by a situation of severe resource constraint. However, it would have been helpful to authorities if the Government had been able to make some longer-term commitment to an increase in resources when conditions allow . . . . if the long-term aims of Court are to be achieved a clearer and more dynamic initiative by Government is required.

An article in *The Times* by Caroline Moorehead was more blunt:

> In his Eleanor Rathbone speech, and in a subsequent DHSS circular (HC(78)5), Mr Ennals accepted the basic Court tenet that the present divided services should be 'welded together into an integrated child health service'. But he did not agree on the form this should take, nor it seems on the desperate need for change of some kind. For though many of his words echo the Court recommendations they lack one essential element: immediacy.
>
> This is what troubles a number of the committee members the most. The agreement is there; the suggestions for discussion are outlined. Any inspired medical officer would, if he searched, find scope — but he would not find direction. In these days of cutback such lack of enthusiasm may effectively mean a clever way of shelving the report altogether. ('What happened to the Court Report?' 4 April 1978)

In July 1979, the Royal Commission on the National Health Service[1] published its *Report* (HMSO, Cmnd 7615). Because of the recent work done by the Court Committee, the Commission did not consider services for children in detail. However, the Report did comment on the Court recommendations:

[1] Set up in May 1976, under the chairmanship of Sir Alec Merrison, the Commission was asked to 'consider in the interests both of the patients and of those who work in the National Health Service the best use and management of the financial and manpower resources of the National Health Service'.

We agree with the general approach of the Court Committee's recommendations though not with their proposals for new categories of staff. Routine school health care seems to be a logical extension of the responsibilities of the primary health care teams; and it would be valuable if post-graduate educational programmes could enable some G Ps to obtain the training needed for them to develop a special interest in paediatrics. To focus attention on, and bring help to, particularly vulnerable families and children at risk will call for close collaboration between general practitioners, health visitors and social workers. (page 68, paragraph 6.54)

Where to find out more

Books

Fit for the Future The Court Report (HMSO, Cmnd 6684, 1976, two vols)

The Reorganized National Health Service Ruth Levitt (Croom Helm, third edition, 1979)

Organizations

The Children's Committee, Mary Ward House, 5 Tavistock Place, London WC1H 9SS (01-387 9681)

Circulars

DES 1/74 The NHS Reorganisation Act 1973: Future Arrangements for the Provision of School Health Services and of Health Advice and Services to Local Education Authorities.

DES 2/75 The Discovery of Children Requiring Special Education and the Assessment of Their Needs.

DHSS HC(78)5 Health Services Development: Court Report on the Child Health Services.

DHSS HC(78)28 Children in Hospital: The Maintenance of Family Links.

14 A New Partnership for Our Schools: The Taylor Report (1977)

Why Taylor was set up

The basic blueprint for how maintained schools should be governed has been in operation for over 30 years. It was set down in sections 17-22 of the Education Act 1944, in a detailed White Paper published along with the Act and called *Principles of Government in Maintained Secondary Schools* (Cmnd 6523), and in an Administrative Memorandum no. 25 (1945) which reproduced a model or blueprint for an instrument of government (which sets out the constitution) and articles of government (which sets out the functions) of secondary schools.

The Act required every maintained secondary school to have a body of governors and every primary school a body of managers. The constitution of these bodies (who served on them) had to be set out in an instrument of government or management; and the functions (what they did) of governors and managers, of local education authorities (LEAs) and of headteachers set out in articles of government or rules of management.

The responsibility for making instruments and articles/rules was allocated between the Secretary of State and each LEA. All instruments and articles/rules were expected to conform to the basic principles set out in the 1944 White Paper. In practice, who served on a governing or managing body was a decision taken by the local education authority. The Act did not stipulate what groups in the community should be represented on these bodies. An LEA could also group two or more schools under a single governing body.

Precisely what a managing body could do — its powers —

was determined solely by the LEA through the rules of management. It could do the same for governing bodies, although the articles of government had to be specifically approved by the Secretary of State. A governing body's responsibilities could range over all or some aspects of the appointment and dismissal of teachers and other staff; the admission of pupils; the internal organization and curriculum of the school; finance; the care and maintenance of the buildings; and holiday arrangements.

By 1975, there was considerable dissatisfaction about the way many of these bodies were operating. A study[1] carried out between 1965 and 1969 (but not published until 1974) found that the intentions of the 1944 Act were, in many cases, being ignored or bypassed. For example, many schools did not have their own separate governing or managing body, but were grouped together with other schools under a single body; and although the Act allowed grouping, its authors had not envisaged groups so large as to negate the purpose for which the governing body was intended.

A high proportion of bodies were dominated by local authority councillors reflecting the political majority of the local council. Parents, teachers and the local community were provided with little information about how a governing body operated, what decisions it was making and how it arrived at them. Some bodies did not become involved with staff appointments; few had any real influence on 'the general direction of the conduct and curriculum of the school'; involvement in financial issues was rare and often went no further than 'rubber-stamping' decisions taken by the local education authority. All these were matters a governing body had a right to be fully involved in. The Taylor Committee concluded from the results of that study:

> ... the extent to which managing and governing bodies carried out the functions assigned to them in rules and articles was slight. The formulation of instruments, rules and articles and the approval of the latter by the Secretary of State were no guarantee that managing and governing bodies would play the roles originally intended for them.

[1] *The Government and Management of Schools* G. Baron and D. A. Howell (Athlone Press, 1974).

The late sixties and early seventies saw four key developments in education: the growth in demand for more participation by more people (consumers and professionals) in educational decision-making; the reorganization of secondary schooling along comprehensive lines; the reorganization of local government; and the gradual, but patchy, development in the way school governing and managing bodies were operating — more along the lines of the original intentions of the 1944 Act. These changes were producing 'a wide variety of practice and purpose'. All of which built up a head of pressure for a proper and detailed appraisal of how schools were, and should be, governed.

In January 1975, the Secretary of State for Education, Reg Prentice, announced the Government's intention to set up an independent enquiry into the management and government of schools in England and Wales. The Committee, under the chairmanship of Tom Taylor, the leader of Blackburn Council, held its first meeting in May 1975 and reported in September 1977. The Committee of 24 contained three parent representatives.

What Taylor was asked to do

Review the arrangements for the management and government of maintained primary and secondary schools in England and Wales, including the composition and functions of bodies of managers and governors, and their relationships with local education authorities, with headteachers and staffs of schools, with parents of pupils and with the local community at large; and to make recommendations.

What Taylor recommended and why

The Committee found that since the 1965-9 study, there had been very significant changes in the 'context and atmosphere' of school government. These changes had been brought about primarily by the four key developments mentioned above. Although some of the practices revealed by the study still persisted in some areas, many LEAs had made their system of school government more effective and efficient. Parental representation was more widely accepted; teacher representatives were more in evidence as well. A few LEAs even provided places for pupils and non-teaching staff. But while changes in the structure and composition of governing and managing bodies were widespread, changes in their functions were not.

A new approach to school government

The Committee concluded that there was a need for the continued existence of a body entrusted with specific responsibility for each school, apart from the head and staff. This was to ensure that each school was run with as much awareness as possible of the wishes and feelings of the parents and the local community. It would also ensure that the parents and community in turn would be better informed of the school's needs, and of the policies and constraints within which the LEA operated and the head and teachers worked.

All those concerned with a school's success — the LEA, staff, parents, and local community — should be brought together to discuss and justify proposals about the work and direction of the school. They should all share in making decisions on how the school was to be run and organized. The Committee believed that this was the most effective way to ensure that every aspect of the life and work of the school came within the ambit of all those interests acting together.

There was a need to clarify who could exercise what decision-making powers. The ultimate responsibility for the running of its schools had to lie with the local education authority that provided them. The LEA should set out general policies and directions for its schools and always have the final say on exercising its statutory duties for schools; the governing body should set out the lines along which its particular school was organized and run; the head and staff should take many of the day-to-day decisions.

The governing body should stand in direct line of formal responsibility between the LEA and the head of the school.

To avoid confusion, all the powers relevant to school government should be formally vested in the local education authority. But the LEA should delegate as much of this power to the governing body as was compatible with the LEA's ultimate responsibility for its schools. In turn, the governing body should give as much discretion to the head of the school as was compatible with the head's responsibility for ensuring the success of the school.

Every school should have its own separate governing body, so the grouping of schools under a single body should cease. Section 20 of the Education Act 1944, which allowed grouping, should be repealed. The terms 'governor' and 'governing body' should in future be used for both primary and secondary schools.

Membership of governing bodies

The effect of the 1944 White Paper was to hand over the composition of managing and governing bodies to the local education authorities:[1]

> In the case of county schools the governing body is to consist of such number of persons appointed in such manner as the local education authority may determine; in the case of voluntary schools the governing body is to consist of such number of persons as the Minister may determine, subject to compliance with the prescribed proportions of foundation governors and of governors appointed by the local education authority.

[1] *Minor authorities* The only interest that the Education Act 1944 stipulated should be represented on managing or governing bodies were 'minor authorities'. These would include parish councils, non-metropolitan district councils and (in Wales) community councils. Section 18 of the 1944 Act stated that where a county primary school served an area in which there was a minor authority, two-thirds of the managers should be appointed by the LEA and one-third by the minor authority. The Taylor Committee recommended that section 18 should be repealed as they believed that the minor authority interest would be taken up within the proposal that one-quarter of the governing body of a primary school should consist of members specifically chosen to represent local community interests. In addition, they recommended that any elected member of a local authority in the area served by a school should be able to stand for election to a school governing body in either the 'LEA' or the 'community' category.

> ... in all schools it may be assumed that the governing body
> will include (i) adequate representation of the local education
> authority (ii) other persons whose qualifications are such as to
> enable them to play a useful part in the government of a secondary
> school.

There was widespread dissatisfaction with the dominance of governing bodies by political parties — a feeling that was reinforced by the fact that not all the L E A representatives turned up regularly at meetings. There was also dissatisfaction with some bodies' failure to exercise effective control over how their schools were run.

Every governing body should therefore have four groups equal in size: representatives from the L E A; the school staff (the head, teachers, and where the size of the body allows, non-teaching staff); the parents (with, where appropriate, the pupils); and the local community.

The maximum number of governors on any body should normally be 24, with a minimum of eight, so there should never be fewer than two members from each of the four types of members. The head should always be one of the school staff members. Every parent governor should have a child at the school and be elected by a vote of the other parents with children at the school. The L E A should draw up and oversee the rules and procedures for parent-governor elections. All elections should be school-based and the procedures should ensure the maximum participation; nominations and voting papers and results should be forwarded to all eligible parents. All communications should be in straightforward language and, where necessary, in more than one language.

The Secretary of State should consider whether the qualifying age of eighteen for pupil governors could be reduced to sixteen, without having to raise the whole issue of minors holding public office. In the meantime, pupils under eighteen should take as full a part in a governing body as the law allowed.

Community representatives should be coopted by the other three-quarters of the governing body, and should have indicated their willingness to be coopted. LEAs should draw up lists of potential governors, to include nominations from

241

local employers and trade unions. The term of office for all governors should generally be within a four-year framework.

Communication and cooperation

Governing bodies could only achieve their full potential if there was close cooperation and good communication with the school's staff, parents and the local community.

Staff (teaching and non-teaching) should be fully consulted and able to express views on the running of the school. Notices, agendas and minutes of governors' meetings should be available in staffrooms, except for matters considered by the governors to be confidential. The governing body should ensure there are adequate arrangements for teachers and supporting staff to discuss and express views with the head on day-to-day matters.

Parents should be encouraged to set up their own organization based on the school and to decide that organization's aims and how it should work, in consultation with head and governing body. They should be provided with the means to publicize their activities and have regular access to the school and its resources. Every school should have proper arrangements for making sure all parents knew about school policy; were involved in their child's progress and welfare; and had ready access to school and its teachers. Every parent should receive a letter from the governing body setting out the linked rights and responsibilities of parent and school towards the children.

Pupils should have proper access to the governors for expressing their views on school matters. If they wanted a school council, the governors should approve it and should make sure it worked effectively. The pupils should, as a general rule, decide the agenda for the council's meetings.

Community links should be encouraged. The governors should keep in contact with local agencies concerned with children's welfare; with other governing bodies over issues of common interest; and with local employers and trade unions. LEAs should always gather opinion from governors on local matters which, directly or indirectly, affected the school.

The concerns of the governing body

Curriculum Every aspect of the life and work of the school should be seen as interdependent. There was no aspect of the school's activities from which the governing body should be excluded nor any aspect for which the head and teachers should be accountable only to themselves or to the LEA. It followed that the responsibility for deciding the school's curriculum, in every sense of that word, ought to be shared by all concerned groups at every level. With this in mind, the governing body, along with the head and the teachers, should set out the educational and social aims of the school and devise a programme for achieving them.

This should include shaping and monitoring the teaching methods, how the school was organized (e.g. timetabling, activities offered), the educational experiences and pastoral care available to the children, and the effects on the children of the schooling provided. The head should supply the governors with an adequate flow of information about what was going on in school.

Guidelines should be set out to encourage a positive and pleasant atmosphere in the school with high standards of behaviour, making only those rules and sanctions as were needed to maintain the standards set. The governors should make periodic reviews of how the school was progressing (including seeing classes at work) and report to the LEA. They should be able to call on the skills and advice of LEA advisers. LEAs should make sure they could provide this service to schools, and if not, should increase the number of advisers accordingly.

Finance LEAs should keep overall control of the financing of schools, since a good proportion of that finance was

243

determined nationally (e.g. teachers' salaries). However, governing bodies should have some influence over the resources to be made available for their school. They should participate in budgeting for the school, prepare estimates for LEA approval, and have a good deal of flexibility over how the approved budget was used in school. Governors should also be fully consulted about decisions on building work, large and small.

A joint working party of the DES and LEAs should be set up to investigate how allowances for schools (e.g. capitation allowances) should be decided and how distributed.[1]

Staff appointments Headteachers should be appointed by a small selection committee comprising equally members of the governing body and LEA representatives, the latter providing the chairman. All other appointments should be the governors' responsibility, with advice from LEA officers and advisers.

Current procedures for dismissing teachers seemed to be working satisfactorily. However, difficulties did exist. Therefore, a governing body should know its LEA's conditions of service for teachers. The Secretary of State should start discussions with LEAs and teachers' unions on what to do about the professionally incompetent teacher.

Admissions to school The LEA should continue to have overall control of the admissions policy for its schools, although governors should be consulted. The principles and criteria on which school places were allocated should always be made public.

Suspensions and expulsions Every LEA should set out clearly defined and well publicized procedures for barring a child from school. No child should be prevented from attending school except in accordance with these procedures. (There would be some exclusions on certain well-defined health grounds.)

[1] This has previously been recommended by the Bullock Committee on literacy skills in February 1975.

244

Parents should always be consulted when a child's persistently bad behaviour made suspension a real possibility. Suspension should not be regarded as a punishment, but rather as a breathing space to find a solution to the problem so as to get a child back into schooling as speedily as possible. While a headteacher should use discretion in dealing with disruptive behaviour, his/her right to suspend a pupil should be limited to a period of up to three days. There should be further safeguards. Full information should be quickly presented to the parents and a record of the suspension and the incident leading to it kept at the school. The governors should be able to extend a suspension, but again for a limited period only. During this time, the relevant people should be brought together to discuss the problem and find a solution. If unsuccessful, the matter should go to the LEA, which should hear and decide on any parental appeals against suspension and should determine whether to expel the pupil or not. The governors should be told of the LEA decision. The LEA would remain responsible for the future education of any expelled pupil. There should be immediate legislation to bring these recommendations into effect.

School premises The governors should remain responsible for reviewing the state of repair of school premises and be able to make urgent minor repairs within a limit set by the LEA. LEAs and governing bodies should work out a general area policy on letting schools to outside organizations. Headteachers should then be able to decide on lettings for their own school, based on the governors' guidelines. The LEA would have the final say in any dispute over the use of a school.

Training of governors

All LEAs should make sure that initial and in-service training courses were provided for school governors, if necessary in cooperation with other institutions and agencies. All governors should undertake such training as soon as was practicable.

245

Procedures for governing bodies

A governor should normally be in office for up to four
years. There should be no compulsory retiring age. No
one should be a governor of more than one school catering
for the same age group. Any governor could be chairman,
except for a paid employee of the school. Meetings should
be held at least twice a term. Clerking arrangements should
be left to the LEA. Governors should not receive an attendance allowance, but they should be able to claim proved
loss of earnings and any travelling and incidental expenses.
This would ensure no one was prevented from membership
because of the cost of attending meetings.

All minutes and papers should go to every governor and
to the LEA. Nothing should be confidential, except what
was decided by the governors. Full information about governors should be made available to parents and others.

Voluntary schools

About 30 per cent of all maintained schools were voluntary
schools, i.e. schools provided by voluntary foundations
(churches and charities) but whose running costs, including
teachers' salaries, were met by the LEAs. Voluntary schools
were either aided, controlled or special agreement schools,
according to how they were funded and run. For the purpose
of school government the differences from county schools
were: in an aided or special agreement school, two-thirds of
the governors were appointed by the voluntary foundation
and one-third by the LEA. This meant that the voluntary
foundation could control the arrangements for the admission
of pupils, the appointment of head and teachers, the use of
school premises, the religious and (for secondary schools)
the secular curriculum, and could make or block significant
changes in the character of the school (such as an LEA
comprehensive reorganization scheme). A controlled school
had only one-third of its governors appointed by the voluntary

foundation and two-thirds by the LEA. In short, a voluntary school was generally much more independent of LEA policy with a governing body controlled by the voluntary foundation.

The Secretary of State had suggested that the Committee should not concern themselves with 'those aspects of voluntary school management and government which reflected the present structure of the "dual system" of county and voluntary schools'. The Committee did in fact receive evidence from religious bodies suggesting changes in how voluntary schools were governed. But they recommended that more detailed consultation should take place between the Secretary of State and the voluntary foundations in order to make the fundamental changes required to bring the voluntary schools more in line with the county schools. Recommendations such as the 'four equal shares' concept of school government were impractical within the existing structure of the dual system. However, some recommendations could, and should, be accommodated into that system by the voluntary schools, such as the abolition of grouping, the training of governors, the payment of necessary expenses, and accepting the LEA's dates for school holidays.

Implementing the Report

Legislation should be brought in quickly to ensure that LEAs carry out the main recommendations on the membership, powers, procedures and training of governing bodies in all county schools within a maximum period of five years. Their progress should be monitored by the DES and further guidance given where appropriate.

The recommendations for a separate governing body for each school (abolishing section 20 of the 1944 Act), for getting rid of the 'minor authority' legal obstacle to the four equal shares in membership (section 18 of the 1944 Act), and for setting up a new suspensions procedure should be legislated for straightaway.

Notes of extension

Several members of the Committee expressed degrees of dissension or a wish to go further than a majority of the members felt able to agree to. In the second category was a 'note of extension' put forward by seven of the 22 Committee members: parents should have the right *in law* to be given information about the school their child attends, regular consultations and reports on the child, and the opportunity to see teachers by arrangement at all reasonable times. They should also have a right of access to information about their child's education, including records kept in a permanent form in the school.

What happened to Taylor

The Taylor Report, published in September 1977, recommended a major shift in educational responsibility. They were saying that local authorities should delegate as much responsibility as possible to the new four-part governing body. School governors would be concerned with how their school was run, what it was costing and who was employed on the staff. But more people, including children over sixteen, would be involved in making those kinds of decisions. The Committee did not suggest anything really new; they were able to point to current practice going on somewhere in the country for every recommendation they made about how governing bodies should operate. Their basic aim was to make best practice the normal practice nationwide.

Indeed, the Committee found that there had already been a significant change in the 'context and atmosphere' of school government, which by 1975 was in a period of 'transition'. Nonetheless a formal and central restructuring of governing bodies was felt to be necessary. While the Committee was sitting, the report[1] of the problems at the William Tyndale

[1] *William Tyndale Junior and Infant School Public Inquiry: A Report to the Inner London Education Authority* by Robin Auld QC (ILEA, July 1976). See also *William Tyndale: collapse of a school — or a system?* by John Gretton and Mark Jackson (George Allen and Unwin, 1976) and *William Tyndale: the teachers' story* by Terry Ellis, Brian Haddow, Dorothy McColgan and Jackie McWhirter (Writers and Readers Publishing Cooperative, 1976).

junior school exemplified the inadequacies that could and still did exist in many school managing and governing bodies.

However, despite the significant changes that had been going on, some of the Taylor Committee recommendations drew strong opposition. The concept of 'four equal shares' in membership was criticized by many LEAs which did not wish to lose their majority representation and by minor authority organizations which did not like losing their specific right to representation. Extending governors' powers brought vehement opposition from both teacher unions and educational administrators. One teacher union (the National Union of Teachers) found the Report, which suggested a relaxation of the control over school affairs (especially over the curriculum) by head and staff, tantamount to 'a busy-bodies' charter'. Another recommendation which drew disfavour was the suggestion that pupils under eighteen should become governors.

This kind of professional opposition, together with the Government's wish to proceed quickly to some kind of restructuring of school government, made the Secretary of State, Shirley Williams, divide the two issues of composition and powers. The latter was put on ice during the usual period of 'detailed and extensive' consultation.

At the end of November 1978, just over a year after the Report was published, the 1974-9 Labour Government published a new Education Bill. This contained five clauses dealing with proposed changes in how schools were to be governed.

The term 'governor' and 'governing body' would be used in both primary and secondary schools. Regulations would be made by the Secretary of State about the size and membership of governing bodies in both county *and* voluntary schools. All governing bodies should include representatives of parents with children at the school and of teachers at the school, and (for county secondary schools) the local community. Local authorities wanting a governing body to serve more than one school (grouping) would have to obtain specific permission to do so from the Secretary of State. All 'grouped' schools should have parent and teacher representation on the governing body serving them.

The Secretary of State also grasped (at least in part) the nettle of the voluntary schools, and proposed that the number of foundation governors at aided schools should be reduced from a majority of two-thirds to an overall majority of two on bodies with up to 18 members, and three on larger bodies. Finally, and surprisingly, it was proposed that a pupil should be eligible to be a governor from the age of sixteen — the unspoken implication of this conflicted with the accepted view of current law.

The subsequent White Paper *The Composition of School Governing Bodies* (Cmnd 7430, December 1978) set out the Secretary of State's proposals about what was to be covered in the regulations referred to in the Bill. The powers of governors were not dealt with, and the Secretary of State explained her position on the whole issue of school government thus:

> There is still no agreement about what the formal powers of governing bodies should be. Most people, in my view rightly, see the nature of the relationship between the governing body and the school as something organic which is individual to each school. Where the relationship works, it does not need any over-elaborate delegation of statutory powers, and where it does not work no amount of formal statutory power will increase its usefulness or its influence. The Bill, therefore, does not contain any provision relating to the specific powers of governing bodies, partly because I believe that the time is not yet right for such legislation and partly because I believe that getting the right people on to governing bodies in sufficient numbers will be enough to do the necessary task on its own.
> (House of Commons debate, 5 December 1978)

The Bill set out that up to half of the total membership of governing bodies would be taken by LEA representatives. The minimum statutory representation for parents, teachers and the local community would vary according to the size of the school: for parents, a minimum of between two and four; for teachers, one and four; for the local community, two. In primary schools, the community places would be taken by minor authority representatives. (Parents and teachers would have similar representation on voluntary school governing bodies.)

Representation for pupils and non-teaching staff would be decided locally. Much of the detail for implementing proposals would be left to local discretion, except for the establishment of national safeguards to ensure elections for governors were properly and effectively conducted. The head should be able to *choose* whether to be a full member of a school's governing body. Grouping arrangements would only be approved in a small number of special cases, such as two schools sharing the same site.

The Government had accepted Taylor recommendations on a single name for all school government (governor and governing body); statutory representation of parents and teachers on governing bodies; statutory regulations on elections of governors and the election by parents of parent governors. The Bill also contained proposals to put a statutory duty on LEAs to provide parents with information on school admission policy and procedures with a promise of further regulations from the Secretary of State on the kind of additional information to be supplied to parents.

However, it differed from the Taylor Report in several fundamental respects: no four equal shares arrangement; no end to minor authority representation; no automatic membership of a governing body by the head; no complete abolition of grouping; no end to LEA dominance.

There were also some significant omissions: no statutory right for parents to form a home-school group or to see their child's school record; no legislation for a Taylor-style suspensions procedure; no proper safeguards for parental participation in the life of the school or for consultation between governors and staff, pupils and the local community[1]; no training requirement for governors; no joint DES/LEA working party on capitation allowances; no formal discussions on the professionally incompetent teacher; and as yet still no satisfactory overall procedure for school admissions, although the Bill did contain some proposals

---

[1] An advisory DES circular had been issued at the end of November 1977 called *Information for Parents* (15/77) which set out the kind of information that schools should be prepared to let parents have. The general principle has been accepted that parents should be given more information about their local schools. But the enthusiasm and conscientiousness with which LEAs and schools go about that task vary considerably throughout the country.

about admissions policy, including the power for LEAs to limit the annual intake of pupils in its schools[1], about parental preference and appeals procedures, and the retention of powers over admissions by voluntary-aided school governing bodies.

In fact, the Bill failed to become an Act. The May 1979 General Election intervened while the Bill was in the House of Commons committee stage of its passage through Parliament. So the *legal* situation remained as it was before the Taylor Report.

The new Conservative Government included five clauses on school government in its Education (no 2) Bill — published in October 1979 — which became the Education Act 1980. They followed the same basic framework as Labour's Bill. The trends towards a separate body for each school and greater representation for parents and teachers were acknowledged and provided for — although grouping was not wholly abolished nor was a Taylor-style partnership specifically legislated for. There was, though, nothing to prevent an LEA from arranging its governing bodies along Taylor lines should it wish.

Some minor improvements were made — for example, including special schools in the arrangements; providing a neater solution to the composition of voluntary school governing bodies. The National Association of Governors and Managers (NAGM) welcomed the fact that there was less central direction in the organization of governing bodies — 'it provides for parents and teachers . . . without complexity, rigidity and over-regulation'. The parents' right to detailed information about local schools (including this time the publication of school exam results) was reiterated — again with the promise of specific regulations to be followed by LEAs. However, the main omissions were similar to those of Labour's lost Bill plus, this time, no reference to pupil governors.

[1] LEAs considered this an essential step in order to enable them to plan more effectively for substantially fewer pupils in school in the 1980s, because of the decline in the birthrate between 1964 and 1977. From a peak of nine million pupils in school in 1977, the number will fall to between seven and seven and a half million by the late 1980s. See DES Report on Education 92 *School Population in the 1980s* (June 1978) and 96 *Trends in School Population* (November 1979) available free from the DES.

Briefly, the new Act provides that:

Both primary and secondary schools will have 'governors' and 'governing bodies' thus dispensing with the terms 'managers' and 'managing bodies'. In general, every school should have its own governing body. All governing bodies must by law have parent and teacher representatives — two parent governors (elected by a secret ballot by parents); at least one elected teacher governor (at least two in schools with more than 300 pupils). All governing bodies must have LEA representatives but the number and proportion of governors representing other interests (e.g., non-teaching staff, pupils, the community) is up to each LEA.

Greater controversy was caused by some of the Bill's other clauses — the reduction in the statutory duties of LEAs to provide school meals and transport; the new arrangements for school admissions and for local appeal committees for parents dissatisfied with the school place allocated to their child; and the proposals for the assisted places scheme which aims eventually to provide central government funding to help up to 100,000 pupils go to independent school.[1]

What then is the current state of the 'partnership' in our schools? A national survey[2] of all LEAs in England and Wales by the Advisory Centre for Education (ACE) at the start of 1979 revealed that some 90 per cent of LEAs already had some form of parent representation and 90 per cent had some form of teacher representation on their governing bodies — either elected or coopted, mainly with full powers but a few with only observer status. Eighty per cent of LEAs had both parent and teacher representation. In most LEAs, the LEA-appointed governors were in the majority. About 30 per cent had some pupil participation, though not always throughout the LEA and often not with full governors' powers. But in well over half the schools, there was only one parent governor on the governing body. Fourteen LEAs allowed no parent representation. Grouping of schools was less common, although 48 per cent of LEAs still did not have individual governing bodies for each school. In short, the survey found

---

[1] The scheme is to begin in September 1981 with eventual funding of £55 million a year. In February 1980, the size of the scheme was cut by half.
[2] *School Governors: Partnership in Practice* Joan Sallis (ACE, April 1979).

'some representation of parents and teachers . . . in an over-whelmingly majority of LEAs, though in most cases in token numbers, on boards with large majorities appointed by the LEA'.

There was also found to be a growing interest in the powers available to governors, with more direct concern in the daily life and work of the school, more discussion of school issues, close involvement in selecting the head. Interest in financial matters remained low. Half the LEAs provided, or had plans to provide, some form of training for their school governors. (The latter is certainly an area of improvement with more LEA-sponsored courses, more commercially-produced training manuals, and an Open University course for school governors funded by a DES grant.) Many LEAs were planning further developments in their arrangements for school government.

A variable system of letting and charging for the use of school premises persists with no set of national guidelines — a situation which consistently makes schools underused resources in the local community.

The Taylor Report had documented, and through its own publication helped to encourage, the recent developments in the way governing bodies were operating — more partici-patory, more involved in the life of the school. But the 1979 ACE survey revealed that much was still in need of reform.

Governments' proposals — in Labour's 1978 Bill and White Paper and in the Conservative 1980 Act — have been criticized for being piecemeal schemes for democratizing school govern-ment which have failed to embrace Taylor's more imaginative and straightforward concept of the four equal shares. They were in effect legislating largely for a situation that was, at least in skeletal form, already in existence or developing, and failing to encourage more fundamentally democratic changes. NAGM criticized[1] both Governments (Labour more than Conservative) because they feared that local initiative to create greater democracy in school government would be

[1] *The Education Bill and White Paper: Analysis and Commentary* by Tony Travers and Tyrrell Burgess (NAGM paper, February 1979) and *Education (no 2) Bill: Commentary* (November 1979 Annual Conference).

inhibited by central regulation. NAGM favoured legislating for the four equal shares and then relying on the existing set of powers and duties already laid down in the 1944 Education Act.

Where to find out more

Books

A *New Partnership for Our Schools* The Taylor Report (HMSO, 1977)

School Managers and Governors: Taylor and After Joan Sallis (Ward Lock Educational, 1977)

Governors' Guide 1979 Barbara Bullivant (Home and School Council, 1979)

School Governors' and Managers' Handbook and Training Manual Tyrrell Burgess and Anne Sofer (Kogan Page, 1979)

The School in its Setting Joan Sallis (ACE, 1980)

Organizations

Advisory Centre for Education (ACE), 18 Victoria Park Square, London E2 9PB (01-980 4596)

Campaign for the Advancement of State Education (CASE), 43 Little Heath, London SE7 (01-317 7213)

Home and School Council, 81 Rustlings Road, Sheffield S11 7AB (0742 662467)

National Association of Governors and Managers (NAGM), 81 Rustings Road, Sheffield S11 7AB (0742 662467)

National Confederation of Parent-Teacher Associations (NCPTA), 43 Stonebridge Road, Northfleet, Gravesend, Kent (0474 60618)

Circulars

No circulars or administrative memoranda have been issued specifically on the governing of schools since AM 25 in January 1945 *Instruments, Articles of Government and Rules of Management*. The Education Act 1980 incorporates changes in the government of county, voluntary and maintained secondary schools. See DES circular 1/80.

Key Regulations or Statutory Instruments (SI) on the standards and general requirements to be observed by schools maintained by LEAs include the Schools Regulations 1959 (SI 364) and the Standards for School Premises Regulations 1972 (SI 2051).

15   Special Educational Needs: The Warnock Report (1978)

Why Warnock was set up

In 1955 there were 52,000 handicapped pupils being educated full-time in special schools. By 1977, there were 135,261. A further 21,674 pupils, who were being taught in ordinary schools, were in classes that had been designated as 'special'. Half a million other children attended groups in primary and secondary schools which had not been officially designated as 'special', but they were in the main children with some kind of learning difficulty, as opposed to additional emotional or behavioural problems. In 1955 there were 623 special schools; in 1977 there were 1,653.

The 1944 Education Act had set out the duties of LEAs towards handicapped children — to ascertain which children needed special educational treatment, and to provide it for them 'in special schools or otherwise'. In 1959, official categories of pupils needing special treatment were set out in *Handicapped Pupils and Special Schools Regulations 1959* (SI 1959 no. 365). Ten categories were listed; by 1974, the DES education statistics listed nineteen separate categories of school for children with a handicap.

The Education (Handicapped Children) Act 1970 brought all handicapped children, however severe the handicap, within the framework of special education. LEAs became responsible for the education of all mentally and physically handicapped children. No child would in future be regarded as ineducable. The category for educationally subnormal children (ESN) was also extended by dividing it into ESN(M) for children with a moderate degree of handicap and ESN(S) for those with a severe degree of handicap.

More of the less severely handicapped children were being catered for in ordinary schools; special schools tended more to cater for the most severely handicapped. In 1975 the DES and the Welsh Office issued a new circular[1] (2/75 and 21/75) to 'clear up uncertainties and confusion which surround the subject of ascertainment, and to provide a fresh statement of what is involved in discovering which children require special education and in recommending the form it should take'. This circular is generally used as the basis for deciding how and which children should be assessed for special educational treatment.

In November 1973, the Education Secretary Margaret Thatcher announced the setting up of a Committee of Enquiry to consider the needs of handicapped children. The Committee began its work in September 1974, chaired by Mary Warnock. This was the first Committee of Enquiry set up by any British Government to review educational provision for *all* handicapped children. The last time anything like it happened was the Royal Commission on the Blind, the Deaf and Dumb and Others of the United Kingdom in 1889.

What Warnock was asked to do

Review educational provision in England, Scotland and Wales for children and young people handicapped by disabilities of body and mind, taking account of the medical aspects of their needs, together with arrangements to prepare them for entry into employment; to consider the most effective use of resources for these purposes; and to make recommendations.

What Warnock recommended and why

The Committee published their Report in May 1978. The 1974-9 Labour Government had pre-empted the Committee

[1] *The Discovery of Children Requiring Special Education and the Assessment of Their Needs* (March 1975).

in one respect by including a section on the education of children with special needs in the 1976 Education Act. Section 10 of that Act stated that, subject to certain qualifications and effective from a date to be appointed by the Secretary of State for Education, handicapped children should be educated in ordinary schools rather than in special schools. The qualifications included whether integration proved impracticable or incompatible with providing efficient instruction, or involved unreasonable public expense. The Committee consequently made recommendations on how best to put the principle into practice.

The Committee saw the educational needs of children in the context of two broad aims: first, to enlarge a child's knowledge, experience and imaginative understanding, and to create an awareness of moral values and the capacity for enjoyment; second, to become an active and responsible member of society, able to achieve as much independence as possible. The task was to consider how teaching and learning could best be arranged wherever there were children who had an obstacle — physical, sensory, intellectual or emotional — to overcome.

The Committee therefore set out to change the whole idea of what we should mean by special education. The traditional idea was to use special methods which fitted a particular category of children. The Committee believed the emphasis should move away from considering a child's handicap to deciding what a child's educational needs were.

The Committee did not investigate the causes of educational handicap; nor the particular problems of highly gifted children; nor how to improve educational provision for each specific disability.

The scope of special education

Children should no longer be seen in terms of two distinct groups — handicapped or non-handicapped. Instead all children should be seen in terms of their individual educational needs. Special education should be seen as an extension (or continuum) of educational provision available either as short-term help over a particular difficulty or as long-term restructuring of the normal curriculum.

Children's medical needs or difficulties might be of little help when sorting out their educational needs; there was no necessary direct link between the two. Applying a rigid medical formula to decide educational provision caused confusion. All the factors relating to how a child progressed educationally should be taken into account — abilities as well as disabilities. Labelling children according to their handicaps should be abolished; instead all children should be considered according to their educational needs. The distinction between special and remedial education should go. Children currently in remedial classes, or who were regarded as educationally subnormal, should be described as 'children with learning difficulties', either mild, moderate or severe. The term 'maladjusted' should be retained.

The concept of special education should therefore include the whole range and variety of additional help, wherever it was provided and whether it was on a full- or part-time basis, by which children may be helped to overcome educational difficulties, including children with emotional or behaviour disorders who were previously considered 'disruptive', and children thought before to need remedial rather than special education.

In future, special educational provision for a child should mean having:

1 effective access to teachers with appropriate qualifications or substantial experience;
2 effective access to other professionals with appropriate training;
3 an educational and physical environment with the necessary aids, equipment and resources appropriate to a child's special needs.

All this should be given legal backing by amending section 8 of the 1944 Education Act which excluded from provision those children whose needs did not arise from physical or mental disability.[1]

[1] Section 8(2)(c) of the 1944 Education Act; section 5(1) of the 1962 Education (Scotland) Act.

It should be assumed that in future about one child in six at any time, and up to one in five at some time, would need special education provision during their school career.

Discovery, assessment and recording

It was vital for a child's education that any special needs should be discovered and assessed as early in a child's life as possible.

Discovery A basic programme of health surveillance should be provided for all children.[1] More information about child development and about sources of expert advice should be available to parents. Health visitors were an important factor in detecting children's disabilities, and (where appropriate) community physicians should receive information about handicapped children from paediatricians and other hospital consultations. Local education authorities should monitor whole age-groups of children at least three or four times during their school life.

As a basic working principle, all educationally relevant information about a child should be shared between professionals, and between professionals and parents. A school should keep a personal folder on every pupil containing progress records and factual information. Parents and pupils should have ready access to this folder. A second *confidential* folder, with access controlled by the head, should contain results of professional consultations and sensitive information which had been given in confidence about a child's social background or family relationships.

Assessment There should be five stages of assessment. The first three would be school-based, relying mainly on the school staff; the last two stages would involve staff from a number of professions and rely on more specialist expertise (a multi-professional assessment team). The results of stages

---

[1] Also proposed by the 1976 Court Report on child health services.

4 and 5 should be carefully documented through the SE forms procedure.[1]

Where district handicap teams have been established (see the Court Report), they should be augmented to carry out assessments. When a child had been assessed the child's progress should be reviewed every year by the LEA's special education advisory and support service.

LEAs should have the legal power to insist on a child having a multi-professional assessment if considered necessary.[2] Others — say, parents — should be able to insist that an LEA did make an assessment if the LEA were unwilling to do so. Parents should be fully involved in all stages and procedures of assessment, for no assessment of a child's needs could be complete without the information parents could supply and no educational programme could adequately meet those demands without parental cooperation.

The SE forms procedure should be improved and extended to include children who have not yet started school.

Recording LEAs should keep a record of children considered in need of special educational provision not usually available in an ordinary school. But no child should go on a record without first being assessed by a multi-professional team. Nor should a placement be made without a completed SE4 form. The SE4 form would act as the basis for an LEA decision on whether or not a child should be recorded as requiring special educational provision.

Parents should have ready access to their child's record, which should contain the SE4 form, a profile of the child's needs, the recommendation for the provision of special help, a note on how the recommendation was being met in practice, and a note of the Named Person[3] for the child's parents

---

[1] This procedure occurs when a child is assessed for special education. There are four forms: SE1 completed by the child's teacher; SE2 by the school doctor; SE3 by an educational psychologist; and SE4 a summary and action sheet completed by an experienced educational psychologist or a special education adviser. The forms are then sent to the LEA's education officer responsible for special education. This is not a mandatory procedure, but one recommended by the DIES in circular 2/75 (Welsh Officer 21/75).

[2] This would mean amending section 34 of the 1944 Education Act.

[3] See section *Children under five* p. 262.

designated by the multi-professional team. The record should be passed on if a child moved to another LEA. Parents should have an explicit right to appeal not only against an LEA's decision that a child *was* in need of special education, but also against a decision that a child was *not*.

Children under five

Parents should be regarded as the main educators of their children in the early years of life. Services which could advise and support parents in this role should be improved and expanded. Children with disabilities or significant difficulties should be detected and helped as early on as possible. There should be no minimum age limit for getting help. (This should be made clear by an appropriate amendment in the law since LEAs were not legally obliged to provide for children under the age of two.)

Explaining to parents that their child was handicapped in some way was a delicate and difficult task. It was often handled badly. Support and information should be readily available to parents at this time.

The cornerstone of this support should be someone — usually the health visitor — who was designated as a Named Person, so parents always know there was someone to turn to for help. They should be able to change their named contact without difficulty if it did not work out well. Parents should have access to information and advice, and to an extended peripatetic teaching service.

Nursery provision should be greatly expanded, with special nursery classes and units. A general expansion would automatically increase the opportunities for nursery education for children with special educational need. Playgroups and opportunity groups should be ready to accept young children with disabilities or difficulties. There should be an increase in the number of combined nursery schools and day nurseries. Whatever kind of pre-schooling was available, parents should always be as fully involved as possible.

Parents as partners

Once a child started school, the Named Person should normally change to the head of the child's current school. Later, in the period of moving from school into adult life, the careers officer should take over as the Named Person.

Parents should always be seen as full partners with the numerous professionals who assessed and provided for a child's special needs. Thus parents could in turn effectively help their child. They should be able to visit regularly and without ceremony their child's school and talk with head and teachers. They should have direct access to the special education advisory and support service. In addition, parents of children with severe difficulties who lived at home should have a variety of short-term relief, including access to special schools kept open during school holidays.

Special education in ordinary schools

Given the wider concept of special education, some 20 per cent of children are likely to be in need of special educational provision (rather than the 2 per cent covered by the existing official definition of special education). Most of this provision would occur in ordinary schools and careful planning was required. Section 10 of the 1976 Education Act was on the statute book and it was necessary to concentrate on the practical requirements for the eventual success of integration. Teacher and parents should be committed to the principle of integration and be well-prepared for the tasks involved; the premises should be suitable; the curriculum well planned; and specialist help readily available.

Where a special class or unit was set up in an ordinary school, one of the school's governors should take on a particular concern for it, and a specialist teacher should be responsible for its day-to-day running. In large schools, a special resource centre (or other supporting base) should be set up. LEAs should provide more staff and resources in ordinary schools which took on a special education role and issue detailed public information about what was available in each school. The Education Secretary should, in turn, issue detailed guidelines to LEAs on how to arrange special educational provision before section 10 of the 1976 Act was brought into force.

Special education in special schools

There were three types of special school in England and Wales: those run by the LEAs, those run by voluntary bodies, and independent schools catering wholly or mainly for handicapped pupils. The scale of education in special schools was likely to decline in the future for three reasons: the fall in the birthrate; the improvements in preventive health services; and the eventual implementation of section 10 of the 1976 Act.

However, special schools would continue to have a vital role in, for example, offering separate provision for children with particular needs; giving intensive specialized short-term help, sometimes at short notice; or developing as resource centres, for all the teachers in the area, for curriculum development and in-service training or possibly concentrating on rare or complex disabilities. Boarding schools could be more flexible in what help they gave and to whom they gave it. Special schools ought to cater either for senior or for junior pupils since all-age schools had too many disadvantages. They should develop close links with local ordinary schools.

Every special school should have its own governing body, which included a handicapped person and which reflected the wider community from which its pupils came. Independent special schools should continue to be officially recognized as 'acceptable' to the Secretary of State. This recognition would be in part dependent on allowing access to LEA officers and on the existence of a governing body which included a member of the LEA.

All education in hospitals should be regarded as special educational provision and a part of the mainstream of special education. Every child should receive education as soon as

264

possible after going into hospital. Hospitals should have buildings or rooms set aside for educational purposes for those children unable to go to school from hospital. Once it became clear that a child needed long-term hospital treatment, his educational needs should also be assessed. There should be joint planning and funding arrangements between health and education authorities to help provide the right sort of resources and equipment.

Community homes should be seen as a part of the regular provision of education for children with special needs. In order to improve the quality of education, teachers in community homes should be employed by the LEA, rather than the social services department.

Home-tuition teachers should have close links with local schools, and particularly with those special schools acting as resource centres. LEAs should make sure they can provide advisory services for both hospitals and home tuition.

The transition from school to adult life

Helping young people over sixteen who had special needs meant not just education, but training, employment and a wide range of supporting services. Arrangements needed to be made to develop their potential to the full, and employers had to be helped to recognize and encourage that potential. A pupil's special needs for adult life should be assessed, with help from a careers officer, at least two years before s/he was due to leave school.

All pupils needed to acquire the basic skills, social competence and vocational interests necessary for adult life, with opportunities to go on to sixth form, to sixth-form college, or to further and higher education college. In turn, these colleges ought to provide (and publicize) special courses and facilities for these young people, including the more severely disabled.

In every special and ordinary school catering for older pupils a teacher should be appointed to have responsibility for the careers guidance of handicapped pupils.

Employers and those national organizations concerned

with employment (e.g. Manpower Services Commission, industrial training boards, Training Services Agency) needed to develop more opportunities for young people with disabilities. Workplaces should cater more for special needs.

The extent and quality of counselling services for adolescents on personal and sexual relationships should be improved.

The Committee would like to have recommended the extension of mandatory grants for handicapped students or of courses which would attract mandatory grants. However, this proved too difficult in terms of defining the particular groups of students and the courses. Instead LEAs should be more generous in awarding discretionary grants and (where students already have a mandatory award) supplementary grants to students with disabilities who stay on at school after sixteen or go on to further or higher education.

More research should go into the design of aids for handicapped people. The mobility needs of young people with disabilities should be urgently considered, particularly with the phasing out of the invalid tricycle — a popular form of transport for this age group.

The curriculum

The skills and knowledge needed to develop the curriculum in special education are thinly spread. Curriculum development in special education should arise naturally out of the work of ordinary and special schools. Teachers should come to see themselves as a source of expertise. Each kind of educational difficulty would have its own curriculum requirements. The aim should be as far as possible to ensure that all children had access to the normal curriculum. The Committee discussed in detail the various curriculum needs of handicapped children. They recommended that resources be made available (e.g. to the Schools Council, to local teachers' centres) to develop curriculum projects for use in special schools and units; that a new section of the Schools Council should be funded to set up and disseminate projects on the curriculum for small groups of children with special needs; and that particular attention be given to developing the curriculum and accompanying materials for children with *moderate* learning difficulties, and to research into the causes of those difficulties.

A child may need to have special means of access to the curriculum, including special teaching techniques; a special or modified curriculum; or a particular social structure or emotional climate in which education took place. These needs should be catered for in one of a continuing line of ten sorts of provision according to the type and severity of a child's handicap: from support and help in an ordinary class to education in a residential special school, and from long-term education in hospital to home tuition.

Teacher education and training

There needed to be considerable advances in teacher training to ensure improvements in special educational provision. This was a top priority. Teachers in ordinary and special schools had to be able to recognize signs of special need, help to operate the five stages of assessment, and to record their observations. They needed to accept the wider concept of special educational need and the practical implications of having some children in a class needing special help.

A special education element should be included in *all* initial training courses for teachers, with most serving teachers going on a short in-service course within the next few years. LEAs should also provide induction programmes for teachers who will be taking on responsibility for children with special needs. In principle, all such teachers should be properly qualified. There should be a range of recognized teaching qualifications in special education, with a salary increment attached, based on one-year full-time courses. Other advanced short courses should deal with teaching methods for special education, management and administrative skills.

More opportunities should be created for people with disabilities to become teachers in both special and ordinary schools, with a right of appeal to the Secretary of State against being classified as medically unfit for teaching at the end of a teacher-training course. Teachers with handicaps

267

themselves could act as a positive encouragement to handicapped children and also show non-handicapped adults and
children the potential of those with handicaps.

Advice and support in special education

Every LEA should build up its 'special education advisory
and support services' made up mainly of existing advisers,
advisory teachers and other specialist remedial teachers,
reinforced by practising teachers.

An education officer should be made responsible for
arranging these services, with a separate committee of the
LEA to oversee special provision for children of all ages.
Each LEA should ensure there was at least one educational
psychologist for every 5,000 pupils, as well as specialist
careers officers, and more ancillary staff for special classes
in ordinary schools. Special training should be set up for
educational welfare officers and for child-care staff in residential special schools.

The health service and the social services

There should be greater coordination between local education authorities, health authorities and social services departments to ensure adequate provision of child health and
personal social services in all ordinary and special schools.
The Joint Consultative Committees had a valuable advisory
role to play in meeting needs, ensuring proper coordination
of services, and deciding priorities. There should be a named
doctor and nurse (with the right kind of experience and skills)
for every school, ordinary and special, who should develop a
close relationship between education and health staff.

Relations between professionals, confiden-
tiality, and the coordination of services

Confidentiality was often used as an excuse for a failure to
communicate. It also tended to inhibit the growth of a

wider understanding of the problems and needs of children and young people with disabilities. There was therefore an increasing need to establish general principles to guide professionals in deciding what information should be passed on to others.

Relevant information should be shared between professionals concerned with meeting an individual child's needs whenever that was in the best interests of the child and his or her parents. The child's interests had always to take precedence.

Parents should be treated as partners in the exchange of information wherever possible. They should be able to see most of the factual information about their child. They should, as a matter of course, be able to see their child's folder contaning records of progress and other facts. The results of professional consultations, however, would be kept in a separate, confidential folder. Whether or not parents were shown the actual reports on their children had to be a matter for the judgment of the professional concerned. The knowledge that parents could see their reports might make some professionals produce less detailed reports.

Professional groups concerned with special educational needs should develop close working relationships — for example, establishing codes of practice for handling confidential information; joint training courses; working groups on the adequacy of the services provided; and regional conferences. A National Advisory Committee on Children with Special Educational Needs should be established for England and Wales, with a separate Committee for Scotland.

Voluntary organizations

Voluntary organizations had a considerable contribution to make in providing for children's special needs. Their effectiveness had been, and would continue to be, in providing specialist services (e.g. aids, research, social work); in pioneering provision and services, including schools, to meet new needs; and in acting as local and national pressure groups, giving information to parents and developing community support. Collaboration between voluntary bodies and statutory services should increase nationally and locally. Local authorities could improve their support for voluntary bodies (helping with funding, resources, and premises) without risking the independence of the voluntary sector.

Research and development

More research was needed into special education, with more top academic posts in higher education (universities, polytechnics and so on) combining research, teacher training and practical work with children. A Special Education Research Group should be set up to agree research priorities and projects and to award research grants. A Special Education Staff College should also be established to train senior staff in special education. Every LEA should have a centre (based, for example, in a special school) where research and in-service training could be carried out and to which local teachers could turn for help.

The Committee concluded by saying that change in the way special education was organized and the injection of more resources were not enough. There had to be a change of attitude by professionals concerned with special education and by the general public. There should also be a general acceptance of the idea that special education involved as much skill and professional expertise as any other form of education, and that in human terms the returns on resources invested in it were just as great.

They were unable to cost out precisely the recommendations made. Some involved considerable expenditure, others could be financed from existing budgets through the consequence of falling school rolls releasing teachers and buildings for new uses. However, following the major developments in all three sectors of education since 1944 — for example, the raising of the school-leaving age, the elimination of all-age schools, comprehensive reorganization, the expansion of higher education, the development of middle schools and tertiary colleges — the Committee believed it was time for a comparable outlay of resources on innovation in special education, in line with the growing demand from parents of children with special educational needs.

The Committee had formulated proposals 'for the development of special education to the end of the century'. But they set out three priorities for action: to improve provision for children under five with special needs (to include a substantial extension of nursery education for all children); to improve provision for young people over sixteen with special needs; and to initiate a new programme of teacher training. They also urged that the necessary legal framework for the new concept of special education outlined in the Report should be introduced without delay and certainly within eighteen months of the Report's publication (i.e. by the end of 1979).

What has happened since Warnock reported

The Warnock Report was published in May 1978. In July 1978, the Education Secretary sent out a consultative document to over 300 organizations asking for their views on 'any aspect of the Report'. The organizations were asked to pay particular attention to the Committee's wider concept of special education and to the order of priorities for action in meeting special educational need — for example, early legislation; provision for the under-fives; provision for the over sixteens; the development of teacher training; establishing a unified special education advisory and support service in each LEA; promoting research and development. Other Government departments — the DHSS and the Department of Employment — were also consulted.

The DES received over 300 major responses to the Report's recommendations. Most reflected basic agreement with the Committee's new concept of special educational need and support for the abolition of the statutory list of handicaps. There was also general support for the principle of integration, although opinions differed on the timing, the kind of preparation and the level of resources needed before implementation.

Mary Warnock herself saw two key priorities as more in-service training for teachers and more cooperation between education, medical and social services.[1] The Association of Metropolitan Authorities (AMA) called for early legislation on replacing the present list of statutory handicaps; on giving powers to local authorities to assist children from birth; on clarifying parental rights; on providing a statutory duty on authorities to draw up development plans; on clarifying the legal basis of the child guidance and school psychological service. Many professional groups were concerned about 'hurried' integration without proper preparation and adequate resources such as improved staffing levels in schools.[2] The National Union of Teachers (NUT) called for adequate and flexible provision and a substantial allocation of resources before integration. The Union believed there should be a significant proportion of a school's activities in which a handicapped child could participate on equal terms with other children and that the nature of the school should not be significantly changed by the integration of handicapped pupils into the school.[3]

The legislative framework for the Warnock concept of special educational needs has yet to be brought before Parliament. There has been little improvement in nursery provision (certainly not 'a substantial extension' of it — nor is there any sign of it in the future) apart from the increase in the funds allocated to the nursery building programme towards the end of the 1974-9 Labour Government's period in office. There have been no official moves on changes in initial and in-service training for teachers, nor in providing for the over sixteens. One significant advantage though, which must underpin the success of all future action, is the official and professional approval of the Report's general principles. Again, though, the detail may create problems.

In 1979, the Advisory Centre for Education (ACE) carried out a national survey of LEA policy and practice towards the education of children with special needs (*Where*

---

[1] Speech reported in *Education* 15 September 1978.

[2] Some LEAs were still not meeting the minimum requirements set out in DES circular 4/73.

[3] *Special Educational Needs: The NUT Response to the Warnock Report* (NUT, May 1979).

147, April 1979). Most of the 78 local authorities which replied were generally in favour of integration and declared that children were educated in ordinary schools 'wherever possible'. In most cases, the proportion of children considered to have special needs was still greater in special schools than in ordinary schools or special units attached to ordinary schools. Children with the more severe handicaps remained in special schools, and only those with the milder disabilities found ordinary schools open to them. For example, only one LEA claimed to educate children considered ESN(S) in ordinary schools.

No LEA had wholly integrated all of its handicapped children in ordinary schools or in special units attached to ordinary schools. None as yet, according to the survey, had any clear plan to do so. Many were reviewing their provision or establishing working parties on both section 10 and the Warnock Report. They were waiting to see whether there would be significant moves by Government in terms of additional legislation and additional resources; and what sort of guidance would be issued after the consultations were complete.

Some interested organizations claimed that the Warnock recommendations could be interpreted so as to leave the way open to a long drawn-out period of inaction, where policy and practice remain far apart. Hence the calls for setting a date for the early implementation of section 10, together with a Government instruction to LEAs to submit plans for a phased programme of integration, plus further legislation obliging local authorities to make educational buildings accessible to handicapped children (in other words, 'activating' section 8 of the 1970 Chronically Sick and Disabled Persons Act).

The Warnock Committee pointed out that the principle embodied in section 10 of the 1976 Education Act was neither new nor revolutionary, but accorded with a consensus of public feeling that handicapped people should, as far as possible, be helped to take their place in the general community.

At the 1979 conference of the National Society for Mentally Handicapped Children, Stanley Segal set out three

273

decisions that LEAs had to make: what special help ordinary schools could provide with reasonable support; in which schools special arrangements would be made; and the variety and severity of needs that they would meet. He concluded that 'the burning issue . . . is less that of integration or segregation, than that of influencing the quality of life within the school and within the society that surrounds the school'. Warnock too made the point that it was not just *where* handicapped children were educated but the quality of education they received that mattered:

> The quality of special education . . . cannot be guaranteed merely by legislation and structural change. The framework provides the setting within which people work together in the interests of children, and the quality of education depends essentially upon their skill and insight, backed by adequate resources — not solely educational resources — efficiently deployed.

In February 1980, the results were published of a survey undertaken in 1978 by HM Inspectorate into educational provision in 21 community homes with education (CHEs) in England and Wales (*Community Homes with Education*, HMI Series: Matters for Discussion 10, DES/HMSO). The Inspectorate found much the same 'difficult' conditions documented by the Warnock Committee. Limited resources, the isolation of both CHEs and teachers from the ordinary school network, and a lack of support services from LEAs mainly because the CHEs' teachers came under social services authority rather than educational services all contributed to the poor quality of education offered by these community homes. The Inspectorate concluded that 'the education provided in CHEs is frequently at fairly low overall standards, in spite of the commitment of many of the teachers. A radical reappraisal of assessment procedures, of methods, and of the curriculum as a whole is required. It is possible that some of the improvements can be made only if a new relationship between the provision of education in CHEs and the LEAs can be worked out'.

The period of consultation ended in the spring of 1979. In March 1980, the Education Secretary, Mark Carlisle, announced in the Commons that the Government accepted the Warnock recommendation that 'defined categories of bodily or mental handicap should be replaced by that of special educational needs of individual children'. The intention is to introduce 'early legislation to enact a new framework substantially on lines recommended in the Report'. This would incorporate provisions designed to safeguard the interests of children with severe or complex special educational needs, including arrangements for more widely based assessment and for the recording of individual needs; define and protect parents' rights to adequate information and consultation about the education offered for their children. A White Paper was promised 'in due course'.

Recommendations on nursery education, teacher training and further and higher education 'have major implications for central and local Government expenditure and their implementation must be considered in the light of the economic situation and the need for restraint which it entails'.

Where to find out more

Books

Help Starts Here: for Parents of Children with Special Needs (NCB, 1976)

Special Educational Needs The Warnock Report (HMSO, 1978)

Meeting Special Educational Needs: A Brief Guide to the Report Mary Warnock (HMSO, 1978)

Wider Definition of Children with Special Needs: A Summary of the Warnock Report (Advisory Centre for Education, 1978)

Integrating Handicapped Children (HMI booklet, DES, 1979)

Organizations

National Children's Bureau (NCB) and Voluntary Council for Handicapped Children both at 8 Wakley Street, London EC1V 7QE (01-278 9441).

Circulars

Key DES circulars on special educational needs include:

11/61 Special Educational Treatment for Educationally Subnormal Pupils

12/70 The Education of Young Children with Defects of Both Sight and Hearing

15/70 The Education (Handicapped Children) Act 1970

Circular Letter Schools Branch II (SE) 1/73 Children and Young Persons Act 1969 — Arrangements for Education in Community Homes

4/73 Staffing of Special Schools and Classes

11/73 The Qualification of Teachers

3/74 Child Guidance

5/74 The Education of Mentally Handicapped Children and Young People in Hospital

2/75 The Discovery of Children Requiring Special Education and the Assessment of their Needs

Regulations or Statutory Instruments (SI) concerning special education include the Handicapped Pupils and Special Schools Regulations 1959 (SI 365) and amended by SI 2073 (1962) and SI 1565 (1966).

16 Conclusion

The future

Two questions arise out of this summary of Reports and their consequences. Have they achieved their basic objective — to change children's lives for the better? Are they a valuable means of enquiry from the point of view of the consumers of education, health and welfare services rather than of the administrators and politicians?

Successive Ministers would claim that Governments, local and central, have responded as effectively as they have been able, given the need to accommodate limited resources, conservative professional bodies with vested interests, and frequent differences of professional opinion over the value, rightness or appropriateness of particular recommendations. They may point out that Latey was comprehensively enacted; that Albemarle won its restructured Youth Service; that Plowden deeply influenced official thinking both on primary education and on the concept of positive discrimination; that Taylor got the best putative deal it could in the face of powerful political and administrative interests within school government, and the advances already underway irrespective of new legislation; that Halsey's work was accepted as a fundamental, but flawed, contribution to the future direction of inner-city aid programmes; that having legislation actually on the statute books — and so swiftly — was a major achievement for Houghton, with its full enactment only held back by the substantial resources required; that the domestic violence and homeless persons legislation could only improve the situations of disadvantaged families — and Government could not be responsible for the way some local authorities and courts interpreted the laws made or sought to evade the spirit of them.

Reforms have not only been delayed or written off on the grounds of cost. Often they have foundered on the unwillingness or political 'impossibility' of over-ruling vested professional, and even voluntary, interests holding to a different view; as happened, for example, with the concept of the general practitioner pediatrician, with the demand for an end to corporal punishment, with the need to give greater protection to children in care. They have also come to grief through a failure to reconcile a conflict of interests — between parent and child and parent and professional.

The Committees themselves are not, of course, always right. Recommendations have been 'trimmed' to suit official and unofficial lobbying or special pleading. Others have been based on misjudgements or on wrongly assuming cause and effect. They have been overtaken by events or by changes in the way society operates and the demands particular groups of people make on it; for example, the Plowden view of pre-schooling would scarcely be relevant today with many more mothers going out to work, a shift in the domestic and parental roles of mother and father, and the rise of the one-parent family. Finer's view, with its emphasis on more statutory and longer-term provision, has moved Plowden off-centre. Neither Crowther nor Newsom allowed for the enormous extension of comprehensive education. Taylor has been criticized for not spelling out precisely what powers school governors should have.

In turn, official action on these Reports has varied considerably. Overall, it can only be seen as a poor record. Bureaucratic delay, inadequate funding, a lack of coordination between central Government departments and between central and local Government, Ministers or Cabinets with a different set of priorities, internal politicking in Civil Service or Parties, a preference for elitist concerns instead of everyday ones — the reasons for lack of achievement are familiar. Some problems remain intractable, despite genuine and consistent attempts at solving them. The question of resources hangs over everything. But using resources is itself bound up with the question of priorities in economic policy as well as social policy; and Governments, and voters, must be prepared to justify their order of priorities, not just in terms of setting, say, Concorde against spending on education or health care, but also of spending on the 'Concordes' within education and health rather than on the more normal forms of 'travel' used by most of us.

But arguments about the problems of administration and the politics of education and health (valid and very real to the decision-makers and the decision-deferrers) do not impress the people about whom these Committees have been enquiring – the children and their parents, and those who teach, nurse and cure them; those who for one reason or another have to do without what society itself has declared to be basic rights: a good education, effective health care, a safe and caring environment.

The Reports themselves promulgated and documented the development of equality of opportunity through to the more robust policies that can be summed up in Plowden's 'positive discrimination'. Few though have suggested a radical realignment of resources or power.

There is no doubt though that more children now have greater opportunities throughout education, from pre-schooling to university. Expectations have risen; standards are generally higher. More children gain essential and not-so-essential qualifications. Health and welfare provisions have also improved. Yet what has been achieved has taken much longer than many anticipated – and much more remains unimplemented. In effect, for many of the children about whom, and for whom, these Reports have been compiled, the results have yielded little benefit.

One of the more dispiriting aspects of these Reports is the way some recommendations, generally well received, have appeared in Report after Report: the need for a massive expansion in pre-school provision; the need to raise the school-leaving age; the need for more parental involvement in the life of school and hospital; the need to end corporal punishment; the need for more joint-decision-making in education and health affairs; the need for grants to help young people stay in full-time education after sixteen; the need for teachers' aides.

Even the achievements are far from safe. Currently, the policies of the new Conservative Government threaten to reverse the trend of non-selection in secondary ecuation, switch resources in favour of the already advantaged, and substantially cut the funding of education and health services. In some areas, pre-school provision has started to contract rather than expand. The advantages to be won from the drop in the school population are likely to be lost. Many of the wheels that these Reports *did* set turning are moving into reverse.

Do Committees of Enquiry have a future? They continue to be set up. The latest one (the Rampton Committee) is investigating the education of children from ethnic minority groups. There have also been suggestions for a major enquiry into pre-school provision (a pre-school Plowden) and into the education and training needs of sixteen- to nineteen-year olds (another Crowther).

In general though Governments frequently claim that such Committees are less important now because Government departments are better equipped to deal with the demands of swift or radical policy changes, to cope with changing circumstance, and more able to provide detailed and valid research and evidence. The Department of Education and Science claims to have a more substantial armoury with improved and more public surveys — particularly from the HM Inspectorate — and the advice of the Assessment of Performance Unit and the Educational Disadvantage Unit. The Department of Health and Social Security, with its clutch of advisory committees and quangos (now being severely pared down by the current Conservative Government) might also make a similar claim. But the often ambiguous and somewhat muted impact of Government-sponsored bodies such as the Personal Social Services Council, the Children's Committee, the National Consumer Council make the option of a more independent form of enquiry attractive. For the keyword *is* independence — and it is that which bodies like those mentioned above do not always seem to have. Of course, a Committee of Enquiry is not immune from the same kind of pressure that can be, and often has been, brought to bear on these advisory bodies.

But it would seem to be better able to combat such assaults. Many of these quangos and statutory advisory bodies are being abolished under the new Thatcherite philosophy. Neither Government nor local authorities will be too sad to see some of them go. For it is all too clear that they are reluctant to fund organizations which can and do criticize their work and policies.[1]

Perhaps the series of 1977 regional educational conferences, billed under the title of the Great Debate, highlighted more than anything else the value of an independent and widely accessible body to investigate issues, receive evidence and opinions, and act as a focal point for reform — a body in fact like the Central Advisory Councils for Education which were never reactivated after the Plowden and Gittins Committees had reported in 1967 and 1968 (this, despite there being a statutory obligation on the Secretary of State to maintain them).[2]

Ironically, the health services continued to have the services of the Central Health Services Council (also set up by Act of Parliament — the Health Service Act 1946). But that has been an infrequent producer of major reports on key issues in health, and it too is to be abolished.

The need for an established and popularly recognized body that can mount, quickly and effectively, detailed enquiries into major educational or social issues concerning children has been canvassed by a wider circle than professional pressure groups and consumers themselves. Some politicians see the gap too. In 1976, a Parliamentary Select Committee[3] concluded that there was 'need for wider and more open review and informed public discussion of educational policy'. They recommended that 'a permanent Standing Education Commission should be set up, having the

[1] A report in *The Times* (23 November 1979) noted that local authorities were not expected to object to the proposal to scrap the PSSC since 'they have been irritated by its critical reports, notably on the quality of care in residential homes for children, old people and the handicapped'.

[2] For the views of two previous Education Secretaries, Anthony Crosland and Edward Boyle, on the Central Advisory Councils see *The Politics of Education* Maurice Kogan (Penguin Education, 1971).

[3] Tenth report from the Expenditure Committee, session 1975-6: *Policy Making in the Department of Education and Science* (July 1976).

authority and resources to contribute an independent view on strategic educational planning for the whole education service. Its membership would aim to bring trade unions, employers and ordinary citizens more formally into the education debate.'

Such a Commission, it is claimed, would ensure there is an independent watching brief over educational issues with the potential for speedy periodic full-scale investigations of specific areas of concern. It might also help to cure the seemingly unbreakable habits of secrecy, cover-up and obfuscation that bedevil Government departments. During the same Select Committee hearings that produced the idea of the Commission, Brian MacArthur (at the time editor of *The Times Higher Education Supplement*) suggested that 'Why should this not be made public?' ought to be stamped on every important DES document.

No doubt though this Select Committee's recommendation will go the same way of so many other recommendations that litter these pages like headstones in a graveyard. In any case, whatever form of Committee of Enquiry is established, the persistent and more fundamental problems of limited resources and the reluctance of Governments to act cannot be overcome by that alone.

Other proposals[1] for establishing an effective voice on behalf of children and their needs, concerns and aspirations have also been canvassed:

A Minister for Children to cut across conventional departmental boundaries to ensure the children's interest is formulated, canvassed and acted on.

A more powerful and comprehensive form of ombudsman to investigate injustice and to develop and disseminate good practice in handling children's affairs.

A separate children's ombudsman service, either independent or Government-funded.

A national children's legal centre (with local branches) to take up national and local issues, bring test cases to court, clarify children's rights and their role in society, and to campaign for new legislation.

The value of Committees of Enquiry does not seem to lie in being able to make Government act promptly and decisively.

[1] See 'Giving Children a voice of their own' (*The Guardian*, 2 October 1979).

The intention may be to influence Government thinking, provide justifications for policy change, for the setting of priorities and the reallocation of resources. But it happens rarely or very slowly even when, as with the Platt and Albemarle Reports, Government readily accepts in principle the main recommendations made. It is also clear that elitist concerns stand a better chance of action.

The publication of a Report then is often only the first stage in the process of achieving social or educational change. What then can be made of them as tools in that process?

Reports can bring together and legitimize radical, progressive or just plain commonsense ideas current within the education or health service world and gain for them a broader professional and public acceptance. They can also highlight for a wider audience what has become common practice within a profession.

They can establish, document, publicize and encourage good practice in schools, hospitals, courts and social services departments — and in the day-to-day dealings between professionals, parents and children.

They can win general consent about the direction in which a part of the education or health systems should be moving — what Anne Corbett has called 'their unique capacity to create a consensus for change'.[1] This of course is not always the case; for example, the Warnock Report did not resolve all the contentious issues that surround handicapped children's special needs; the Houghton-inspired Children Act of 1975 did not resolve the conflict of interests between parental and local authority claims over the custody of children considered to be at risk. But as vehicles for consent they do have few equals.

They can receive and absorb a range of evidence and opinion and undertake detailed research, and thereby become definitive documents on a particular service (the Plowden Report became a bestseller; and if you want to know all about child health services, go to the Court Report). Consequently, they have an educative role, spreading ideas and attitudes and straight information, quite uninhibited by the

[1] *Much to do About Education* Anne Corbett (Macmillan, fourth edition, 1978).

baleful influence of a niggardly Government response. Many teachers have read and absorbed the Bullock Report on literacy skills and translated school-based recommendations into reality. The Plowden Report gave a vital boost to the cause of parental involvement in schools and the Taylor Report did the same for increased democracy in the government of schools. The Platt and the Court Reports both developed a heightened public and professional awareness of the health and emotional needs of children; the Select Committee Reports on violence in the family were key factors in bringing the problems of child abuse into the open.

They can be invaluable, powerful and cheap[1] blueprints for pressing for change in who gets what share of the resources available, in the attitudes of those who administer services and make the decisions that affect the lives of children, in the awareness of parents about what they should demand of those services and of themselves in ensuring the best for their children.

Reports like those featured here can help to spread knowledge, develop awareness, focus debate, create consensus, establish priorities, extract commitments, exert pressure, force change. They may be poor substitutes for an enlightened Government, for legislation, for more or better-directed resources. But in a time when these will be thin on the ground, it would be a pity not to use the weapons that these Reports do put into our hands.

---

[1] The cost of the work of the fourteen Committees of Enquiry plus the publication of their Reports amounted to just over £1 million spread over 23 years.

General Information

Books

In addition to the books and organizations mentioned at the end of each section, the following would be useful for reference:

The Law on Education G. Taylor and J. B. Saunders (Butterworths, eighth edition, 1977)
Consumers' Guide to the British Social Services Phyliss Willmott (Penguin, fourth edition, 1978)
Guide to the Social Services (Family Welfare Association/ Macdonald and Evans, 1979)

Education Year Book 1980 (Councils and Education Press)
Social Services Year Book 1980 (Councils and Education Press)
Where to Look Things Up: An A to Z of the Sources of All Major Educational Topics (Advisory Centre for Education, second edition, 1980)

Official Government Reports, Circulars and Statistics can be bought from HMSO bookshops and shops which act as agents for Government publications.

Addresses

(Government departments)
Department of Education and Science (DES), Elizabeth House, York Road, London SE1 7PH (01-928 9222).
Department of Health and Social Security (DHSS), Alexander Fleming House, Elephant and Castle, London SE1 6BY (01-407 5522).
Home Office, 50 Queen Anne's Gate, London SW1H 9AT (01-213 3000).
Department of the Environment (DoE), 2 Marsham Street, London SW1P 3EB (01-212 3434).
Office of Population Censuses and Surveys (OPCS), St Catherine's House, 10 Kingsway, London WC2B 6JP (01-242 0262).

285

Welsh Office, Crown Building, Cathays Park, Cardiff CG1 3NQ (0222 825111).

Welsh Education Department, Government Buildings, Ty Glas, Llanishen, Cardiff CF4 5PL (0222 753271).

Organizations

A large number of organizations now exist to give information, advice and counselling on the specific areas covered by these Reports. These are just a few which can help, or pass enquirers on to an agency that can.

Children's rights: Children's Legal Centre, c/o 61 Denman Drive South, London NW11 (01-458 2679)

Civil rights: National Council for Civil Liberties (NCCL), 186 King's Cross Road, London WC1 (01-278 4575).

Consumer representation: National Consumer Council (NCC) Supports Desk, 18 Queen Anne's Gate, London SW1 (01-222 9501).

Education: Advisory Centre for Education (ACE), 18 Victoria Park Square, London E2 (01-980 4596).

General: Citizens' Advice Bureaux (CABx) — local offices, addresses in the phone book or from the local library; National Association of Citizen's Advice Bureaux, 110 Drury Lane, London WC2 (01-836 9226)

National Children's Bureau (NCB), 8 Wakley Street, London EC1V 7QE (01-278 9441)

Health: Community Health Councils (CHCs) — local offices, addresses in the phone book or from the local library; Association of Community Health Councils in England and Wales, 362 Euston Road, London NW1 (01-388 4814).

King's Fund Centre, 126 Albert Street, London NW1 (01-267 6111)

Housing: Shelter Housing Aid Centre (SHAC), 189a Old Brompton Road, London SW5 (01-373 7276).

Welfare rights: Child Poverty Action Group (CPAG), 1 Macklin Street, London WC2 (01-242 3225).

Index

Bold type indicates whole chapters or the main treatment of a subject.

Parliamentary Acts will be found under Acts of Parliament.

violence: advice centres, 199,
211; courts and, 198; effects
of ROSLA, 73-4; family,
150-1, 153, 171; in marriage,
196-9, 204-5, 209; one-parent
families, 168, 171; police
role, 198-9; refuges, 198,
204-5; *see also* child-battering,
family breakdown
vocational training, 11, 19-20,
69-70, 265-6; *see also* industrial training
voluntary organizations: adoption
societies, 141, 143, 147,
151-2, 153; children in care,
149-52; family crisis centres,
205; pre-school playgroups,
98, 175-6; refuges, 198,
204-5; schools, 246-7, 250;
special schools, 264, 269-70

Waddell Committee, 14-15
wardship and children's cases,
110-12, 114-15
Warnock Report, **256-75**
welfare tests, 145, 149, 153
West Indian Community, The
(1978 White Paper), 138
Wing Report, 232
Women's Aid Centre, Chiswick,
196, 204
work experience projects, 20, 70,
73, 76

young persons, *see* adolescents
youth and community work,
59-61, 63-4
Youth Opportunities Programme,
20
Youth Service: activities/facilities,
54; age range, 52, 59, 62-3;
building programme, 54, 57,
58, 70; community service,
60-1; education and, 9-10,
70; finance, LEA-run, 50-1,
60, 64; role of, 49-50, 53, 54,
58-60, 62-4; social changes
and, 49-51, 62, 64; staffing
and training, 54-5, 57-8, 61,
63-4; ten-year programme,
52, 56-7; voluntary-run,
50-1, 53
Youth Service Development
Council, 52-3, 55, 57, 59-61